The Logic of Ethnic and Religious Conflict in Africa

This book explains why conflicts in Africa are sometimes ethnic and sometimes religious, and why a conflict might change from ethnic to religious even as the opponents remain fixed. Conflicts in the region are often viewed as either "tribal" or "Muslim–Christian," seemingly rooted in deep-seated ethnic or religious hatreds. Yet, as this book explains, those labels emerge as a function of political mobilization. It argues that ethnicity and religion inspire distinct passions among individuals, and that political leaders exploit those passions to achieve their own strategic goals when the institutions of the state break down. To support this argument, the book relies on a novel experiment conducted in Côte d'Ivoire and Ghana to demonstrate that individual preferences change in ethnic and religious contexts. It then uses case illustrations from Côte d'Ivoire, Nigeria, and Sudan to highlight the strategic choices of leaders that ultimately shape the frames of conflict.

JOHN F. MCCAULEY is Assistant Professor of Government and Politics at the University of Maryland. His research focuses on ethnic and religious conflict, economic development, and informal political institutions in Africa. He has published articles on these topics in the *American Political Science Review*, *Comparative Political Studies*, *Political Psychology*, and *Political Science Research and Methods*, among others. His research has been supported by the National Science Foundation, the John Templeton Foundation, and the Bradley Foundation. He has conducted field research in Burkina Faso, Chad, Côte d'Ivoire, Democratic Republic of Congo, Ghana, Madagascar, Niger, and Nigeria.

D1496491

The Logic of Ethnic and Religious Conflict in Africa

JOHN F. MCCAULEY

University of Maryland

CAMBRIDGE
UNIVERSITY PRESS

CAMBRIDGE
UNIVERSITY PRESS

University Printing House, Cambridge CB2 8BS, United Kingdom

One Liberty Plaza, 20th Floor, New York, NY 10006, USA

477 Williamstown Road, Port Melbourne, VIC 3207, Australia

4843/24, 2nd Floor, Ansari Road, Daryaganj, Delhi – 110002, India

79 Anson Road, #06–04/06, Singapore 079906

Cambridge University Press is part of the University of Cambridge.

It furthers the University's mission by disseminating knowledge in the pursuit of education, learning, and research at the highest international levels of excellence.

www.cambridge.org
Information on this title: www.cambridge.org/9781107175013

DOI: 10.1017/9781316796252
© John F. McCauley 2017

First published 2017

Printed in the United States of America by Sheridan Books, Inc.

A catalogue record for this publication is available from the British Library.

ISBN 978-1-107-17501-3 Hardback
ISBN 978-1-316-62680-1 Paperback

For Phyllis and Michael McCauley
and to the memory of James B. Reilly

Contents

Figures

Tables

Abbreviations

AFRISTAT	L'Observatoire Economique et Statistique d'Afrique Subsaharienne
AG	Action Group, a political party in Nigeria
ASWAJ	Ahlu Sunnah wal Jama'aah, a Muslim group
BBC	British Broadcasting Corporation
CONSORT	Consolidated Standards of Reporting Trials
DIAL	Développement, Institutions et Mondialisation
FMG	Federal Military Government, the government regime in Nigeria
FN	Forces Nouvelles, a rebel group in Côte d'Ivoire
FPI	Front Populaire Ivoirien, a political party in Côte d'Ivoire
IMF	International Monetary Fund
MPCI	Mouvement Patriotique de Côte d'Ivoire, a rebel group in Côte d'Ivoire
NCNC	National Convention of Nigerian Citizens, a political party in Nigeria
NIF	National Islamic Front, a religious-political organization in Sudan
NPC	Northern People's Congress, a political party in Nigeria
OIC	Organization of the Islamic Conference
PDCI	Parti Démocratique de Côte d'Ivoire, a political party in Côte d'Ivoire

RDR	Rassemblement des Républicains, a political party in Côte d'Ivoire
RNC	Royal Niger Company, a colonial-era commercial enterprise in Nigeria
SPLM/A	Sudan People's Liberation Movement/Army
SUTVA	Stable Unit Treatment Value Assumption
WCC	World Council of Churches

Preface and Acknowledgments

My introduction to sociopolitical life in sub-Saharan Africa came as a high school teacher in Pama, a small village tucked in the southeastern corner of Burkina Faso. In Pama, my closest friends were a Muslim, a Catholic, a Protestant, and a traditional religionist, each of a different ethnic group. Together, we rarely missed an ethnic or religious feast in the village, and as teachers and civil servants, we delighted in the lessons of Gulmanché and Mossi elders. By virtue of the atypical mixing that happened to define the population there, many events were open to all, diverse, and rich in laughter, teasing, and celebration. That experience stood in stark contrast, however, to the news that unfolded around us in the early 2000s. I followed stories of ethnic violence over oil reserves and of religious violence over Shari'a law in Nigeria. I watched as migrants described alternately as Muslims, northerners, and Dioula flooded back to Burkina to escape violence in neighboring Côte d'Ivoire. I struggled to understand the Ituri conflict between ethnic groups in the Democratic Republic of Congo, and the expanding Islamic insurgency in parts of Mali, Niger, and elsewhere. Trying to square my own experience of inter-group harmony with these nearby episodes of ethnic and religious strife, I asked more questions than anyone could have been expected to answer for me.

Later, as a Ph.D. student at UCLA, I used that taste of identity group relationships in Africa as the basis for my studies. I sought to understand why ethnicity and religion sometimes serve as the foundations of peace and sometimes as the sparks of violence. Returning frequently to West Africa, I was particularly struck by a puzzle that emerged from the conflict in Côte d'Ivoire. By all accounts, the conflict began as a result of tensions related to immigrant rights and control of resources. Yet, some who described the conflict and its early foundations referenced hatreds and discrimination between ethnicities, the southern Akan groups and the northern Malinké, in particular. Others, by contrast, saw religious hatreds between Christians and Muslims, particularly as the conflict progressed. How could a conflict having nothing to do with ethnic or religious substance per se come to be labeled in those identity terms? Why would a conflict perceived at one stage as "tribal" later come to be seen as a fight in the name of God? This book constitutes an effort to answer those questions.

That the identity frames of the Ivoirian conflict could change suggested to me a choice, either in the labels that key players employed or in the policies and strategies they used to evoke one identity type or the other. This, of course, is far from unique to Africa: from U.S. presidential campaigns to European responses in the face of refugee crises, political elites frequently mobilize support with pointed messages or targeted policies, the outcome of which is often a perception of political contest-ation through sharp and divisive identity lenses. In addition to the stra-tegic choices of elites, however, I also recognized – perhaps from those feasts in Pama – that ethnicity and religion seem to affect people in different ways. Put in one or the other of those settings, we seem to want different things, to favor different priorities, and to associate differently. My reading of the ethnic politics literature in political science suggested that, too often, this second feature – the constitutive differences in ethni-city and religion that affect individuals in unique ways – was missing. Thus, you will find as you read the book that my theoretical explanation for the emergence of conflict frames in Africa brings together the strategic choices of elites and the passions and preferences of individuals in ethnic versus religious contexts.

The research for this book required help and support from countless sources; needless to say, I incurred many debts along the way. I want to first acknowledge the Ivoirians, Ghanaians, Burkinabé, and Nigerians who shared their time and stories. In some instances, they did so even as the political institutions around them failed and their own sense of personal comfort and security was anything but certain. As survey respondents, participants in experiments, focus group discussants, and interview subjects, they gave me a better understanding of the logic of ethnic and religious conflict in Africa. I am deeply indebted to them.

This book began as a doctoral dissertation in political science at UCLA. I would like to acknowledge the unwavering support I enjoyed from my dissertation committee there. I thank Barbara Geddes for always pressing me to explore the observable implications of my claims and for dedicating so much of her time to my written work. I thank Ed Keller for inspiring a love of African politics and for keeping me honest about the complex patterns of sociopolitical relationships on the ground. Ted Miguel at UC-Berkeley, whose passion for understanding and reducing civil conflict in Africa is contagious, provided great encouragement and a new way of looking at problems. I owe a special debt of gratitude to my advisor, Dan Posner. He has been a great mentor and a great friend, and a set of eyes that saw things I could not. Our collaborations continue to shape my thinking.

Many other colleagues and friends left imprints on this work. I benefited from conversations in the field with Jeremy Horowitz, Nahomi Ichino, Staffan Lindberg, and Kristin Michelitch. Claire Adida, Leo Arriola, Tom Bassett, Jeffrey Conroy-Krutz, Thad Dunning, Don Green, David Laitin, Amanda Robinson, and Keith Weghorst have been invaluable sources of advice and feedback. At UCLA, Joseph Asunka, Mac Bunyanunda, Liz Carlson, Kim Dionne, Koji Kagotani, Eric Kramon, Peter Krause, Jeff Paris, Oliver Proksch, Tyson Roberts, Jae-Hyeok Shin, Dave Shullman, and Robbie Totten provided support and helped in various ways. Halsey DiSario was a superb research assistant. Special thanks go to Bob Archibald and Marc Trachtenberg.

Colleagues and friends in West Africa made the field research possible. In Côte d'Ivoire, I am indebted to the Centre Multitudes at the University of Cocody-Abidjan and to its director, Michelle Tanon-Lora. Adama Coulibaly, Abdramane Koné, Jacques N'Goran, Yaya Soro, and the entire team of research assistants worked tirelessly and contributed greatly to the project's success. Karim Tondossama deserves special thanks for opening his home to me, offering the contacts I needed in Bouaké and the north, and coordinating the research team. In Ghana, Emmanuel Gyimah-Boadi and the staff at the Center for Democratic Development were incredibly generous with their time and resources. I benefited greatly from conversations with Sheikh Mohammed Kamil Mohammed, Roland Owusu Ansah, Rev. Nathan Samwini, Marie Renée Wyseur, and Al-Hajj Al-Hussein Zakaria. Issahaku Al-Hassan, Joseph Owusu-Gyamfi, Mildred Wryter, and the entire research team went beyond the call for me. I am particularly grateful for the support I received from Francis Gomado and family, who welcomed me as a full-fledged member of their own tight-knit group. In Nigeria, Rev. Danny

McCain opened doors. In Burkina Faso, Taladidia Combary, Ibrahim Compaoré, Ibrahima Ouattara, and the Sana family have been irreplaceable to me.

It would not have been possible to undertake three major field research trips and to dedicate myself to the writing without generous financial and institutional support. For that, I owe several debts of gratitude. The UCLA Graduate Division, the UCLA Globalization Research Center-Africa, the Lynde and Harry Bradley Foundation, the National Science Foundation, the John Templeton Foundation, the University of Maryland's Graduate Division, and the UMD Dean's Research Initiative all provided critical support. The Center for Religion and Civic Culture at the University of Southern California introduced me to a diversity of scholars and provided key backing; I thank Don Miller for making that happen. Prior to joining the faculty at Maryland, I served on the Initiative on Religion in International Affairs at Harvard University's Kennedy School of Government. That opportunity provided me with the time and space to move the project forward, and I thank Monica Toft for making that possible. The Working Group on African Political Economy has been a steady source of intellectual support and ideas. Workshop participants at Berkeley, Harvard, Arizona State, Maryland, and Yale have helped refine the project at various stages. My debts to all involved are immeasurable.

I have had the great fortune of finishing the book in an incredibly supportive environment at the University of Maryland. I thank my colleagues – particularly Hanna Birnir, Sarah Croco, Irwin Morris, and Margaret Pearson – for their advice, support, ideas, and in some cases countless readings of papers and chapters. Allyce Chen and Julia Marra provided outstanding assistance, and Maneesha Sakhuja read multiple drafts. My graduate and undergraduate students have been inspirational.

Robert Dreesen, the senior editor for politics and sociology at Cambridge University Press, shepherded the book through production with patience, professionalism, and efficiency. He offered practical advice and steady encouragement through the process. I am thankful to him and his colleagues, and to the anonymous reviewers of the manuscript.

Finally, I want to thank some friends and family. Alain Balmaceda, Mara Castillo, Roger Duthie, Dave Haffner, Alice Ham, Jonathan Renshon, Lei Shishak, and Kim Varzi supported my work but also created a world for me outside of it, and I never took that for granted. Moira and Darren, Anne and Dominik, my twin brother, Steve, and my big brother, Dan, showed an enthusiastic interest, provided intellectual and personal guidance, and helped me from one stage to the next. I am lucky to have siblings like them. My parents, Phyllis and Mike, have been my biggest inspiration. They gave me everything I needed, and they always taught us to work diligently, to pursue our passions, and to be curious about the world outside St. Mary's County, Maryland. This book is for them.

PART I

I

Introduction

On December 4, 2000, in Côte d'Ivoire's capital of Abidjan, sixty-year-old Bakary Kaba was gunned down in the presence of his family as he performed the ablutions of foot washing in preparation for prayer.[1] Mr. Kaba was a Muslim, and human rights reports indicated that he was killed at the hands of Christian military police officers who shot him simply because of the Muslim robes he wore. Though tragic, Mr. Kaba's killing was not isolated – it came on the heels of a massacre of fifty-seven Muslims on the outskirts of Abidjan, the burning of churches and mosques throughout the country, and the murder of several prominent priests and imams. Thrown into turmoil by a December 1999 coup, and unhinged once more by failed elections in October 2000, Côte d'Ivoire at the time of Kaba's death found itself in the throes of violence that would ultimately lead to a decade-long civil conflict and that would turn this once proud and united nation into a setting for inter-religious violence, or so it was described.

Mr. Kaba's clothes marked him as a Muslim, but he was not just a Muslim. He identified with the Malinké ethno-linguistic group (or "tribe").[2] He was an immigrant, having migrated to Côte d'Ivoire years earlier from Guinea in search of stable employment. Though living in

---

[1] For a summary account of the killing, see U.S. Department of State (2001).
[2] I refer to ethno-linguistic groups as "ethnic groups" rather than "tribes" due to an association of tribe with backwardness (Southall 1970) and colonial control (Campbell 1997). Ethnic groups and tribes are sometimes used to refer to different levels of community, so I lose some degree of precision. I also realize that my labeling decision introduces the risk of confusion between broad and narrow ethnicity. Throughout the book, where I use "ethno-linguistic group" or "tribe," they are synonymous with "ethnic group."

Abidjan at the time of his death, Mr. Kaba was in many respects a
northerner, owing to his kinship ties and previous residence in the north
of the country. He was thought to be a supporter of the Rassemblement
des Républicans (RDR), an opposition political party that would later
come to power. Of the many groups that Mr. Kaba represented (Malinké
ethnicity, immigrant, Guinean, northerner, RDR supporter), why did his
religion doom him? Why, in a country divided along ethno-linguistic as
well as religious lines, was this violence defined in Christian-Muslim
terms?

    In this book, I seek an answer to those questions. Stated more gener-
ally, why do Africa's "ethnic" conflicts sometimes emerge along ethno-
linguistic lines and sometimes along religious lines? During the Rwandan
genocide, majority Hutus launched a 100-day attack against minority
Tutsis that left more than 800,000 dead in a shocking case of ethnic
violence (Prunier 1995). Yet Rwandans are not only members of the
Hutu and Tutsi ethnicities; they are also members of religious groups
and other social identities. Why was the Rwandan genocide not a different story of majority Catholics launching an attack against minority
Muslims? In Sudan, a north–south civil war was at one period a matter
of Arabs fighting black Africans and at another period a matter of
Muslims in conflict against non-Muslims (Deng 1995). In Nigeria, conflicts like the Ogoni uprising in the 1990s occurred between ethno-
linguistic groups; clashes in Jos and other northern cities in the 2000s
occurred between Muslims and Christians; and the 1967–1970 civil war
in the Biafra region began as an ethnic group conflict and ended with
attention on religion without the participants ever changing. Across
Africa, recent violence in the Central African Republic, South Sudan,
the Democratic Republic of Congo, Mali, Burundi, Chad, and elsewhere
has implicated either ethnic or religious actors. Even beyond the African
region, conflicts in Sri Lanka, Myanmar, Northern Ireland, India, and the
Middle East are often viewed through either ethno-linguistic or religious
lenses, yet current theories in comparative politics are not equipped to tell
us whether there is something about ethnicity and religion that shapes
those lines of conflict. I suggest that there is.

    The question of why conflicts in Africa are sometimes ethnic and
sometimes religious is not an esoteric one. According to Sambanis
(2001), fully 73 percent of civil wars worldwide are counted as ethnic/
religious in nature; the remaining 27 percent are coded as revolutionary
wars, though even then ethnicity or religion is frequently exploited for
divisive purposes. Fox (2012) puts the share of religious wars alone at

62 percent of all conflicts, up from about 30 percent in the 1960s. In the African context, where ethnic and religious identities color much of life's quotidian interactions and many of its social and political divisions, conflicts *not* described in ethnic or religious terms prove to be the exception.

Of course, the notion of ethnic and religious wars can be understood in multiple ways. Toft (2007) makes the distinction between conflicts in which identity is *central* versus those in which it is *peripheral* but nevertheless plays a role simply by virtue of the two sides representing opposing labels.[3] Svensson (2007) describes *incompatibility wars*, in which opponents fight over the actual content of identity differences, and *identity wars*, in which other factors drive conflict but the opponents' labels happen to differ. Pearce (2005) calls this an *issue-oriented* division versus an *identity-oriented* division. These distinctions are critically important for determining the cause of conflicts. In this book, my goal is somewhat different: I aim to understand why conflicts, once they have begun, take on one label versus another – a "tribal war," for example, versus "religious killings."[4] This is a question of conflict frames. Sometimes, the cause of a conflict and its frame are closely related; at other times, conflict frames have little to do with the cause of violence itself. In virtually all cases, I argue, the choice of frames is ultimately a political one.

Accounts in the political science literature of how identities such as ethnicity and religion become important follow three distinct paths. First, the now outdated primordialist perspective suggests that certain types of identity (usually the ethno-linguistic group) have greater intrinsic or objective importance than other types and are thus more likely to be at the root of conflict, as groups in close proximity cling to innate differences and deep-seated hatreds (Douglass 1988; Geertz 1973). Second, contemporary instrumentalist and constructivist views instead treat identities as the fluid and situational choices of instrumental actors (Barth 1969; Kasfir 1979; Posner 2004; Young 1976) – in the limit, simply as "interest groups" that form in a strategic effort to accumulate resources (Bates 1983).[5] In this context, there are frequently no functional differences in

---

[3] These scholars refer specifically to religious conflicts, but the distinctions they make apply equally well to ethnic ones.

[4] The tribal war citation refers to South Sudan (see *New York Times* 2015); religious killings refers to Nigeria (see *Evening Standard* 2012).

[5] Instrumentalism highlights choices made in the self-interest of actors, while constructivism underscores the importance of narratives created for a social group or community (see Stewart 2008). While some scholarship falls distinctly into one or the other camp,

mobilizing according to religion, ethnic group, language, race, or other ascriptive identity types – the particular lines along which ethnic conflict happens to emerge are instead a matter of the relative sizes of groups, institutional factors that favor one group over another, and the manner in which political entrepreneurs exploit those differences to their advantage. Finally, a third set of scholars focusing exclusively on conflict in religious terms prioritizes the characteristics of particular religious groups, suggesting that, for example, the language, organizational structure, history, or tenets of Islam shapes Muslim relations with other religions (Badie 1987; Huntington 1996; Kalyvas 2000; Lewis 1990; Sanneh 1994; Stark 2001; Toft 2007).

The argument that I make lies between these approaches. Like the contemporary constructivist approach, I argue that the salience of ethnicity, religion, or any other social identity is context dependent and that political entrepreneurs make strategic calculations regarding the identity type they wish to politicize. What distinguishes my argument from others in this camp, however, is my view that ethnicity and religion offer different baselines from which those strategic calculations must be made. Like the scholars of religion and politics, I suggest that something is indeed different about religion (and ethnicity) that merits scholarly attention from political scientists. Where my argument differs is in placing emphasis not on the tenets or other characteristics of specific traditions, but rather on the social impact of ethnic and religious identities writ large that inspire different priorities and preferences. These broad differences between ethnicity and religion (among other possible identity choices) affect the calculations of political entrepreneurs, regardless of their particular ethnic or religious stripes.

The central argument in this book is that individuals have multiple identities, each of which evokes distinct preferences. Political entrepreneurs understand this and seek to mobilize supporters in terms of the identities that have the most useful behavioral consequences, vis-à-vis the leader's own strategic goals. They do this by altering the frame of conflict, either exploiting policies that mobilize an optimal identity or mobilizing an identity type to generate support for an optimal policy. In this sense, the argument offers a new explanation for why identities like ethnicity and religion become salient in conflict settings, and thus why fighting occurs along one identity line rather than another: it is not because some

---

I conflate those camps here to focus on the context-dependent nature of political identities under both accounts.

identities are innately more important to people (as primordialists might claim) or because certain identity groups possess characteristics that increase the likelihood of conflict (as some scholars of religion and politics may argue). It is also not simply a matter of optimally sized identity coalitions (as constructivists or instrumentalists might suggest), because ethnic and religious divisions sometimes provide no clear numerical advantage. Instead, conflicts become ethnic or religious because those identity types evoke distinct preferences that can be exploited for political ends.

How do ethnicity and religion in Africa differ? Ethnic groups in the region do not have formal behavioral guidelines but instead draw socio-political relevance from narratives of descent and from historical ties to well-defined geographic areas overseen by a chief or traditional authority. Ethnic groups, in this sense, are land-based identities. The impact of world religions in Africa is quite different: they inspire only weak ties to land and instead rely on imported sets of behavioral guidelines to maintain social and political relevance and to serve group members. As a convenient shorthand, I refer to them as rule-based identities. I argue that these features generate *mobilizational differences* – ethnicity inspires preferences for control of the land and local resources, whereas religion inspires preferences for protecting moral lifestyles and voluntarily accepted rules, particularly with transnational influence. Thus, although the instrumental interests of the political entrepreneur remain unchanged, his calculations do not, owing to the fact that his support base(s) will mobilize collectively around different concerns in ethnic versus religious contexts. In this view, the choice of which identity type to politicize is a matter not simply of relative group size but of the precise outcome the political entrepreneur hopes to achieve. Efforts to protect or accumulate local resources are associated with mobilization of the ethnic identity. If, conversely, the political goal calls for developing ties beyond the local land or highlighting matters of moral legitimacy, the political entrepreneur would do best to politicize religion. Applied to contentious political situations, the uniting of mobilizational differences and political goals has strong implications for how we view cases of "ethnic" conflict. In case after case in the African region, the evidence supports this approach.

The value of the argument, however, goes beyond the intellectual exercise of classifying conflicts as ethnic, religious, or otherwise. Understanding why conflicts are seen through an ethnic versus a religious lens generates insights into the sources of aid and alliance available to parties in conflict. It sheds light on the targets of violence and the potential for retaliation and may also help to predict the severity of conflict. Perhaps most important, distinguishing ethnic from religious conflict frames can put us in a position to better identify strategies for mitigating future tensions between adversaries.

BOUNDARIES OF THE ARGUMENT

I do not intend to explain why conflict begins. Instead, taking political and economic competition over scarce resources as a broader, fundamental cause of conflict,[6] I ask which labels groups employ when they come into conflict. Why does competition take place along some lines rather than others? Given individual attachments to several identity types, when should we expect ethnicity or religion to be evoked in the course of conflict? Focusing on these questions puts me in position to set aside the myriad moving parts that complicate stories of conflict onset and to do what those arguments do not – account for the mobilizational differences between types of identity that political entrepreneurs can use to their advantage in contentious political circumstances. My goal, then, is to construct a more complete understanding of conflict in Africa by going beyond the question of why conflict emerges to ask why, when groups come into conflict, the same people sometimes fight in the name of "tribe" and sometimes in the name of God. I maintain the view that these labels rarely serve as the cause of conflicts per se, but rather as incredibly powerful tools wielded in the course of conflicts.

The frame, or identity lens through which political activity is seen, is determined by several factors. First, the *actors* involved in a conflict – including political entrepreneurs, violence "specialists," and community members on both sides – announce themselves as members of an ethnic group, religion, or other social group. Second, the *targets* of violence in civil conflicts affect the lens through which that conflict is seen. The burning of churches and mosques, the murder of priests and imams, and the killing of religiously sacred animals (e.g., cows in Hindu regions) shape conflict as religious; attacking party headquarters frames conflict in political party terms; upsetting traditional shrines, destroying crops farmed by an agriculturalist ethnic group, or killing animals associated with a pastoralist group marks a conflict as "tribal." Third, the *rhetoric*

---

[6] Competition over resources underlies explanations rooted in both opportunity (Collier and Hoeffler 2004) and grievances (Gurr 1970). For summaries of the literature on conflict cause, see Brubaker (2004, chapter 4) and Blattman and Miguel (2010).

used by actors in a conflict to make demands and incite participation contributes to the framing of conflict as ethnic, religious, or other. When, for example, an opposition political figure makes the public announcement that he is not permitted to take part in elections because he is a Muslim (an example described in Chapter 6), the conflict is more likely to take on a religious tone. Finally, the *reporting* of incidents during conflict influences the lens through which that conflict is seen. Paul Brass (1997) uses the example of a dispute over a young girl, coincidentally between Muslims and Hindus, as an illustration of the power and danger that reports can have on the frame of ethnic or communal conflict. To those affected by conflict, however, the frame is not simply a choice of labels but often a deeply felt cause for which to raise arms.

Why should we care about the frame of Africa's conflicts? As the example from Brass illustrates, frames can be notoriously fickle and subject to manipulation (e.g., from a state press interested in cultivating an outcome or image favorable to the government). That is not to say, however, that the frame does not matter; Brass's very point is that how a conflict is viewed has important consequences for how it proceeds. First, there is the matter of targets: Mr. Kaba in Côte d'Ivoire may not have been gunned down in front of his family had the Ivoirian conflict not taken on a religious frame. Second, some evidence suggests that the frame of conflicts – as religious, ethnic, or otherwise – has consequences for the outcomes and severity of violence. Wilkinson (1999) suggests, based on data from India, that conflicts over religion tend to be more violent; Fox (2004) presents cross-national data over a fifty-year period to demonstrate that wars in the name of religion are both longer and bloodier than non-religious wars. Sambanis (2001) notes an association between ethnic and religious conflicts and a lack of democracy. There are thus reasons to suspect that the frame of conflict – shaped by the actors involved, the targets, the rhetoric, and the reporting – affects the longer term trajectories of those conflicts. My objective is to explain why that frame is sometimes ethnic and sometimes religious.

Even in cases where the roots of a conflict appear obvious – say, in the imposition of Islamic Shari'a law for criminal matters in northern Nigeria – we should still ask why elites chose the particular strategy they did to mobilize supporters. In that instance, what is often described as a political power grab (Mu'azzam and Ibrahim 2000) could have targeted Hausa-Igbo ethnic divisions instead. Why might political leaders push a policy like Shari'a law if it divides society? The answer I propose is that doing so alters the salience of identity types in systematically useful ways.

Insofar as identity types have unique effects on individuals, political entrepreneurs can filter those individual-level preferences through their own strategic goals to achieve different ends.

To develop this argument, I focus on ethnicity and religion in Africa, for the following reason. The project begins with the fairly pedestrian view that something changes for individuals when they are placed in different identity contexts. To test that hunch, I sought an environment where multiple social identities are equally strong and potentially politically salient. In sub-Saharan Africa, ethnicity and religion are appropriate foils: over 90 percent of respondents to surveys in the region indicate that religion is important in their lives, and the same surveys indicate that the ethno-linguistic identity is the primary form of self-identification.[7] Together, religion and one's ethnic group are the most common social identity responses to the question, "how do you identify yourself first and foremost?" There is also a history of conflict in the region that has emerged along both ethnic and religious lines, generating sufficient variation in the outcome of interest to allow for the construction of a causal argument linking the mobilizational differences of identities to the lens through which conflict is seen. At the same time, Africa can be taken as a harder context in which to demonstrate mobilizational differences between ethnicity and religion, precisely because both are such central aspects of most individuals' lives, and they are often difficult to separate. Thus, to the extent that mobilizational differences do appear in the African context, I will have chosen a conservative environment in which to make the case that those differences affect political choice over the identity frames of conflict.

The argument is not intended as a universal explanation of all identity conflict. Different theories may be needed to explain the role of nationalism, class, or other identity types in conflict situations. Furthermore, as I develop in Chapter 2, ethnicity and religion should take on different meanings across distinct geographic regions. The categorization of religion as inspiring weak ties to land but strong commitments to rules, for example, may be accurate at the geographic peripheries of world religious communities, but less so at their geographic cores. Though Islam had spread across Africa by the tenth century, and Christianity had established pockets by the fifteenth century, their widespread impact is in many

---

[7] See data from Rounds 1 and 2 of the Afrobarometer public opinion surveys, in which questions regarding primary modes of self-identification were asked. Data available at www.afrobarometer.org/data.html.

respects quite recent, having advanced significantly only during the 1800s (Clarke 1982). Attachments to land in Africa had by this point taken on different meaning, under traditional structures of authority. Religion as an identity type in the Middle East, by contrast, where sacred sites unite religious rules with territory and nationalism, should be expected to evoke a different set of concerns. Similarly, in Africa, where little congruence exists between ethnic boundaries and national borders, ethnic identity may function very differently from that in Japan, where ethnicity, land, and national political identity converge. What I present in this book is an argument that mobilizational differences exist across identity types, and that these differences help to explain why certain identities become salient in cases of African conflict. I make the case by focusing on two identity types – ethnicity and religion – that are especially important in this particular setting. Identities will serve different functions in other settings, but by understanding ethnicity and religion in one important context, we might gain improved insight into their roles in other contexts.[8]

The principal subject of this book is the communal and civil conflicts, past and present, that so frequently take on ethnic or religious frames in Africa. Of late, observers have devoted special attention to the recent wave of religious-motivated terrorist attacks in the region (see Munson 2016 as an example). Those cases of violence occupy a separate analytical class, often more galvanizing to Western audiences but also much smaller in scope, so they are not a central focus of the book. Nevertheless, insofar as terrorist group leaders may have incentives to mobilize support in the same way that political elites mobilize collective action during communal conflict, some lessons from this argument may be applied to religious terrorism in Africa, as I aim to demonstrate with an application to Boko Haram in the concluding chapter.

DEFINING CONCEPTS

To this point, I have used quotation marks in referencing the broad concept of "ethnicity" or "ethnic politics," as distinct from ethno-linguistic

---

[8] This claim may run counter to patterns of globalization, which might suggest either an increasing universality of religious and ethnic meaning or the absence of any behavioral patterns in religion and ethnicity at all. Yet, so long as some regional specificity in identity types remains, space exists for arguments that both explain patterns in one context and shed light on distinctions with other contexts. See Cox (2010) for a description of religious globalization.

(or "tribe") groups in Africa. The term *ethnic* requires special attention, as its complications serve in some sense as the very purpose of this study. In contemporary political science, the trend for many has not been to address religious or ethnic group conflict as problems in their own right. Instead, competition between all forms of ascriptive identity types – language, ethno-linguistic, racial, religious, and so on – is treated under an umbrella definition of "ethnic politics." Here, for example, are working definitions of "ethnicity" culled from some of the leading studies in comparative politics:

> Birnir (2007: 610): "Ethnicity is self-identification around ... language, race, or location. Other characteristics such as religion and culture qualify as well."
>
> Chandra (2004: 2): "I take the term 'ethnic group' to refer to the nominal members of an ascriptive category such as race, language, caste, tribe, or religion."
>
> Horowitz (1985: 53): "Ethnicity easily embraces groups differentiated by color, language, and religion; it covers tribes, races, nationalities, and castes."
>
> Kasfir (1979: 365): "The concept of ethnicity ... may be fundamentally ethnic, class, religious or – it is worth stressing – a combination of these identities."
>
> Posner (2005: 14): "Linguistic, tribal, and religious communities ... are all 'ethnic options.'"
>
> Rothchild (1997: 3): "Ethnic groups – formed along ethnic, racial, religious, regional, or class lines – have distinct origins and appeals, but they share common features ..."

As several of these definitions reveal, there is unfortunate ambiguity between the umbrella definition of ethnicity and a more constricted use of the term. The semantic confusion has not gone unnoticed – Varshney (2002: 4) notes that ethno-linguistic traits count as "narrow" ethnicity, while other ascriptive groupings form the foundation of "broader" ethnic politics. Brubaker (2004: 136) also acknowledges the problem of "ethnic ambiguity" in reference to the use of the same term to describe both narrow, descent-based communities and broad, cultural groups (which include all of the identity types mentioned above – religion, race, region, caste, etc.).

There is, nevertheless, a straightforward rationale for the umbrella definition of ethnicity: preferences and behaviors across all identity types are assumed to be constant. Thus, the calculus of political entrepreneurs need not include information about the characteristics of different identity types per se (or about the different outcomes those identity options might elicit), but only about the general characteristics of identity groups as groups, such as their size. There is no room for differential affect across identity types in these arguments, nor for a psychological pull that might be stronger under some identity types than others, nor for unique, non-material benefits that might accrue to group members under certain types of identity. One umbrella term works because political entrepreneurs can expect their support bases to pursue group-level advantages in the same way, regardless of whether contests occur in the name of their ethnicity, in the name of their religion, or in the name of any other social identity type. In other words, according to proponents of the broad definition of ethnicity, a group is simply a group. Differences between specific identity types within that conception of ethnicity are treated as a black box.

My aim is to get inside that black box, to understand whether specific types of identity elicit distinct preferences that can then be exploited differentially to serve precise political aims. The case for doing so – for treating ethnicity and religion as distinct political forces – hinges on whether there are theoretical grounds on which to expect behavior in the name of ethnicity to differ from behavior in the name of religion. To adopt an argument structure proposed by Helmke and Levitsky (2004) in reference to formal and informal institutions, if ethnic politics (EP) with ethnicity as its focus generates preferences similar to ethnic politics centered on religion, there would be no need to move beyond the umbrella definition of ethnic politics:

$$EP_E \; = \; EP_R = X$$

However, if political appeals to ethnicity and religion have distinct consequences for mass preferences and behaviors, a case for treating ethnic politics as distinct from religious politics is strengthened:

$$EP_E = X$$
$$EP_R = Y$$

In the latter case, relying on an umbrella understanding of ethnic politics has clear limits: it prohibits us from differentiating between ethnic politics (narrowly defined) and religious politics. Thus, for two reasons – both to overcome the semantic confusion surrounding "ethnicity" and to facilitate the substantive disaggregation of identity types and their effects, I refer to broad categories of "ethnicity" as *identity types*. They are the social categories that have potential political salience: religion, ethno-linguistic groups, race, language, caste, region, and so on; what Sacks (1992) would call *identity categories*, and what Posner (2005) refers to as *ethnic cleavages*. Within each identity type are any number of social *groups*: Christians, Muslims, Buddhists, Hindus, and Jews; Dioula, Fulani, and Yoruba; blacks and whites. I reserve the label of *ethnic* for the narrower conception, Africa's ethno-linguistic groups.

A fuller description of ethnic groups takes place in Chapter 2. In short, I use the term to refer to social groups whose members typically share a story of common descent, a language, and lifestyle norms (e.g., marriage and burial traditions). However, both in the construction of theory and in the empirical evidence that I gather, I leave it to the individual to determine the ethnic group to which he or she belongs and the boundaries of that group. Some may label themselves part of what are considered agglomerations of several clans or smaller ethnic groups; others may consider their ethnic group to be a subset of the larger ethno-linguistic grouping. For the purpose of this introductory chapter, I simply note the common identification of people in sub-Saharan Africa along ethnic lines, and the perceived importance of this identification for political issues. Hence, ethnicity counts as one of the handful of identity types along which political leaders in Africa can mobilize supporters, making Hutu, Yoruba, Dioula, and Kikuyu relevant in ways that, for example, tall, short, thin, and obese are not.

Evidence of ethnic identities being constructed or manipulated should not undermine the use of the narrow ethnic group as a politically relevant identity type in contemporary studies. Many, such as the Ashanti in present-day Ghana, the Zulu in present-day South Africa, and the Wolof in present-day Senegal, existed as well-organized kingdoms long before colonial intrusion, and the geographic and definitional boundaries of those groups have changed little over time. Furthermore, the fact that narrow ethnic groups have been combined, adjusted, and wholly invented should not be taken as an indication that contemporary Africans do not feel a deep-seated or innate attachment to their own narrow ethnic identity; many – and, judging by statistics from nationally representative surveys, most – actually do (see Afrobarometer Round 1, 2001). Even in cases where a particular ethnic group was the result of social construction in some time period $t = 1$, at a future time period $t = 2$ its members may nevertheless perceive of their own ethnic identity as deep-seated and blood born, a phenomenon Brubaker (2004: 38) refers to as "self-sameness over time." Thus, despite historical tinkering with what ethnic groups are and where their boundaries begin and end, it is impossible to overlook their relevance in contemporary political Africa.

The concept of religion also deserves mention at the outset. Broadly speaking, religion is the term for a cluster of beliefs, shared by a group of individuals, that includes a story of human origin, explanations for the unknown, and a set of behavioral guidelines for attaining a favorable personal outcome, such as salvation (Weber 1922; Zinnbauer 1997). In this book, I focus on the political role of world religions in Africa – that is, Islam and Christianity, which account for almost 90 percent of the region's inhabitants.[9] The principal alternative to these religions in the region is African traditional religion, which I incorporate for comparative purposes at times in the study but otherwise treat as a distinct type of identity, based on the relevant features of (world) religion that I elucidate in Chapter 2. As is the case in the context of ethnicity, it is not necessary that I make judgments about what is or is not a religious group or religious beliefs. Theologians may take issue, but to know the answers to those questions as they pertain to this study, I need only to rely on the self-categorizations and stated views of religious group members and believers. Finally, because the primary focus of this project is on the distinctions between ethnicity and religion that contribute to the broader frames of conflict as either "tribal" or "religious," I focus little on the particularities of specific ethnic or religious groups. Nevertheless, where these distinctions are empirically insightful or helpful in addressing alternative explanations for the findings I present, I share them.

ASSUMPTIONS

To argue that political entrepreneurs have the ability to manipulate individual-level preferences by prioritizing different identity types implies, first and foremost, that individuals have multiple social identities whose salience can vary. This is particularly true in cases of overlapping identity types, where one's ethnic identity tends to reveal his or her religious identity and vice versa. The assumption of malleable identity salience rests at the heart of this project.

That identities are flexible and context dependent is now a matter of convention among social scientists: Southall (1970) explains that one can choose to be a Luyia, a Kenyan, or an African, none of which existed as

[9] For religious data, see the World Christian Database (2016).

political labels before the late 1800s; Crawford Young calls identity "fluid and ... constantly in flux" (1976: 98); several others demonstrate how political conditions affect the salience of one identity type versus another (Chandra 2004; Eifert, Miguel, and Posner 2010; Laitin 1986). Yet it is important to note a complexity in the notion of malleable identities. Changing *across* identity types is a simple affair, explaining a reprioritization among a set of potential options (Brubaker 2004; Chandra 2006; Posner 2005). To take a simple example, one may be Catholic on Sunday, a political scientist on Monday, and Irish on St. Patrick's Day. Changing groups *within* one identity type is a different matter. To alter one's racial self-definition, for instance, may be exceedingly complicated, and so, in most cases, is changing ethnic groups (setting aside the social construction of new ethnic identities, which would typically affect individuals only over a generation or more). Changing groups within the identity of religion can be quite easy as a de jure matter – requiring little more than a personal attestation – but potentially quite difficult in the face of social constraints. Regional, national, and political party identities can be altered fairly straightforwardly (though perhaps not without expense), whereas identities within certain types of physical characteristics (height, eye color) cannot.

My argument applies to changes *across* identity types. The set of choices is potentially innumerable – as the psychologist William James wrote in the late nineteenth century, a person "has as many different social selves as there are distinct groups of people about whose opinion he cares" (1890 [1950]: 294). Practically speaking, however, the list is constrained to a handful of identity types that inspire collective action. Horowitz limits that list to five factors: race, religion, caste, ethnolinguistic group, and region. Critical, of course, to the potential salience of any identity type is the presence of an "other." As social identity theorists have noted, social recognition of one's own group is determined with reference to specific other groups (Tajfel and Turner 1986: 16), such that, for example, being of the Yoruba ethnicity in Nigeria has meaning only with knowledge of the existence of Hausa, Igbo, or other ethnic groups. In this study, I am particularly interested in changes that enhance ethnic or religious salience, from whatever baseline individuals begin.

Coupled with the notion of malleable identities are some propositions regarding human behavior. Individuals seek utility in both material and non-material forms, from formal and informal sources; they desire resources from the state, but they are also pulled by concerns over self-worth, lifestyle, kin, and their place in the world. To overlook those sources of utility is to ignore, for example, the sociopolitical importance of bloodlines, ancestors, and traditional chiefs and to discount the widespread practice of self-flagellation among some Shiite Muslims in the Arab world and Opus Dei Catholics in the United States, the asceticism that some Buddhists believe alleviates suffering, and the practice of tithing among some Christian traditions that is repaid only in an afterlife. Attachments to ethnic and religious identities, in short, alter utility functions by introducing important non-material interests. Our theories might more accurately describe collective human behavior, then, if we find ways to incorporate these interests as a function of different identity contexts.

My argument is not in contradiction to the rational, instrumentalist logic that underpins many contemporary studies of political behavior. Those arguments explain political choices as efforts to maximize individual utility, given a set of exogenous, fixed preferences. The maximization of individual utility is also the centerpiece of political behavior in my argument, only with two caveats. First, I test empirically what those preferences actually are, in ethnic versus religious contexts. Demonstrating that ethnicity and religion evoke different sets of preferred actions underscores the consequences of mobilizing groups along different identity lines. Thus, whereas the extant constructivist literature has shown convincingly that identities can change, the contribution of this study is to explain how that matters. Second, I make room in the theory for those non-material benefits that can accrue differently under the guises of ethnicity and religion, in the form of righteousness, salvation, honor, blood ties, and so on. In this sense, I am adding an additional motivating factor to studies of ethnic politics that rely only on group size as the explanation for competition over resources.

The argument requires additional assumptions about political entrepreneurs and their incentives. First, political entrepreneurs may be formal office holders or opposition figures, but they need not be: in Rwanda, the voices of the Milles Collines radio program who instigated violence, as well as the Hutu military leaders who organized that violence, may be considered political leaders. In the ongoing war against terrorists, actors such as Osama bin Laden and the leadership of groups such as Boko Haram, the self-proclaimed Islamic State, and Al Qaeda in the Islamic Maghreb would certainly qualify as political entrepreneurs, despite the fact that their efforts to mobilize collective action do not occur through formal political channels. I assume that the broad goal of political entrepreneurs is to gain and maintain political power and that their calculations are purely instrumental in pursuit of this broad goal. In other words, political entrepreneurs are not subject to the same non-material, psychological incentives that can motivate the masses. Finally, I assume that political entrepreneurs are knowledgeable about the incentives and preferences of individuals. Whether that knowledge results from a rational choice assumption of perfect information or a process of successful learning, it is this assumption that allows elites to exploit the community-wide salience of identity types in pursuit of their own favored outcomes when institutions break down and conflict reigns.

Given these assumptions, we might expect the strategic calculus of a political entrepreneur to incorporate the following concerns. First, what do ethnicity, religion, race, or other identity types mean to individuals? By asking this question, the political entrepreneur begins an exploration of the preferences that mobilizing one identity type over another might elicit among followers. Second, what are the political entrepreneur's own political interests? Does she see an opportunity to take the reins of political power, or the potential for wealth accumulation by seizing territory? Would her standing improve if social policies could be changed, or might she benefit from increased international attention on her supporters? This question, coupled with the preferences that different identities elicit, forms the basis of political choice. Third, what identity types are plausible sources of cleavage in the region, and might any of several identity types be exploited? Do those identity types overlap, leaving the political entrepreneur with the same support bases irrespective of the identity card she plays? Finally, given individual-level preferences in different contexts, the entrepreneur's own political interests, and the opportunity to manipulate the frame of ongoing tensions, what tactics might leadership employ to ensure that followers act collectively? The goal would be to mobilize supporters to act in committed defense of their identity group, in such a way that their support strengthens the political entrepreneur's own probability of political success. These questions serve as the foundation for specific hypotheses presented later in the book.

By drawing together the utility calculations of both elites and masses, this study follows Kalyvas (2006) in problematizing a relationship for which one side is often assumed away. Studies that demonstrate why rebels engage in conflict or why communities support a violent movement teach us much about mass interests (see Weinstein 2007). Likewise, scholarship that explores why leaders take their troops to battle or refrain from doing so reveals important lessons about elite decision-making (Huth 1988). The subject of this study – why conflicts become ethnic or religious – differs in the sense that the story can be completed only by considering the interests of both elites and masses, as well as the inter-actions between them. Doing so complicates the argument, but also creates an opportunity to explain cases in which coalition size alone yields no apparent political advantage.

It would be naïve, of course, to suggest that the size of support coali-tions does not matter in the course of conflict. Certainly, such a calcula-tion is the first consideration of both instrumental elites and their rational supporters, and, consistent with my argument, it may well be the motiv-ation for political leaders to mobilize the identity groups that they do. But what motivates the entrepreneur's mobilization decision when the identity groups to which she might appeal are not of clearly different sizes? Understanding the behavioral differences that identity types elicit allows me to construct an answer to that question. Ethnic attachments to land and religious attachments to geographically unbounded rules may work in tandem with size advantages where ethnicity and religion offer different-sized coalitions. Where the same cast of supporters constitutes a leader's ethnic coalition and her religious coalition, however, an argu-ment rooted solely in group size is ill-equipped to explain why one or the other becomes the focus of conflict. An argument rooted in the mobiliza-tional differences of ethnicity and religion is equipped to explain both circumstances.

The same logic could be applied beyond the context of conflict, to vote shares or the provision of public goods, for example. The study is par-ticularly well suited, however, to explain choices that elites face in conflict settings, outside formal political channels. In these contexts, formal insti-tutions break down and create an open space with exceedingly high stakes. To apply the concept of mobilizational differences in these settings is thus to wrestle with perhaps the paramount concern of inter-group competition: why individuals in certain situations are exceedingly devoted to their identity groups, and why the result is often the most profound, violent type of inter-group discord.

My approach represents a departure from the "group is a group" study of ethnic politics and may thus be met with skepticism by some readers. Five objections may be raised. The first is that one cannot construct systematic theories of social science on a foundation of impos-sible-to-measure, non-material preferences associated with different identity types. Not only are those attachments too arbitrary and amorph-ous to explain the aggregate behavior of groups in any meaningful way, the objection would go, but they also matter little for the choices that people make in sociopolitical settings, where material and power incentives rule. But this concern should not dissuade us from exploration. It is an empirical question, after all, as to whether or not systematic differences exist in the preferences evoked by ethnicity, religion, or any other identity type. Those differences may complicate our theoretical understanding of ethnic politics, but they do not adulterate it; on the contrary, if differences across identity types exist, our theories will be stronger to the extent that we find ways to incorporate those differences. Several scholars have made efforts to do so: Crawford Young (1976) notes that, in addition to being a social identity, religion uniquely offers a world view. David Laitin (2000) shows that religious groups differ from language groups in that they have shorter transition periods. Grim and Finke (2007: 653) explicitly state that "we need to recognize that religion and ethnicity are separate concepts." How these and other evaluations matter for our understanding of conflict in Africa requires further exploration, which is the goal of this project.

According to the second objection, my argument essentializes ethnicity and religion, imposing fixed characteristics, and thus perhaps outcomes, to a changing world. There is far too much evidence of religion associated with both violence and peace – think of the use of Buddhism as a tool for conflict in Myanmar and healing in Cambodia, for example – and the same could be said for ethnic group labels. Imposing distinctions would thus represent a reversion to primordialist thinking. In this book, I take pains to stress that the elements of distinction may change over time and place, but in a given political context, some ethnic and religious norms must persist, on average, so that it makes sense to speak of Punjab as distinct from Hindu, or Roman as distinct from Catholic. For Laitin (2000), it is the transition period; in this argument, it is a foundation of land versus a foundation of rules. These features, I argue, shape human behavior and preferences in predictable ways in given contexts; the differential outcomes we see are then explained by the political exploitation of ethnic groups and religion for instrumental purposes.

Quite apart from concerns of essentialism, a third potential objection is that my argument fails to account for clear historical patterns that make *certain* religious or ethnic groups more prone to conflict and violence. In other words, I may not be essentializing enough when it comes to distinctions between particular religious and ethnic groups. In the last several years, acts of terrorism perpetuated by radical groups in the name of Islam have for some observers distinguished Islam per se from other world religions (Bar 2004). Similarly, ethnic groups such as the Lobi of Burkina Faso and the Zulu of South Africa are often labeled "warrior tribes" (Mazrui 1975), having developed violent defenses against marauding neighbor groups. In this project, I do not deny that different behavioral patterns exist among specific ethnic and religious groups, but I raise two arguments in defense of tabling those distinctions in favor of the meta distinctions between ethnicity and religion. First, it is well documented that the norms, behavioral patterns, and even specific teachings of religions and ethnic groups vary over time and place. Islam has undergone substantial changes over time and across regions (Zubaida 1993), and Crusades supported by the Catholic hierarchy during the eleventh century are not in keeping with the teachings of Catholicism today (O'Brien 1994, chapter 17). So I do not wish to stamp any particular ethnic group or religion with present-day perceptions or exigencies. Second, despite those changes in what it means to be Muslim, Catholic, Lobi, or Zulu, I argue that some basic commonalities can be used to describe ethnic groups and world religions in Africa, the former rooted in perceived inheritances of land and the latter in sets of geographically unbounded moral guidelines. Incorporating this claim into the way we frame conflict will represent a contribution to the social science literature, so I constrain the focus of this research agenda to the broader distinction.

Fourth, some may object to my argument on the grounds that its empirical outcomes cannot be distinguished from those of more straightforward explanations relying solely on the relative size of groups. In Rwanda, the Hutus may have been prompted to consider their attachments to land, but they were also a larger group desiring the reins of political power. Thus calculations in coalition size can sometimes explain much of the story. While this is true, an argument that recognizes identity-specific preferences may be in closer keeping with actual human behavior. Furthermore, what political elites desire is sometimes not a neat political calculation of head counts but an opportunity to mobilize supporters collectively during conflict, particularly when group sizes do not provide a clear advantage. My argument accounts for how that can happen.

Finally, some readers will note that this study entails little close analysis of the formal institutions of the state, which typically occupy a central place in political studies. That choice is by design, given the objective of explaining the role of ethnicity and religion in conflict settings. Conflict implies by necessity at least some degree of institutional breakdown, along with the opportunity for political outsiders to counter the state's monopoly on violence (see Blattman and Miguel 2010); as such, a focus on sides in conflict rather than on formal institutions should prove fruitful. Furthermore, ethnic and religious groups constitute key *informal* political institutions that shape outcomes in ways often as important as the more formal rules of politics (Helmke and Levitsky 2004). Finally, the concept of conflict frames has most relevance to the elites who mobilize and the masses who follow. Those actors may or may not function within the constraints of formal political institutions, but their interactions are nevertheless a matter of central political importance.

METHODS AND RESEARCH

I use two principal methods in the construction of my argument. First, to explain the preferences of individuals in a systematic manner, I rely on a randomized experiment conducted in the field. Druckman et al. (2011) note that experiments constitute an improvement over observational data due to the exogenous variation – which is both randomly assigned and clearly understood – in the explanatory variable of interest (in this case, the subject's primary identity: religion or ethnicity). More important, because essentially all individuals in Africa have both ethnic and religious identities, I had little choice but to employ experimental techniques to tease out the effects of each. Observational studies could control for specific ethnic and religious group membership and for degrees of commitment to each, but they would provide little leverage in distinguishing between behaviors based on ethnic commitments and those based on religious commitments. In particular, I am interested in testing the effects of ethnic and religious contexts on the political preferences that individual Africans hold. To do that, I administered ethnic and religious treatments and measured their effects (against each other and a control group) among hundreds of participants, most often in their homes. This is admittedly messier than a laboratory experiment would be. The advantage, however, as Gerber and Green (2000) argue, is that experiments conducted in naturalistic settings actually tell us something about causal relationships in the real world. For this reason, a growing list of studies rely on experiments conducted in the field, particularly in Africa (Blattman and Annan 2016; Dunning and Harrison 2010; Habyarimana et al. 2007; McCauley 2014; McClendon 2014; Michelitch 2015; Wantchekon 2003). Experiments often can tell only half the story – about an effect, not necessarily the mechanism explaining why that effect occurs – but they still take us much closer to the production of clear causal inferences that rests at the heart of scientific exploration.

Second, to understand the complex dynamics that shape conflict as ethnic in some circumstances and religious in others, I rely on recent historical case studies of conflict in the African region. There are things that case studies will never be able to tell us, such as the proportion of variance across cases that is explained by the included set of variables. But there are also important sociopolitical questions that can be answered only by tracing processes closely in a handful of cases. One reason is the complex causal progression that leads to the frame of conflict as either ethnic or religious; it unites different levels of analysis and evolves in sometimes obtuse ways as political incentives shift. In this study's cases, I take pains to demonstrate the predominant frame of conflicts through their actors, targets, rhetoric, and reporting, while also explaining why those frames emerged. That such steps are required, and that the answers I present may still be subject to debate, is an indication of the complexity of the research question. To rely on brute classifications of variables and outcomes in order to force the relatively small set of cases into a quantitative model may thus do more harm than good with respect to finding empirical answers.

Field research for the study was conducted in the West African states of Côte d'Ivoire and Ghana, with additional interviews and archival work in Nigeria. The testing of individual-level political preferences in ethnolinguistic versus religious contexts could, of course, be done almost anywhere in the world. Why here, in Côte d'Ivoire and Ghana? The book project began as an effort to understand why religion became a caustic divider during the Ivoirian conflict, despite the fact that the conflict itself had nothing to do with religion. I explain the conflict in Côte d'Ivoire more fully in Chapter 6, but a brief description here will provide helpful context for the chapters that follow. Ethnic and religious divisions had been kept largely at bay in Côte d'Ivoire through decades of economic growth and redistribution, but that all changed in the mid-1990s: with resources becoming increasingly scarce and a presidential race looming, leaders of the incumbent, southern-based political party introduced a policy known as *Ivoirité*, or Ivoirianness, which created advantages for those perceived as pure or native Ivoirians, at the expense of those who immigrated later – and who also happened to be largely Muslim and of northern ethnicities such as the Senoufo and Malinké. Overt ethno-national discrimination followed, limiting rights and opportunities for those perceived as not pure Ivoirians. When a northern presidential candidate – the current president eventually installed in 2011, Alassane Ouattara – was excluded from running and discrimination seeped into the military, a rebellion coupled with widespread popular backlash divided the country into north and south, and the decade-long conflict was under way. The puzzle came in the shift from ethno-national divisions to a religious frame: while no substantive religious concerns were ever presented as a source of dispute, the targets, actors, rhetoric, and reporting soon focused on Christian–Muslim differences. As observers note, "a high level of religious violence" ensued (Vüllers 2011: 19). The goal of the research, then, is to understand that puzzle and others like it across Africa, where ethnic and religious conflict frames emerge and change, despite the conflicts themselves not being about ethnicity or religion per se.

Ghana offers an appropriate alternative context from which to gather individual-level data. First, Ghanaians are equally committed to their ethnic and religious identities. Second, as I demonstrate in Chapter 3, both countries have predominantly Muslim populations in the north and predominantly Christian populations in the south, as well as ethnic divisions that follow similar lines. By basing the empirical study of individual preferences along this divide, I put myself in a position to vary the ethnic and religious contexts within each country. Most important, the national political contexts differ significantly: whereas Côte d'Ivoire suffered through a decade of recent conflict, Ghana stands out as one of the region's few peaceful and stable democracies. Missing from Ghana is the institutional breakdown and widespread violence that led to identity exploitation in neighboring Côte d'Ivoire.

In short, the study design allows me to account for alternative explanations. Had the data for this project been collected only in a Muslim area, for example, the findings would be subject to the criticism that what I am labeling a "religious effect" is really just a "Muslim effect." Had they been collected only in an Akan ethnic region, they could be construed as an "Akan effect" rather than an "ethnic effect." And had I limited the research to Côte d'Ivoire, the effects of ethnicity and religion on individual preferences could be lost in the claim that Côte d'Ivoire is simply peculiar because of the conflict. Instead, using a multi-religious, multi-ethnic, and multi-national study design, I am able to distinguish the effects of ethnicity and religion per se from the effects of the conflict in Côte d'Ivoire. I then leverage the case of Côte d'Ivoire later in the book to provide evidence of the interplay between ethnic and religious preferences and elite mobilization tactics. Other cases from Sudan's protracted civil wars and Nigeria's Biafran War reinforce my claim that patterns in ethnic and religious conflict frames – even within the same conflict, and even when the cast of supporters remains constant – can be explained systematically.

PLAN OF THE BOOK

The book comprises two main parts. Part I (Chapters 1–4) is devoted to distinguishing between ethnicity and religion, insofar as they shape individual-level behaviors and preferences. In Chapter 2, I develop the first theoretical component of the argument. I begin by describing communities in Africa to elucidate features of ethno-linguistic versus religious identities in the region, and I then present a model to link these features to the utility functions of individuals in either ethnic or religious contexts. Chapter 3 presents findings from the experiment conducted in Côte d'Ivoire and Ghana in which I randomly and artificially evoked either the ethnic or the religious identity among subjects and then evaluated their political preferences. The data suggest distinct preferences in ethnic and religious contexts, which I link to the land-based nature of ethnic groups and the rule-based nature of religion in the region. In Chapter 4, I explore the implications and the external validity of the experiment, using "real-world" data drawn from followers of an Ashanti ethnic group association, a Charismatic-Pentecostal Christian group, and a *Wahhabi* Muslim group, as well as from bi-ethnics.

In Part II (Chapters 5–8), I construct an explanation for how those differences in identity types are exploited by political leaders, thus shaping African conflicts as either religious or ethnic. Chapter 5 develops the second theoretical component of the argument. Given that ethnicity and religion generate different preferred actions, how do elites make use of that information to serve political ends during conflict? Those choices, I will show, are strategic ones that build on the preferences that ethnicity and religion inspire. In Chapter 6, I explain how the argument fits the recent, decade-long conflict in Côte d'Ivoire. I begin the chapter by explaining the incentives of elites following a power vacuum that emerged in the 1990s, and I document how, as those incentives changed, the actors, targets, rhetoric, and reporting of the conflict shifted from ethnic to religious. Chapters 7 and 8 trace similar processes in the civil wars in Sudan and in Nigeria's Biafran War.

Chapter 9 is the concluding chapter in which I consider the implications of the argument for how we might understand two other cases of conflict with ethnic or religious frames: the Rwandan genocide and the ongoing Boko Haram Islamic insurgency in Northern Nigeria. The chapter also considers the practical consequences of conflict frames, including the possibility that frames can alter the duration and intensity of conflict, and it explores what the study of "ethnic politics" gains by incorporating a recognition of mobilizational differences between identity types.

2

A Theory of Mobilizational Differences in Identity Types

In this chapter, I develop a theory to account for mobilizational differences across identity types.[1] I ask, why should we expect the preferences of individuals to change systematically in different identity contexts? Why might someone who emerges from a mosque, church, synagogue, or temple view the world in a fundamentally different way than she does when seated at the feet of a tribal elder or in an ethnic association meeting? What explains this variation, independent of any political manipulation? Answering that question constitutes the first step in understanding how political entrepreneurs mobilize supporters in different ways pursuant to precise political aims. To develop this account of ethnic versus religious preferences, I divide the chapter into four parts.

First, I explore the foundations of ethno-linguistic groups in the region and highlight the central features that characterize (narrow) ethnicity as a land-based identity in Africa. Second, I undertake the same process for world religions in the study area. Painting with admittedly broad strokes, I examine the historical foundations of Islam and Christianity in Africa and underscore the key elements that make religion a landless, rule-based identity in the region. Third, I develop a model for individual-level preferences that takes into account the identity context in which people operate. Increasingly, social scientists are recognizing the role of micro-level and psychological motivations for broader political outcomes (see, e.g., Blattman 2009; Sambanis and Shayo 2013; Smelser 2007); here, I build on the foundations of ethnicity and religion to explain how preferences are

---

[1] This account builds on the theory advanced in McCauley (2014).

27

molded by those identity types in systematically different ways. Finally, I present hypotheses that should explain the individual-level preferences that emerge in ethnic versus religious contexts in contemporary Africa.

ETHNIC GROUPS IN AFRICA

Studies frequently take narrow ethnicity, ethno-linguistic differences, and ethnic diversity not only as central to African politics but also as responsible for many of Africa's political shortcomings. To cite just a few, Easterly and Levine's (1997) seminal study of Africa's long economic tragedy puts ethnic diversity at the center of those ills; Horowitz (1985) argues that ethnically divided societies are prone to conflict since those ethnic groups look inward with entitlement and outward with suspicion; and Diamond (1988) suggests that the ethnic foundations of patronage politics have contributed to undermining the process of democratization. What is more, journalists and other observers often embrace the ethnic story as the principal story describing Africa, a "tribal" continent where politics and society are dictated by ethnic attachments (see, e.g., *Economist* 2012). Finally, citizens themselves, in response to nationally representative survey questions regarding self-identification, regularly place "tribe or language" atop the list of identity options (with religion not far behind).[2] Ethnic identity is indeed ubiquitous among Africans, and classifications of ethnicity include more than 2,000 distinct groups (Blench 2006), ranging in size from the very small (the Hadza of Tanzania, for example, who number around 1,000) to the very large – the Igbo of Nigeria, for instance, who number up to 30 million (MacEachern 2000). It is all but impossible, furthermore, to be African and not acknowledge membership in one ethnic group or another: Harden (1990: chapter 3) recounts the incredulity from all sides that a young man testifying at his father's burial dispute endured in claiming to be "only Kenyan" with no attachment to an ethnic group. To demonstrate that individuals are mobilized differently depending on the identity context, then, I want to begin with what is popularly construed as the defining social cleavage in African politics.

Historically, the presence of distinct ethnic groups in Africa emerged through longstanding community and kinship networks, as well as social-psychological reconstructions of those networks. Though some research

---

[2] This claim is based on a comparison of responses to the question, "What group do you identify with first and foremost?", asked on Rounds 1 and 2 of the Afrobarometer Public Opinion Surveys. www.afrobarometer.org/data.

prioritizes genetic sequencing as a biological method for deciphering the processes of ethnic group formation in Africa (see, e.g., Bosch et al. 2000), much in the history of African ethnicities is not captured genetically. On the other hand, a fair appraisal would also not suggest that ethnicities are purely constructed concepts created from a tabula rasa during the colonial era (Mafeje 1971). A more appropriate historical interpretation lies somewhere in between: groups that developed distinct languages and ancestral lines occupied social spaces but also interacted across those spaces for purposes of economic exchange as well as territory and resource extraction. The more powerful and efficient among them, typically organized as kingdoms or chiefdoms, claimed authority over territory and often taxed the more acephalous groups by demanding tributes or slaves (Cohen and Middleton 1971). Ultimately, the stronger *sociétés englobantes* took over the weaker *sociétés englobées*, such that, in the pre-colonial period, well-established kingdoms as well as subgroups within those kingdoms existed (Amselle 1985). In other cases, smaller, acephalous groups had reason to unite of their own accord, and local slave raiding and trade ties created still more layers of complex social group membership ostensibly related to lineage. Languages and local customs were markers of membership in both broad groups and their subgroups, explaining the nested nature of what are frequently referred to as subtribes, tribes, and language groups (and the extreme difference in the sizes of ethnic groups) in Africa today.

During the colonial period, often for reasons of political expediency, kingdoms and subgroups were reified, further combined, or divided. The goal of colonial powers in doing so was typically to facilitate the creation of administrative boundaries and to establish a local political hierarchy with which to work: examples include the favoring of the Tutsi as a chosen elite in Rwanda (Prunier 1995) and the agglomeration of smaller groups into the Tonga in Zambia (Posner 2005). Use of the term "tribe," which both described the identity type and carried a connotation of primitiveness and exoticism, became commonplace (Southall 1970).

This brief history of ethnic identity formation in Africa suggests that ethnicity has both quasi-biological roots and psychological elements based on social constructivism. As Chandra (2006) notes, however, it is the *myth* of an ethnic identity – its perceived history among members and the narrative of a consistent legacy – that underpins identity in contemporary sociopolitics. In this light, the ethnic groups that exist today may *feel* very real and historically entrenched to their members; recall Brubaker's (2004) description of constructed identities as generating "self-sameness over time," or what Fearon and Laitin (2000a: 848) describe as the fallacy of "everyday primordialism." The narrative that persists in this case is typically one linking families and their land to chiefs, kingdoms, and ancestors before them. Ethnicity thus appears to have a unique foundation in African politics, replete with the distinct features that I outline below: common descent, social norms, and local land ties.

First, ethnicity is not experienced as a voluntary identity type; its narrative is instead one of common descent. During an interview I conducted with a local Dida chief in southern Côte d'Ivoire, he explained the meaning of his ethnicity by repeatedly gesturing to the veins in his arms, indicating that his blood was "Dida blood." Early anthropological analyses of African culture followed cues like this one, relying on language differentiation, the inheritance of physical features, and the obligation to pay "blood wealth" as markers distinguishing social groups as distinct ethnicities (Evans-Pritchard 1940). Contemporary scholarship less frequently cites physical markers or social obligations but nevertheless distinguishes ethnic groups on the basis of perceived lineage and common descent (Chandra 2006; Laitin 1998). As Fearon and Laitin suggest (2000b), when it comes to one's narrow ethnic group, you are what your parents are, end of story. The implication is that, to the individual, ethnic identity is not a matter of choice. A social identity type based in this way on common descent, and lacking the possibility to voluntarily convert, might understandably generate baselines for behavior distinct from those that emerge in more voluntary contexts.

Second, the ethnic identity is perpetuated through systems of social norms, rather than formal doctrine. Without question, those norms in some cases maintain the force of law: when Jacob Zuma fathered a child out of wedlock in 2009, Zulu custom mandated that he pay a financial penalty to the family of the child's mother, an obligation that even he, as President of South Africa, could hardly circumvent (*Telegraph* 2010). Absent from social norms such as this one, however, is the raison d'être beyond the maintenance of a well-functioning community. These norms may persist as means for sanctioning behaviors that potentially undermine the community, but they do not serve broader goals, such as salvation. Furthermore, to stray from the ethnic group's established social norms is not to stray from the ethnic group itself: a Kusasi farmer who tills his field using an Akan-style hoe is only a local oddity; he is not an Akan. Ethnic group members thus face little in the way of sine qua non as it relates to behaviors constituting membership in the group. Instead, norms develop between chiefs and communities, and between community members over time, to regulate a number of social dilemmas, among them death (Goody 1962), inheritance (Cohen 2013), and the land that ostensibly corresponds to one's ethnic blood (Njoh 2006).

Finally, following from settlement patterns over time and those social norms governing land rights is the fact that ethnic identity in Africa is closely related to geographic territory.[3] Colonial powers placed administrative trust in ethnic groups for precisely this reason, leading scholars of the time to define "tribes" as cultural groups with "political unity, speech uniformity, and *geographical continuity*" (Wissler 1923, emphasis added). Geographic areas, native villages, and traditional city-states are thus synonymous with ethnic identities for many groups (Laitin 1986; Staniland 1975). Contemporary instrumentalists also acknowledge the importance of geography to the ethnic identity; Bates (1974: 464), for example, suggests that it is the "clustering in space" that explains the salience of ethnicity in politics, as physical proximity to the resources of power and modernity generates winners and losers. Historically, chiefs, headmen, and land priests in the traditional hierarchy have overseen the distribution of land for farming, creating a quasi-official link between ethnicity and land (Lawry 1990). As national governments become increasingly involved in the oversight of land ownership and use rights, co-management strategies with traditional ethnic leadership are often prioritized (Adams et al. 1999; Lawry 1990), and governments in some cases cede their control to traditional chiefs (Baldwin 2014), a further sign of ethnic group identification with local lands. Boone (2014) argues, in fact, that local land tenure regimes produce and reinforce ethnic identities.

The narratives of common descent, norms rather than doctrine, and inherent ties to land form the foundation for a social identity that can be described in shorthand as a land-based identity.

RELIGION IN AFRICA

The history of world religions in Africa – Christianity and Islam – highlights two important trends: one of an exogenous, imposed identity in the region and one of relatively recent sociopolitical influence.

---

[3] African diaspora communities emigrate but sustain an identity with the land and group they left. That some pastoralist ethnic groups in the region – the Tuareg and Fulani, for example – are labeled nomadic or semi-nomadic only reinforces the narrative of ethnicity as an identity type tied to the land; these groups are viewed as exceptional in reference to their own itinerant relationship with the land.

Christianity's spread through the region occurred in four distinct phases. Owing to a lifestyle reliant on farming, water, and slaves, the early Christian Coptics and Abyssinians (in Egypt and Ethiopia) were ill-suited to carry their religious beliefs and lifestyle across difficult terrain, and Christianity made little progress in Africa for centuries. Then, in the fifteenth century, Portuguese slave ships circumvented the terrain of Northern Africa to deliver Catholic priests to the west and south of Africa during missions to accumulate gold and slaves. Despite the 1534 establishment of a diocese in São Tomé that included much of West and Central Africa, however, Christianity in the region was generally limited to small coastal and southern enclaves – a fort in Elmina, Ghana, and a foothold in the converted Chief Mani Soyo's coastal territory of central Kongo, for example (Hastings 1994). The third and most influential phase of Christianity in Africa occurred alongside colonization in the nineteenth century. In fact, the initiative to open up the interior of Africa (to Europeans) came not from colonial administrators but from Christian missionaries, who relied on local catechists, imported Caribbean Christians eager to Christianize Africa, and traditional African chiefs who accepted the prestige of international relations in exchange for allowing religious freedom among their subjects (Groves 1954). Colonial trading companies helped to advance the combination of "commerce, Christianity, and civilization" to replace African institutions and to raise standards of living (Livingston 1868), and by 1970, a religion practiced by just 9 percent of the population in 1900 was accepted by 40 percent of Africans.[4] Christianity's fourth phase has been driven by the Pentecostal Christian renewalist movement, which has fused spirit-based healing with American-style evangelism, particularly in the former British colonies (Gifford 1994). Today, approximately 47 percent of Africans label themselves Christian (World Christian Database 2016).

Islam was itself established over three phases in Africa. Its introduction to sub-Saharan Africa was gradual and peaceful: Lydon (2009) describes Arab and Berber traders as able to succeed where Coptic Christians had failed, carrying Islam south on the backs of camels during caravans to long-distance trade outposts.[5] By the ninth century, those traders had passed Islam on to the Soninke of the Sahelian region (just south of the Sahara), who in turned passed it along to Dioula traders of southern West

---

[4] Data from the World Christian Database. www.worldchristiandatabase.org/wcd/.
[5] Those camels were constrained from traveling further south by the prevalence of tsetse flies, which carry a disease harmful to both humans and draft animals, in the Gulf Coast region (see Fukuyama 2011).

Africa (Levtizon 1994: 208).[6] The success of early Islam in Africa was a function of both its adaptability and its scholarship. Traditional chiefs maintained identities distinct from Islam but were nevertheless often won over by a system that provided access to goods from afar. Prayer, rather than dedication to Qur'anic verse, became the key manifestation of Islam among sub-Saharan African practitioners (Levtzion 1994: 214), and local customs were often blended with their new religion to form what some scholars refer to as African Islam (Soares and Otayek 2007), or *Islam Noir* (Monteil 1964). Yet Islam in Africa maintained what Levtzion (1994: 333) describes as a "fixed, stable core, engraved into the rock of doctrinal legal literature," which reduced many of the parochial aspects of Islam and established a new form of identity in the region.

The second phase of Islam in Africa prioritized the fixed, stable core of doctrine, beginning with the nineteenth-century *jihads* across the northern stretch of sub-Saharan Africa. Those offensives – orchestrated not by outsiders but by African ruralists who viewed the elite, urban leadership as complacent in their religious practice, too cozy with European traders, and unwilling to sacrifice decadence – ended the peaceful, adaptive process of Islamization that had gone on for nearly 1,000 years (Trimingham 1970). Famously, Usman dan Fodio would orchestrate a self-proclaimed jihad against the Muslim *uluma* of northern Nigeria, transforming the region into a Hausa–Fulani Islamic caliphate (Trimingham 1970). Across the French-colonized regions, Samory Touré carried out jihads to break emerging ties between colonial authorities, traditional leaders, and "status quo" Muslim elites (Kane and Triaud 1998). These revolutions moved Islam from the periphery to the center of sociopolitics in the region and generated a disruption in local Islamic practice that would favor the rigid legality of Islamic law over its previous adaptability. The most recent phase of Muslim change in the region is marked by a new form of internal tension: indigenous Africans who pray in Arabic and follow widespread Islamic norms for dress and behavior consider their own practice to be a "pure" form of Islam, yet foreign-born or -influenced *Arabistes* advocate for a continued separation from traditional norms (Brégand 2007).[7]

---

[6] The relationship between trade and Islam in the region was symbiotic: just as ancient trade routes opened new communities to Islam from the North, Islam provided the written word and legal institutions that would allow long-distance trade to flourish.

[7] The tensions do not follow Muslim subgroup lines: the vast majority of both camps are Sunni, although Sufism is a more common form of Sunni Islam among the indigenous. Saudi Arabian and Libyan Muslims are particularly active in supporting "missionary" projects in sub-Saharan Africa (see Hunwick 1996).

Those tensions have informed the strategies of violent Muslim extremist groups, some now with indigenous African leadership, discussed in the Chapter 9. In either case, Islam in Africa has since its early spread achieved greater distance from – not congruence with – traditional, local customs.

Other world religions have left historical, social, and economic marks on the region. Jews maintained a widespread presence in the West African trade markets as late as the nineteenth century, typically partnering with Muslim traders and investing in trade caravans but also establishing oases as far south as Timbuktu in present-day Mali and in the Ghana kingdom (Lydon 2009). Beta Israel Jews historically populated Ethiopia prior to emigration to Israel (Kessler 1982), and communities of Jews – both Ashkenazic immigrants and those claiming Hebrew descent – populate southern Africa (Beinart 1996). Indian laborers of the British colonial era brought Hinduism to East and Southern Africa, where communities continue to thrive (Vertovec 2000), and converts to the Baha'i faith and Buddhism are found in small numbers across the continent. Yet the impact of Islam and Christianity has been vastly superior to that of other world religions in the region, both in terms of sheer numbers and with respect to their sociopolitical importance. Today, approximately 90 percent of Africans list themselves as either Muslim or Christian,[8] and where inter-religious conflict has emerged in Africa, it has almost invariably occurred along Christian–Muslim lines. The character of world religious identity in Africa stems unquestionably from these two sources.

These histories of religion in Africa explain the emergence of features that can quite understandably be associated with religious membership in the region but that are ill-suited as descriptions of other identity types such as the narrow ethnic group. I highlight three such features whose social and psychological effects are critical, I argue, in shaping preferences in the name of religion as distinct from preferences in the name of ethnicity or other identity types.

First, religion in Africa is a voluntary, not purely ascriptive, identity.[9] Notwithstanding the threat of social sanctioning and the supply of

---

[8] The proportions are approximately 47 percent Christian and 45 percent Muslim. See World Christian Database, www.worldchristiandatabase.org/wcd/.

[9] Chandra (2006) argues that religion is in some cases "ethnic" and in some not, depending on whether the identity is passed down through family or adopted via conversion. I acknowledge this complexity in the social nature of religion and recognize that it may vary by family or individual.

religious places of worship that can constrain practical choices among religious group options, one can in theory belong to any religion and adopt its system of beliefs. Furthermore, changing from one confessional religion to another in Africa can be done with relative facility, owing to the fact that conversion is in many instances achieved on no more than personal profession and minimal doctrinal education (Rambo 1993).[10] One participant in my field research labeled herself a Mormon "as of this month," explaining that she had taken a liking to Mormon missionaries, invited them back a few times, and was baptized and converted. Even language groups, setting aside the kinship elements of ethnicity, are much different: they require time and effort to transition, generating different strategic concerns for elites interested in mobilizing support along language versus religious lines (Laitin 2000). Voluntary membership is particularly characteristic of religion in most communities of sub-Saharan Africa, where competition for new members continues to reshape local religious composition and where new branches of Islam and particularly Christianity emerge regularly.[11] In the dataset that I introduce in Chapter 3, fully 25 percent of respondents reported changing their religious group since birth – in some cases from traditional African religion to Islam or Christianity, in other cases from one branch or denomination to another within Islam or Christianity, and in a smaller but not insignificant number of cases between Islam and Christianity, a choice made frequently enough to explain the existence of groups such as the Christian Association of former Muslims in Ghana (Gifford 2004). Yet this process of religious "churning" (Putnam and Campbell 2010) is not unique to Africa but suggestive of the general nature of membership in religious groups; recent studies in the United States suggest that as much as 30 percent of Americans have also changed their religious group since birth (Putnam and Campbell 2010). Voluntary identity types provide members with at least the perception that their membership in any particular group is an individual choice. With choice comes an implied process of ranking based on superiority (otherwise, why choose one over another?), the effects of which I explore in the hypotheses below.

---

[10] Here again, I limit the claim to the world religions widespread in Africa: Christianity and Islam. Both achieved mass followings by virtue of having congregational and evangelical elements. The description would not fit Judaism or Hinduism, for example.

[11] The World Christian Database lists more than 40 active Christian denominations and more than 10 branches of Islam in Africa. www.worldchristiandatabase.org/wcd/.

Second, the religious identity is underpinned by formal doctrine in ways that other identity types are not. Laitin (1978: 572) proposes a helpful framework for understanding how:

> First is the pure doctrine as it would be analyzed by theologians. Second is the practical religion, or religion in its sociological sense, which emerges out of the interaction of doctrine and social origins of the ideas. And third, the interaction of the practical religion with the cultural conditions of the community of converts from a different culture yields a practical religion of the converted.

The lessons that Laitin's framework provide for an argument based on mobilizational differences across identity types are twofold. On the one hand, a practical religion of the converted provides theoretical justification for the region-specific approach to world religious identity that I have advocated. Islam is no less Islam in Nigeria than in Iran or Indonesia; it is simply Islam practiced in a different social context. Conversely, the practical religion and the practical religion of the converted make sense to us only because pure doctrine exists to provide the basic outlines of broad religious traditions in any regional context. Doctrine, to return to Levtzion's description, is the pure, stable core of religious traditions that link their historical foundations to the contemporary pull they exert on adherents. As Dr. Al-Hajj Haziz Al-Hussein Zakaria, of the Maryam Centre for Interreligious Dialogue in Tamale, Ghana, puts it, "Tidjaniyya and Wahhabi Muslims may have different interpretations, but at the end of the day we are people of the same book."[12] Ethnic group leaders can make no such appeals.

Giving a central place to the existence of religious doctrine of course raises the question of what doctrine counts as legitimate doctrine. In this book, I table distinctions in specific doctrine to focus on the commonality, across major religious traditions, of written doctrine intended to shape individual behavior and to provide a worldview linking that behavior to the divine (Berger 1999; Young 1976). Religious doctrine has greater structure than local customs or social norms but is also distinct from, say, political party manifestos, in terms of purpose: to adopt the language of Durkheim (1912 [1995]), religion is the social identity that addresses the "sacred," or things set apart, rather than the "profane." A key sociopolitical role that doctrine plays, therefore, is to provide a platform linking in-group members that otherwise lack the perceived myth of shared descent. Otherwise stated, doctrine creates

---

[12] Personal communication, January 14, 2009.

in-group members outside the local political context, and out-group members both at home and abroad.

Third, world religions are exactly that – they are transnational identities unlike any other social identity type. More than twenty countries, some in Africa and others in the Middle East and Asia, are Islamic states or recognize Islam as a state religion; approximately fifteen (primarily in South America and Europe) list some form of Christianity as an official religion, and many more around the world have traditions of Islam and Christianity underpinning their laws and sociopolitics.[13] The freedom of religion from geographic constraints is particularly the case in Africa, where no sacred site – no Mecca, Jerusalem, Rome, or Varanasi – exists to fight over, protect, or worship. World religion is thus, in a constitutive sense, a landless identity type in Africa.[14] To be sure, places of worship for religious practitioners in Africa may be as indivisible and honored as any church, mosque, or temple elsewhere, yet the lands on which they rest are not imbued with the religious history and meaning that would create religious ties to land.[15] The upshot from a sociopolitical perspective is that coordination can occur among in-group members across national borders, absent any shared local incentives. Individuals form special ties with religious communities owing nothing to the lands they live on, the languages they speak, or their biological lineage, and states use religious identity as a criterion for political alliance both historically and contemporarily. During my own field research among Muslims and Christians in Côte d'Ivoire and Ghana that I describe in detail later in the book, foreign co-religionists were an occasional presence at places of worship: Americans, French, Koreans, and others strengthening relationships with Christian leaders and communities, and, inter alia, Saudi Arabians,

[13] Data drawn from the U.S. Department of State's 2014 Report on International Religious Freedom. www.state.gov/g/drl/rls/irf/2009/index.htm.

[14] This may seem counter to the notion of predominant Muslim and Christian zones on which the research design presented in Chapter 3 is based. Scholars disagree as to whether those "worlds" are breaking down (Cox 1995) or are increasingly rigid and at odds (Huntington 1993). Across sub-Saharan Africa, the religious divide that formed as a function of geographic constraints on northern Muslim traders and their southern partners (Lydon 2009) was reified by the establishment of Islamic emirates and by colonial policies that forbade Christian overlap with Muslim-administered regions. Social sanctioning also militates against widespread religious change (Berger 1999). Thus, we should expect the change that comes with voluntary, easily adoptable status to occur incrementally and person by person, though traditional chiefs have at times led large-scale conversions. In any case, overlaps, changes, and significant religious minorities exist across religious fault lines.

[15] See Hassner (2013) for an explanation of the indivisibility of sacred religious grounds.

Libyans, Egyptians, and Iranians fulfilling the same role among Muslims. The influence of religious transnationality, furthermore, is not unidirectional: Lighthouse Chapel International, a Pentecostal Christian Church founded in Ghana, has spread to more than fifty countries, including the United States.[16] Other types of social identity in Africa – ethnicity, region, language, and caste – lack this transnationality. A transnational identity type like religion, I argue, transforms the bounds of group membership, thereby generating unique individual-level concerns that can be activated independent of any political mobilization.

On the basis of these three features – being voluntary, based on a foundation of formal doctrine, and transnational – I categorize religion as a rule-based identity in Africa. As noted, of course, religious rules are subject to interpretation and change (Zubaida 1993). I use the concept of rule-based identity simply as shorthand to convey the relatively easy adoptability of an identity rooted in codified guidelines. The label is largely unique to religion, and its implications are critical for understanding individual-level preferences: to follow the sacred is to demonstrate a broad set of predictable preferences.

To this point, I have ignored the issue of traditional African religions, which, though in precipitous decline (from approximately 58 percent of the sub-Saharan population in 1900 to somewhere between 3 and 10 percent today),[17] continue to influence views of the sacred and to qualify attachments to the world religions in the region. A common refrain in Senegal, for example, is that its population is "95 percent Muslim, 5 percent Christian, and 100 percent animist."[18] It is precisely the heavy influence of traditional religious beliefs and practices on world religion that has given rise to the concepts of African Islam and "domesticated" Christianity (Sanneh 2003). In this study, however, I treat traditional African religions as an identity type distinct from the world religions; they simply do not share the features that I argue are central to world religions as sociopolitical identities in the region. Traditional religions, for instance, do not rely on formal doctrine, and the belief system that does underpin specific traditional religions is not typically adoptable by outsiders. Furthermore, traditional religions are linked to locality and the

---

[16] For a brief history, see www.lighthousechapel.org/.

[17] World Christian Database. www.worldchristiandatabase.org/wcd/.

[18] Personal communication with Dr. Moustapha Tamba, professor of sociology at the University Cheikh Anta Diop in Dakar, Senegal, March 27, 2009. The term "animist" is often used to describe traditional African religions, owing to their characterization of ascribing healing powers to inanimate objects in nature.

land, emphasizing natural locations such as hills, springs, and prominent trees, and sacred periods of the year that generally correspond with harvest seasons (Onaiyekan 1983). Finally, membership in the corresponding ethnic group ("tribe" in the quotations that follow) is a quasi-necessary criterion for membership in a traditional religion: Barrett notes that traditional religions amount to "a system of rites aimed at strengthening the fellowship of the tribe ... and increasing its power" (1968: 123), and Onaiyekan describes traditional deities as having "no claims to sovereignty beyond the land and members of the tribe" (1983: 239). That traditional religions are defined more by land ties than by doctrine makes the notion that (world) religion and ethnicity are distinguishable types of identity all the more defensible. I do include the traditional religious perspective in the empirical analysis that follows in Chapter 3, and the results suggest that, when it comes to mobilizational differences between ethnicity and religion, traditional African religion represents a special case that gives added leverage to the argument I advance in this book.

Before outlining the preferences that follow from these distinct identity types, it is important to recognize how complex the construction and definition of ethnic and religious groups are, lest the distinction in land versus rules become too stultified. Ethnic and religious groups emerge, change, and are redefined frequently in the service of members' or leaders' interests. Group size is far from pre-determined, not simply because of entry and exit but also as the meaning of labels changes and what constitutes a "Muslim" or a "Yoruba" evolves (see Posner 2005). Ethnicity in the African context is historically tied to land, but, as I have noted, ethnic groups are not devoid of behavioral regulations or rule-based proscriptions. Similarly, religious identities in some contexts serve as channels for local economic development, and religious leaders can play key roles in controlling land and guiding local production, as is the case for the brotherhoods that oversee peanut production in Senegal (see Cruise O'Brien 1977).

I should thus stress two important elements of the history and definition of identity groups in Africa. First, their meanings evolve historically, and that is as true of the broader identity types as it is of the specific groups therein. Historical patterns linking ancestry to local lands, and ethnic channels of patronage to local development, suggest a general association between ethnic identity and homelands. Different historical patterns that saw Islam and Christianity introduced with doctrinal texts from foreign traders or missionaries intimates a tendency to prioritize those geographically unbounded rules and ties. Whether their origins as distinct identity groups in Africa are centuries old or only since the onset of colonialism, those historical patterns once established create norms sticky enough to shape the priorities of future members in important if subtle ways. The second element worth emphasizing is that this description characterizes preferences on balance, in a context of evolving interests among both groups and individuals. The key to understanding the exploitation of ethnicity and religion is to recognize that even subtle differences in preferences, built on sticky historical norms that develop in a region, can tip collective action in the favor of a political leader – even to the point of engaging in violence – if the right mobilization strategies are employed.

In the case study chapters that follow in Part II, I detail the historical processes by which ethnicity and religion became particularly prominent social identities in those national contexts, reflecting patterns that persist across the region. The stickiness of historical norms allows contemporary political elites to then exploit ethnicity and religion to further their own strategic interests, though we may always find unique local circumstances that redefine both the interests of actors and the identities themselves.

PREFERENCES BASED ON THE DISTINCTIONS BETWEEN RELIGION AND ETHNICITY

I proposed in the introductory chapter that ethnicity and religion are somehow different. This walk through their histories and features in Africa suggests how: ethnic groups are land-based identities rooted in a narrative of historical lineage, thereby emphasizing common descent, shared norms, and locality, whereas religions are rule-based identities that can be adopted, highlighting their voluntariness, their formal doctrine, and their transnationality. These images are stylized extremes. Yet if we were to place all identity types along a two-dimensional space corresponding to the land-based and rule-based characterizations that I have developed (as in Figure 2.1), ethnicity in Africa would fall around point A, toward the land-based endpoint and quite low on the rules axis. Traditional African religions would also fall near point A. World religious identities in Africa, conversely, would be located closer to the rule-based maximum and low on the land-based axis, around point B. These general distinctions shape the baselines from which individuals in Africa act and

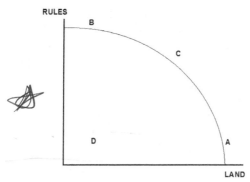

FIGURE 2.1. Conceptual space of land and rule priorities for identity types.

political entrepreneurs in the region calculate strategies for preferred outcomes. Thinking of identity types in a conceptual space like this one also helps to elucidate the distinctions between ethnicity and religion in Africa and the role that identity types play in other parts of the world. We might imagine, for example, that religion as a political identity type in the Middle East would fall near point C, emphasizing the importance of both land and rules. Political party identities in the United States prioritize neither land nor doctrine in a constitutive sense; they might fall closer to point D in this particular conceptual space.

This chapter so far has served as a reminder of Chandra's (2006) important insight that ethnicity and religion in Africa function differently from how they do elsewhere, and I have added some considerations as to how. In what follows, I present a model of behavior to explain how those features of ethnicity and religion in Africa can be linked to systematic variation in individual-level preferences.

First, I assume, in the tradition of social identity theory, that identities take on meaning where there exist comparable alternatives – "others" – in a social setting. In the region of southern Maryland where I was raised, an ethnic group known as the "Wesorts" emerged when freed African American slaves, Piscataway Native Americans, and poor whites in the area were pushed to the same undesirable lands and inter-married. Their name, of course, distinguishes them from "you sorts." It makes sense to say that I am a political scientist only because one can identify occupationally with other disciplines, not to mention with occupations outside academia. The implication is that identity distinctions are not primordial, as essential as one's own identity might feel. Rather, they are a matter of consciousness as a result of the fact that, in some measurable ways, there are groups of people not quite like us. That realization forms a basis not just for group recognition, but for competition and conflict (Tajfel and Turner 1979). The first step in that process of identifying with one group as opposed to another is to send signals interpretable to in-group members, via symbols or behavior in social settings. Thus, we have a preliminary understanding of how identity types can shape behaviors in systematic, identifiable ways.

Unlike social identity theorists, however, I argue that distinct identity types like ethnicity and religion generate exogenous norms that shape members' behavior and preferences, irrespective of the status of the group or competition between groups. Shayo and his colleagues (Hogg 2006; Shayo 2009; Tajfel and Turner 1979), for example, draw on social identity theory to suggest that political preferences are shaped by the perceived benefits of belonging to a coalition of like members. Thus, wealthy members of a poor group tend to prefer higher rates of redistribution than wealthy individuals who belong to a higher status group (Klor and Shayo 2010), and factors that bolster the status of nations strengthen attachments to the national identity over attachments to ethnicity (Sambanis and Shayo 2013). Yet from that perspective, identity types are content free: they explain political preferences only endogenously, as members aim to fit in with like individuals and in higher status groups. Arguments of this sort are thus helpful in elucidating one aspect of affective behavior – belonging – but less helpful in clarifying how one identity type might generate systematically different preferences than another. Instead, based on the distinct histories and norms of ethnicity and religion in the region, I argue that these identities are constitutively distinct, and thus that they impact individual-level preferences exogenously when they are mobilized.

A limited literature does seek to address differences in identity types writ large. Sambanis (2001) distinguishes ethnic from nonethnic conflict, and Esteban and Ray (2008) argue that ethnic conflict differs from class conflict as a result of in-group economic heterogeneity. Baldwin and Huber (2010) note that groups differ both culturally and economically and that the economic distinctions between them better explain variation in public goods provision. The choice between ethnic and national identities may be a matter of institutional constraints (Penn 2008), and support for political party identities over caste identities may be a function of the channels through which resources flow to constituents (Dunning and Nilekani 2013). These studies, however, focus little on the characteristics of identity types themselves; like Shayo (2009), they rely on who one's co-members are rather than on what the identity category is.[19]

Next, I assume that actors seek to maximize their individual-level utility and that utility accrues differently in ethnic and religious contexts. The utility they seek to maximize, moreover, may come in both material and non-material forms (Opp 1989; Simon 1985). I argue that in religious contexts, the narrative of voluntarily adopted rules promoting a world-view reshapes payoffs toward long-term, non-material alternatives. The suicide bombers of September 11, 2001, wrote of seeking the reward of virgins in paradise (Lester et al 2004). Ascetics forgo luxuries and nourishment for the hope of pleasing the divine in an afterlife.[20] In religious contexts, then, we might expect preferences to accumulate around non-material interests, like the psychological comfort of choosing right over wrong, of perceived divine approval, or of potential immortality. The presence of guiding texts, relatively unique among social identities, should more generally inspire individuals in religious contexts to prioritize goods that are behavioral rather than geographically local, related to concerns such as morality, world views, salvation, and justice – broadly put, focused on proper living.[21] We might also expect that their incentives to engage politically would be stronger when ties to exclusive doctrine or behavior-based policies are evoked. Finally, given the nature of the "other" in religious contexts as unconstrained geographically, empathy for in-group members extends well beyond one's home region to political contests framed in religious terms in different parts of the world. This will have important implications for the findings presented in Part II.

Given the landless nature of religious identity, however, religious group members – that is, individuals subjected to mobilization along

---

[19] Bormann et al. (2013), Chandra (2006), Fearon and Laitin (2000), and Laitin (2000) constitute some of the few examples of studies that endeavor to disaggregate narrow ethnicity from other ascriptive groupings based on characteristics of the identity types themselves.

[20] Causality may also work in the opposite direction. Norris and Inglehart (2004) demonstrate that residents of regions affected by poverty, inequality, and danger – features of "existential insecurity" – empirically have the strongest attachments to the divine, seeking tranquility in religion rather than waiting for solutions to the very real threats they face in the present. This would suggest that a lack of material comfort can inspire religiosity, whereas the examples above suggest that religiosity can drive individuals away from the material and toward other, non-material payoffs. These arguments are not incompatible.

[21] Many religious entities provide local club goods, such as schools, health programs, and community space. This study suggests that actors nevertheless place a relative priority on moral matters when the religion is mobilized.

religious lines – might place less emphasis on club goods like development, preferring to free-ride rather than engage in political contestation over those matters. Instead, their incentives to engage politically would be stronger when ties to exclusive doctrine or behavior-based policies are evoked.[22]

In contexts where ethnicity is the preeminent identity, individuals are subject to different utility calculations. The narrative of common descent, for example, places a premium on family and in particular on respect for elders, chiefs, and ancestors. In some instances, elders have cultivated new ethnic group myths for precisely this reason (Lentz 1995). Furthermore, the geographically bounded nature of ethnicity implies a special, lineage-based entitlement to local territory and resources in the ethnic group's stronghold. Psychologically, scholars suggest that the ethnic identity increases feelings of territoriality, rooted in emotional attachments to land perceived as property of the group (Dustmann and Preston 2001; Green 2006; Toft 2005). Those effects, moreover, extend beyond protection of the land to concerns over local development: because African socioeconomies maintain a heavy reliance on local markets and an informal economy, ethnic groups become the loci of local economic progress (Barkan, McNulty, and Ayeni 1991). Barkan et al. (1991) describe ethnic groups in Africa as providing development assistance and local public goods as a function of individual-level attachments to place. Thus, despite widespread understanding of African ethnic groups as constructed, individuals in those groups feel attachments that evoke special concern for land and local development.

That feature of ethnic identity suggests that, when placed in a context in which ethnicity is salient, members are more likely to prioritize matters related to local resources: club goods of low rivalry and high excludability, such as local development projects and community improvement. Ethnic group members – or, more appropriately, individuals subjected to mobilization along ethnic lines – should therefore extract relatively greater utility from defending and improving their club goods, preferring to free-ride on questions of moral or transnational nature.

Finally, I assume that individuals bring their own experiences, background, and character to bear in either of these contexts, so that the salience of ethnicity or religion on a broader scale and the relevance of

---

[22] Political elites may exploit this feature of religion not only to mobilize supporters to optimal outcomes domestically but also to generate support from in-group members abroad.

those identities to the individual interact to shape preferred outcomes. A devoutly religious person would have preferences that differ from those of her neighbor who is devoted to his ethnic group, irrespective of the politically and socially relevant identities around them.[23] A model of mobilizational differences across identity types should account for these individual priors while demonstrating the effects of context. In short, the broader preferences of each identity type remain stable, even as individuals emphasize them differentially and reprioritize them.

Formally, the effects of context on individual-level choices can be modeled in decision theoretic terms. For simplicity, I model one half of the argument: the choice between religious preferences and the status quo, which may be ethnic-oriented preferences or otherwise.[24] One might model ethnic preferences, or those of other identity types, similarly.

Assume first that individual i chooses an action, $A \in \{S, Z\}$, where S is a "sacred" action and Z is a non-religious outcome. A simple example would be the choice to adhere strictly to the dictates of Shari'a law or not. Assume, furthermore, a predominant identity context, $I \in \{R, E\}$, where R is a religious context and E an ethnic one. These contexts are independent and exclusive and are determined by political entrepreneurs (modeled here as nature's choice, N) with probabilities p and $(1 - p)$, respectively. I model the individual choice regarding actions as coming first; this is consistent with an everyday life choice to engage in religious or ethnic activities. The exogenous mobilization of religion or ethnicity at the community level follows. Because the individual does not have complete information regarding the incentives of political entrepreneurs, who shape the identity context, the alternative states of nature are viewed with subjective probability.[25]

Let V represent the benefit that accrues to the individual from performing sacred acts – for simplicity's sake, we might call it salvation. Let c represent the cost to the individual of performing sacred acts: being perceived as "radical," opportunity costs incurred by presenting oneself

---

[23] In rare instances, we can imagine individuals staunchly committed to both their religion and ethnic group (Hardin 1995: 7). However, their preferred actions would be no different theoretically than someone of middling or even weak attachments to both – sometimes they would be inclined toward one behavior set and sometimes to the other.

[24] A more complex model would distinguish both sacred/religious preferences and ethnic-oriented preferences from the status quo and determine the payoffs for each.

[25] Alternatively, nature could be modeled as the first mover, followed by an information set for individual i, who does not know which context (ethnic or religious) nature has provided. Payoffs to the individual would not change.

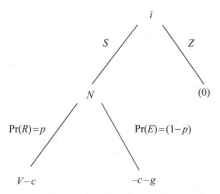

FIGURE 2.2. Expected utility from religious behavior.

as exclusive and unwilling to blend, and so on. Let g represent the punishment for failing to act in accordance with the identity context – for example, ostracism from one's own group due to the performance of non-religious acts in a religious world, or vice versa.

Following Figure 2.2, the expected utility that accrues to each individual from performing sacred acts, with the utility of performing non-religious acts normalized to zero (the status quo), is:

$$Eu_i(S) = p(V-c) + (1-p)(-c-g)$$

Individuals also have natural predispositions toward their religious or ethnic identities in the absence of any identity considerations at the community level. Thus, we can characterize the benefits of sacred acts distinctly for religiously inclined people and those inclined toward ethnicity:

$$V(R,E) = v_R x + v_E(1-x), \quad v_R > v_E$$

where x is a ratio, between 0 and 1, defining personal attachments to religion versus ethnicity. The value of those religious acts (e.g., leading to salvation) is assumed to always be greater for religious people than for the ethnically inclined. Thus, expected utility from performing sacred acts can be rewritten as:

$$Eu_i(S) = p(v_R x + v_E(1-x)-c) + (1-p)(-c-g)$$
$$= p(v_R x + v_E(1-x))-c)-(1-p)(g)$$

Because the performance of non-religious acts is treated as providing net utility equal to zero, individuals will choose to perform sacred acts when

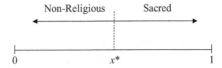

FIGURE 2.3. The equilibrium point between non-religious and sacred acts.

$$p(v_R x + v_E(1-x)-c)-(1-p)(g) > 0$$

$$x > \frac{c + (1-p)g - pv_T}{p(v_R - v_E)}$$

The right-hand side of the above equation can be defined as x^*, the equilibrium point for holding sacred or non-religious preferences (see Figure 2.3).

Simplifying terms,

$$x^* = \frac{c + g - p(g + v_T)}{p(v_R - v_E)}$$

$$= \frac{c + g}{p(v_R - v_E)} - \frac{(g + v_E)}{(v_R - v_E)}$$

Note that as p (the probability of nature providing a religious world) increases, the first term on the right-hand side of the equation decreases in size. Thus, the first derivative of x^* with respect to p is less than zero:

$$\frac{\partial x^*}{\partial p} < 0$$

In other words, as society becomes more religious, the individual is more likely to hold sacred preferences (x^*, the equilibrium point for performing religious behaviors, decreases). This holds true irrespective of the distribution of x. The implication is that individual predispositions toward sacred and non-religious behavior shape preferred actions but that those actions are constrained by the identity context: in a religious world, individuals of all types are more likely to prefer the sacred action, whereas in an ethnic world, those same individuals are relatively more likely to embrace priorities related to ethnicity.[26]

---

[26] Note that the cost of performing sacred actions (c) works in the opposite direction: as c increases, the equilibrium point for deciding to perform sacred acts increases. The hypotheses I present focus primarily on the effects of changing the identity context, not the costs.

HYPOTHESES

The model illustrates that changes in the salience of identity types can elicit different preferences among the same individuals. Here, I outline a few issue areas where we might expect to see evidence of such divergent preferences. To return to the language of the model above, the task is to present issues around which we might expect sacred behavior to be distinguishable from non-religious behavior, or ethnic preferences to differ from non-ethnic ones. Identifying some practical areas in which preferences differ will not only help to ground the argument but may also provide insight into the types of issues that political entrepreneurs can exploit to achieve diverse political aims. In order to generate testable hypotheses, I propose three such domains.

One place to explore differential preferences across ethnic and religious contexts is with respect to political leadership. Land-based identities and rule-based identities, if indeed they are constitutively different, would presumably generate distinct preference orders regarding decisions of governance: on social issues, development strategies, defense spending, and so on. Thus, we could anticipate that when ethnicity and religion are mobilized, voters would look with favor on different types of political leaders, in terms of how they handle those decisions of the state. Individuals placed in an ethnic context, where land and local club goods are prioritized, would likely favor political leaders who promote platforms of development, material well-being, and perhaps clientelist exchanges of goods for loyalty.

Individuals placed in a religious context should favor a different kind of political leader. As a landless, rule-based identity type that elicits concerns over moral behavior and lifestyle guidelines, religion should inspire preferences for leaders who double as moral guides, or at least who make moral and social policy a centerpiece of their political platform.

Hypothesis 1: Ethnic contexts evoke preferences for local development-oriented political leaders. Religious contexts intensify preferences for political leaders who focus on moral issues.

Remember, individuals face competing sociopolitical influences and harbor any number of identities whose salience may come and go. Irrespective of context, moreover, people simply have stronger or weaker attachments to one identity than to another (captured by x in the model of religious context above). What the features of identity types outlined earlier suggest is that, ceteris paribus, adjusting the context toward ethnicity or religion should cause a relative reprioritization of policy concerns, independent of other unobserved influences.

A second domain in which we might expect to find differential preferences when ethnicity and religion are mobilized is the socioeconomic and political character of one's community. Prioritizing land and local club goods, as I suggest individuals in Africa tend to do in ethnic contexts, would have as a consequence the material improvement of the community. As Barkan et al. (1991) note, ethnic associations often form to explicitly serve this goal. Thus, it should follow that mobilization along ethnic lines is associated with a relative interest in being part of a prosperous local community. Rather than free-riding on local matters, individuals for whom ethnicity is made salient maximize their utility when their own homeland area is made better off.

Based on the features of religion and the corresponding preferences that I outlined above, we should expect individuals in a religious context to prefer a much different type of community. Improvements in local well-being are relatively less important when religion is mobilized, so it may make sense for the religious-minded to free-ride on initiatives related to material improvement and club goods. Instead, a community in which moral probity or lifestyle guidelines is the centerpiece would constitute a more valued setting when a landless, rule-based identity type such as religion is made salient.

Hypothesis 2: Ethnic contexts intensify preferences for a materially well-off community. Religious contexts elicit relative preferences for a morally strong community.

Finally, policy preferences constitute a third domain in which to explore differences in the effects of ethnicity and religion. What may be a less consequential policy priority to constituents in one context – say, when ethnicity is on their minds – may be of critical importance to those same supporters in a different context, when their religious identity is salient. Think, for example, of the urgency with which some Christian evangelicals in the United States oppose same-sex marriage, and how, as "southerners," "whites," or "blue collar workers," that urgency might shift to a different concern. Given that dispute over policy priorities serves as a common foundation for political mobilization and protest (Lipsky 1968), understanding potential differentiation in policy preferences in ethnic versus religious contexts is also important.

According to the argument outlined above, we should expect the ethnic minded – that is, individuals placed in contexts where ethnicity is most salient – to prioritize policy concerns that reinforce or accentuate their material standing or that of their local community. Leeway for the direct exchange of goods, for example, may be of relatively greater concern than transparency or respect for the rule of law. Keeping patronage channels open may be more important than formal institutional guidelines.

As a rule-based identity, world religions in Africa rely on codified guidelines for behavior and on worldviews as critical dividers between coreligionists and non-coreligionists. Furthermore, they promote rewards for adherence to those guidelines and worldviews. As a result, we should expect that individuals placed in a religious context will prioritize policy matters that explicitly address lifestyle, integrity, and the protection of moral codes. In some cases, such as the implementation of Shari'a law or the use of prayer in public contexts, members of different religious groups may hold starkly different views on what, exactly, that policy should be. Concerning other matters, such as corruption or promiscuity, specific policy preferences may converge. I suggest only that the identity context shapes the priority of broad policy concerns and that decisions governing lifestyle and morality should occupy a central place for the religiously minded.

Hypothesis 3: Ethnicity evokes preferences for policy that results in material improvement. Religion elicits a stronger relative preference for morality and lifestyle policies.

At this stage, I present these hypotheses as broad expectations of what we might see when otherwise identical individuals are placed in ethnic versus religious contexts. In subsequent chapters, I operationalize the hypotheses in order to move from the general theory of mobilizational differences to the rigorous testing of claims.

CONCLUSION

The argument presented in this chapter requires something of a balancing act: it dismisses the notion that identity types are primordial or fixed, yet I have also sought to recognize and account for underlying differences in ethnicity and religion that have emerged as a result of their histories in the region and that, critically, shape cognitive preferences independent of contemporary political manipulation. In addition, I argue that individuals act instrumentally, but that, because of the identity context (shaped by ethnicity or religion), they do so from different baselines, which generate systematically different priorities. These are the challenges that come with getting inside the black box of broad "ethnicity."

The chapter suggests that, as a land-based identity, ethnic contexts evoke a relative preference for homelands and local material well-being. Conversely, because religions are rule-based identities in Africa, a context in which religion is salient evokes preferences, ceteris paribus, for moral policy that is absent local bias. These patterns emerge as tendencies in the complicated world of African identity configuration, definition, and implementation over time. They are not deterministic or black and white in their consequences, but they do constitute mobilizational differences in ethnic and religious groups. Those mobilizational differences provide opportunities for political entrepreneurs, by virtue of manipulating the identity context, to mobilize supporters around distinct goals. In the next chapter, I present novel evidence in support of these claims.

3

Evidence from Côte d'Ivoire and Ghana

If the logic underpinning this book's argument starts with mobilizational differences between ethnicity and religion, we should expect to see evidence of those differences among individuals in Africa. Do people indeed demonstrate distinct preferences in ethnic and religious contexts? In particular, do we observe patterns in keeping with the claim that ethnic salience inspires greater attention to matters of land and local development while religious salience generates a relative preference for moral probity and rules unassociated with local geography? These questions have little to do with violence, but they suggest preferences that might be exploited by political leaders in the course of violence and conflict.

Observational evidence from around Africa supports these claims. Using data from the Afrobarometer public opinion surveys, which include responses from more than 20,000 individuals across multiple countries in the region,[1] I find important correlations between identity attachments and policy preferences. In particular, in comparing those who self-identify in ethnic terms versus those who list religion as their most important identity, three relevant differences stand out. First, those who prioritize ethnicity are 50 percent more likely to view land disputes as a principal source of conflict (14 percent vs. 9.6 percent, $p < .001$ in a paired t-test). Second, those ethnic self-identifiers are also about 10 percent more likely to participate in local community meetings where local club goods like

---

[1] Data available at www.afrobarometer.org/data/round-2-merged. The key question regarding self-identity was removed after the second round of Afrobarometer surveys in 2002, so the data are drawn from that wave, which included 16 African states. See the Appendix for more details.

land tenure and development projects are typically planned (66 percent vs. 60 percent, $p < .01$). Third, respondents who list religion as their most important identity are 15 percent more likely than those who prioritize ethnicity to believe that fighting corruption is a priority for government (48 percent vs. 42 percent, $p < .01$). These findings hold true even when a number of demographic control variables – including gender, age, education level, and socioeconomic status – are held constant; see Appendix A for multivariate regression analyses and a description of variables. Each of these findings should be anticipated given the mobilizational differences between ethnicity and religion outlined above.

Those observational data suggest systematic patterns across a breadth of countries, but they are also subject to well-documented shortcomings. Green and Gerber (2003) argue that the field of political science has been too optimistic in its assessment of the evidentiary value of such data, owing to the fact that researchers who use them have little means of ensuring that the estimates they produce are unbiased. Morton and Williams (2010) stress that if understanding causal relationships is the objective, observational methods often fail us by obscuring the cause of effects from the effects of causes. And Arceneaux (2010) outlines how the strategic nature of political processes can generate serious selection effects, whereby individuals segregate into unobserved but systematic groups that alter the outcomes we seek to explain. All of this is true. One particular challenge in this study is that it would be exceedingly difficult to determine simply through observational means whether it is one's attachment to ethnicity or to religion – both of which almost all sub-Saharan Africans have and treat as personally important – that is activated when politically important choices are made.

In order to argue that political leaders exploit ethnicity and religion in different ways to mobilize followers in the course of conflict, then, I must do more than the observational data allow. In short, I must demonstrate that, when ethnic or religious identities are made salient, otherwise identical individuals, and even the same individual placed in different contexts, will have preferences that vary systematically. Only then can we be confident that the patterns described so far result from fundamental differences in the effects of ethnicity and religion at the individual level, and not from unobserved factors that correlate with both identity attachments and political preferences.

A meeting I conducted in northern Côte d'Ivoire summarizes the challenges to generating the kind of evidence I would need. Having made arrangements for a morning visit with Sheikh Ali Sanogo, the imam of an orthodox Muslim mosque in Korhogo, I arrived at his family compound just before nine in the morning. After customary greetings, his family explained that Sheikh Ali would arrive momentarily, as he had spent the early part of the morning in his fields. Imams in the region, unlike many of the Christian priests and pastors, receive little in the way of remuneration for their leadership services and must rely on other activities to supplement their income; since Sheikh Ali is also a farmer, the news that he was in his fields came as no surprise. Moments later, he arrived by moped, wearing what one would expect of a farmer in northern Côte d'Ivoire: comfortable, traditional pants and shirt, sandals, and a hat. The hat, a wide-brimmed circular one that rose to a point at the top, not only protected Sheikh Ali from the sun but also announced very clearly that its wearer was a "Senoufo man"; it was of a style customarily worn by members of the Senoufo ethnic group, as Sheikh Ali is. Apologizing for his tardiness, he requested a few minutes to prepare himself before our meeting. Emerging shortly from his quarters, Sheikh Ali was transformed: he carried a Qur'an and prayer beads and wore Muslim robes, *khussa* shoes designed for prayer sessions, and a *taqiyah*, the prayer hat typical among pious Muslims in the region. With an air of hospitality and comfortable authority, Sheikh Ali led me through a series of greetings and then opened our more formal discussion by asking, simply, what I would like to know.

What I was most interested in knowing was something that Sheikh Ali likely could not tell me. I wanted to know, when he removed his Senoufo hat and replaced it with a Muslim hat, how did he change? Are his priorities, attitudes, behaviors, and preferred outcomes – particularly with respect to local club goods versus moral probity and transnational allegiances, the key measures of interest in my study – different when he wears his religious hat as opposed to when he wears his ethnic hat?

The reasons why Sheikh Ali could not have answered this question are numerous. First, as I noted earlier (and my meeting confirms), individuals have several social identities, the salience of which is fluid and constantly affected by both personal and environmental factors (Bates 1983; Laitin 1986; Young 1976). In sub-Saharan Africa, ethnicity and religion are the most notable social markers, but determining which of the two motivates individual actors at any given time is problematic. One possible solution would be to examine the preferences of the staunchest adherents from each set, such as a group of regular churchgoers or imams like Sheikh Ali, on the one hand, and an association protecting tribal protocols, on the other. As this story suggests, however, even the staunchest of religionists occasionally plow their fields and undertake other more traditional activities, and even the most committed ethnic group members may sometimes appear at Christian or Muslim ceremonies or otherwise delve into their religious life. More troubling is the fact that relying on responses from fervent religious and ethnic group members raises the risk of endogeneity in the research design: it would be impossible to know whether certain preferences led individuals to become staunch adherents of those groups or whether membership in those groups generated certain preferences. Finally, if the solution were simply to inquire about both the religio-political preferences and the (distinct) ethno-political preferences of the same individual, such as Sheikh Ali, the problem of interdependent preferences would arise; it is not clear that an individual could voluntarily and accurately distinguish his preferences in the name of religion from those in the name of ethnicity, much as he might try.

To address these challenges, I make use of results from a micro-level, experimental field study. Using research sites in the north and south of both Côte d'Ivoire and Ghana, I artificially evoked either the religious or the ethnic identity among a random selection of more than 1,300 individuals, a strategy intended to manipulate the salience of the two identity types on an individual scale. To apply the metaphor I stumbled into during my meeting with Sheikh Ali, I forced participants to temporarily wear either a religious hat or an ethnic hat. I then evaluated political preferences using an extensive survey instrument that gauged priorities over local club goods and morality.

The findings confirm the hypotheses I presented in Chapter 2. In ethnic contexts, individuals are relatively more likely to prioritize land, material concerns, and local development. Otherwise identical individuals placed in a religious context demonstrate a relative propensity to favor lifestyle- or integrity-based options over material development ones, owing to the landless, rule-based nature of religion in the region. The research also helps to explain the mechanism distinguishing ethnic preferences from religious ones: it is not a result of relative group size or a desire for belonging, but rather that the geographic boundedness of ethnic groups inspires an interest in local club goods, while the geographic expansiveness of (world) religions in the study area elicits preferences for less restricted, behavioral goods. These empirical findings refine our understanding of *ethnic politics*; they imply that political leaders and cultural entrepreneurs must consider substantively different individual-level preferences when mobilizing supporters along ethnic or religious lines.

This component of the study is novel in several respects. First, it allows for differential outcomes, among an otherwise identical population, based on exposure to either ethnicity or religion. This is a departure both from scholarship that assumes static preferences across different politicized identities and from work that analyzes political outcomes solely through the lens of ethnicity, religion, or any other single social identity. Second, by controlling for the effects of political leaders and sociopolitical contexts, the study highlights the features of ethnicity and religion per se as explanations for political preferences – not based on essentialist labels, but because their meanings differ in the eyes of group members in the region. Third, while the project's primary aim is to distinguish between ethnic and religious preferences, the research design also brings new evidence to bear on the question of civilizational divides and Muslim versus Christian politics: by situating the study not only in two national political contexts but also astride one of the longest Muslim–Christian fault lines in the world, I can evaluate empirically whether preferences differ across the "Muslim world" and the "Christian world." Finally, the project adds to a growing list of studies that employ laboratory-like experiments in the African context. While others have imposed experimental treatments in a single political context (Dunning and Harrison 2010; Habyarimana et al 2007; Wantchekon 2003) or have used cross-border political contexts as the treatment itself (Cogneau and Moradi 2014; McCauley and Posner 2017; Michalopoulos and Papaioanno 2014; Miguel 2004; Miles and Rochefort 1991; Posner 2004), this study in a sense does both: it replicates the same experiment in multiple research sites across both a political divide (Côte d'Ivoire–Ghana) and across ethnic and religious divides (in the north and south of each country) to account for a wealth of alternative explanations.

RESEARCH DESIGN

Sites

Testing preferences in ethno-linguistic versus religious contexts could be done anywhere in the world. As noted in the introductory chapter, I selected Côte d'Ivoire and Ghana because both are ethnically and religiously mixed with predominantly Muslim populations in the north and predominantly Christian populations in the south.[2] As neighboring

---

[2] In Côte d'Ivoire, the population is 33 percent Christian, 40 percent Muslim, and 12 percent traditional (CIA World Factbook 2015). In Ghana, the proportions are 68 percent Christian, 16 percent Muslim, and 9 percent traditional. However, those figures are disputed by

coastal countries at similar latitudes on the Gulf Coast of Africa, Ghana and Côte d'Ivoire also share similar climates, topography, agriculture, and access to sea; as a result, they have inspired a number of comparative studies (Alpine and Pickett 1993; Crook 1990; Langer 2008; MacLean 2010; McCauley 2013a; Nordås 2014).[3] Yet they differ in a critical respect: Ghana is in the midst of a period of democratic consolidation and sustained peace – no widespread violence characterized in religious terms has been registered during Ghana's independent history and, aside from localized skirmishes in the north, ethnic tensions have been minimal.[4] In Côte d'Ivoire, conversely, identity-group tensions that were once nonexistent became a focal point of the conflict that enveloped the country beginning in the late 1990s and that was only resolved in 2011. The research design controls for these national political factors by drawing individual-level data from both contexts. This design permits me to evaluate the substantive effects of ethnicity and religion more generally, before exploring how those differences were exploited during Côte d'Ivoire's conflict (as I do in Chapter 6).[5]

Within each country, I employed a design aimed at systematically replicating the research protocols across the most diverse contexts possible, locating one enumeration area in the predominantly Muslim north and one in the predominantly Christian south. In Ghana, those sites are Tamale and Cape Coast, respectively, and in Côte d'Ivoire I established research posts in Korhogo in the north and Divo in the south. In view of the close link between ethnic groups and geographic

the Muslim community, and even the Catholic Church in Ghana puts the proportion of Muslims at 30 percent. The figure for traditional religionists in both countries is subject to debate.

[3] It should be noted that Ghana and Côte d'Ivoire have different colonial histories, Ghana having been colonized by the British and Côte d'Ivoire having been subject to French rule. That difference is unlikely to explain the exploitation of identities at the heart of this book, since in both countries the colonial powers relied on traditional and religious (Muslim) institutions to ease the administrative burden in the north (see McCauley 2013a).

[4] A 1994 ethno-political conflict took on religious undertones as ethnic groups predominated by Christians and traditionalists sought external support from religious bodies (Lentz and Nugent 2000). Since that time, religion has not been incorporated into sociopolitical conflicts in Ghana. Episodes of violence between ethnic groups in the north, particularly the Mamprusi and the Kusasi, occurred periodically since then but have remained limited in scope.

[5] With a sample size of only two countries, rigorously testing national-level variation is not possible in this study. The design nevertheless accounts for the alternative that national-level factors matter and allows for corresponding causal mechanisms to be explored in a qualitative manner, as I do in Chapter 6.

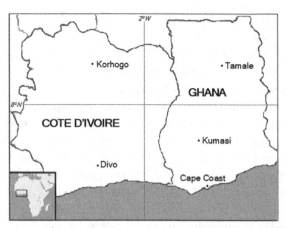

FIGURE 3.1. Research sites.

Notes: Korhogo is predominantly Muslim religiously (68 percent in the data for this study) and Senoufo/Malinké ethnically. Divo is predominantly Christian (67 percent) and Dida. Tamale is 74 percent Muslim and the territory of the Dagomba ethnic group. Cape Coast is 83 percent Christian and predominantly Fante. Kumasi is a cosmopolitan city included in the study for the purposes of a robustness check.

territory, the design also ensures variation in terms of ethnicity: Korhogo in northern Côte d'Ivoire is home predominantly to the Malinké and Senoufo groups; in southern Côte d'Ivoire, Divo is the territory of the Dida; Tamale in northern Ghana is the land of the Dagomba; and the Fante predominate in the Cape Coast area of southern Ghana.[6] Although the northern and southern research sites have predominant religious and ethnic groups, there is sufficient mixing and minority presence so as to distinguish between the effects of predominant religion, individual religious affiliation, predominant ethnicity, and individual ethnic affiliation.

In each enumeration area, participants were drawn from the provincial capital itself and from up to four surrounding rural villages to ensure urban/rural variation. In Ghana, in addition to the sites in the north and south, I added a cosmopolitan research site – Kumasi, the country's second largest city located in the central part of the country – for purposes described in Chapter 4. Figure 3.1 maps the research sites.

---

[6] The research area of Korhogo in northern Côte d'Ivoire is somewhat unique in that two ethnic groups of important relative size inhabit the area.

Subjects and Treatments

Approximately 300 participants were selected from each of the four major enumeration areas, with an additional 118 drawn from central Ghana. Using household maps of urban areas and household estimates from officials in rural villages, research teams[7] developed intervals for household selection to ensure a random sampling of the targeted population. Within each selected household, a second level of randomization took place to select individual participants: enumerators compiled a list of eligible adults in the household and then selected one name via a random draw. The sampling procedure stratified subjects by gender, alternating between male and female from one household to the next.[8] To be clear, the sample was not designed to be nationally representative, but precautions were taken to ensure that it was representative of the populations in the research areas where the work was based.

Participants were exposed to one of two treatments, the intention of which was to artificially prime either the ethnic or the religious identity. Priming an identity experimentally provides two benefits: it isolates preferences along different dimensions in a way that respondents may be unable to truthfully do themselves, and it minimizes contextual factors that could generate noise. For these reasons, priming experiments have gained traction, and have proven to be an effective means of varying inputs, in other political studies (Banks and Valentino 2012; Dunning and Harrison 2010; Iyengar, Peters, and Kinder 1982; McCauley 2014; Sachs 2010; Weber and Thorton 2012). Assignment of subjects to one of the two treatment groups (or to a control group, which I explain below) was also done randomly, ensuring balance in demographic characteristics across the two treated groups and the control group.[9] A descriptive summary of covariates by treatment and control groups is presented in Table 3.1, along with results from Hotelling joint tests of balance that compare the control group to each of the two treatment groups. F-tests fail to reject the assumption of balance, so systematic differences in the outcomes from subjects across the treated and control groups can therefore be attributed simply to being exposed to the ethnic or religious treatments. More detail on the randomized trial procedures

---

[7] Teams included the author and three or four research assistants in each enumeration area.

[8] Procedures mirrored the sampling protocols used by the Afrobarometer survey. www .afrobarometer.org/sampling.html.

[9] Assignment was predetermined via a stratum based on observation number.

TABLE 3.1 *Descriptive Statistics and Covariate Balance across Treatment and Control Groups*

	N	Mean	Std. Dev.	Min.	Max.
Urban					
Religion treatment	446	0.751	0.433	0	1
Ethnic treatment	450	0.731	0.444	0	1
Control group	388	0.691	0.463	0	1
Male					
Religion treatment	446	0.498	0.501	0	1
Ethnic treatment	450	0.482	0.500	0	1
Control group	388	0.526	0.500	0	1
Age					
Religion treatment	446	37.40	13.73	18	80
Ethnic treatment	450	38.23	12.98	18	80
Control group	388	39.84	13.64	18	95
Education					
Religion treatment	446	2.859	1.377	1	6
Ethnic treatment	450	2.931	1.388	1	6
Control group	388	2.825	1.374	1	6
Standard of living					
Religion treatment	446	3.072	0.778	1	4.75
Ethnic treatment	450	3.111	0.778	1	5.00
Control group	388	3.053	0.790	1	4.75
Muslim					
Religion treatment	446	0.460	0.499	0	1
Ethnic treatment	450	0.433	0.496	0	1
Control group	388	0.438	0.497	0	1

Religion-Control 2-group Hotelling	$F_{(6,827)} = 1.7885$
	$\text{Prob} > F_{(6,827)} = 0.0985$
Ethnic-Control 2-group Hotelling	$F_{(6,831)} = 1.0465$
	$\text{Prob} > F_{(6,831)} = 0.3936$

Notes: Education was measured on a scale from 1 (no formal education) to 6 (post-university). Standard of living was calculated as a composite measure based on five-point scales for (1) access to necessities, (2) household amenities, (3) a subjective measure of one's relative socioeconomic well-being, and (4) job status.

can be found in the CONSORT checklist for design-based inference, located in Appendix B.[10]

The best priming treatments are subtle ones; participants should not be able to guess the intention of the treatment, which might inspire Hawthorne effects – whereby individuals alter their behavior in recognition of the fact that they are placed in a studied environment – or strategic or untrue responses (Iyengar 2013). In this case, the treatments consisted of five-minute radio news reports regarding Ivoirian/Ghanaian society, followed by a series of questions regarding the content of the reports. The news reports, which subjects listened to on handheld digital audio players, were performed by professional radio personalities; they were realistic yet concocted solely for the purposes of the experiment.[11] In keeping with the experimental requirement that subjects' responses to treatments not depend on their knowledge of treatments to other subjects,[12] participants were not made aware of the existence of alternative treatments until the completion of activities.

The subtlety came in a simple manipulation of the content of these reports: the two treatments were perfectly identical, only with changes in the names of groups mentioned in the reports. Those receiving the Ethnic[13] treatment heard references to ethno-linguistic groups in their society, and those receiving the Religion treatment heard mention of religious groups in their country. The hired radio reporters simply read the same report twice, switching out the names of ethnic groups for the names of religious groups. A third set of participants, the control group, did not receive exposure to a report on local social identity groups.[14]

To develop content for the reports, focus groups were first organized to ascertain salient issues affecting both ethnic and religious groups, in order

---

[10] The CONSORT statement is a multidisciplinary initiative to improve the reporting of randomized controlled trials. See Schultz et al. (2010).

[11] The reports were recorded in a total of eight different languages, listed later in the chapter.

[12] The problem of treatment spillover is referred to as a violation of the Stable Unit Treatment Value Assumption (SUTVA). See Morton and Williams (2010) for more detail.

[13] I capitalize the treatments throughout this chapter, to distinguish them from more general reference to identity types.

[14] Some control group members listened to music and content-free radio banter in place of the reports on social groups, and others were not provided with any listening treatment. This approach was used to test the exposure effects of listening to radio (regardless of content) as a determinant of outcomes. No differences in outcomes were observed between the two types of controls.

to develop a report that would appear realistic and timely to listeners of either report. The reports, the transcripts of which are located in Appendix C, focused on four key points:

1. The active roles that both leaders and group members play
2. Disagreements between groups over a key policy domain (education was chosen)
3. Occasional mistrust between groups and the ever-present potential for conflict
4. The general feeling that religious/ethnic diversity is necessary and important

The content of the reports was designed to be group-neutral; the aim was not to favor one group over another or to manipulate inter-group (i.e., Muslim–Christian or Baoulé-Senoufo) views themselves. Rather, the objective of the experiment was to manipulate the salience of either religion or ethnicity and to then measure priorities in each of those contexts. To return to the metaphor from above, receiving the treatments forced subjects to wear either a religious hat or an ethnic hat, regardless of their predispositions toward religion or ethnicity in their everyday lives. Subjects assigned to the control group were assumed to respond from the standpoint of whatever social predispositions they typically maintain, absent any manipulation.

Table 3.2 provides summary statistics of the data across research sites. The statistics reveal an even distribution across Ghana and Côte d'Ivoire, across the north and south, and among pooled Muslims and Christians. There is a clear difference in the religious composition of northern and southern sites – the former are on average 71 percent Muslim and the latter 75 percent Christian – which suggests that the sites were appropriately chosen to capture views across the Muslim–Christian fault line. This divide mirrors north–south ethnic differences. Some bias in the research design exists in the favor of urban residents, which may weaken potential moderating effects from rural dwellers and traditional religionists, who are found in greater numbers in rural areas. On the other hand, the proportion of traditional religionists matches the proportion reported in representative surveys in Ghana,[15] and the data include an adequate sample of traditional religionists to help address causal mechanisms (later in the chapter).

---

[15] Afrobarometer results indicate that 3 percent of Ghanaians self-identify as traditional religionists. Afrobarometer data is available at http://afrobarometer.org/data2.html.

TABLE 3.2 *Summary Statistics of Sites, Participants, and Experiment*

| | Côte d'Ivoire | | Ghana | | |
	North	South	North	South	Pooled[a]
Sample size	300	300	299	294	1311
Percentage urban	80	72	71	69	73
Percentage male	50	50	50	50	50
Average age	37	39	37	39	38
Percentage Muslim	68	25	74	15	44
Percentage Christian	21	67	21	83	49
Percentage traditionalist	04	04	05	01	03
Religion treatment (N)	106	100	103	105	456
Ethnic treatment (N)	106	101	102	105	456
Control group (N)	88	99	94	84	399

[a] Pooled data include 118 observations from an enumeration area in Central Ghana (Kumasi). The disaggregated Kumasi figures are not shown to preserve visual clarity.

An important question to ask is whether or not the treatments actually had the desired effect on subjects; in short, did the treatments "take"? Evidence from the survey (independent from the actual outcomes that I seek to measure) suggests that they did. Subjects were asked, post-treatment, a variant of the Afrobarometer question on self-identity that inquired which of their various identity groups – nation, religion, ethnicity, gender, occupation, and so on – they feel that they belong to first and foremost.[16] Figure 3.2 illustrates that the treatment a participant received had a notable effect on his or her tendency to prioritize certain identities: whereas just under 30 percent of respondents in the control group (who did not listen to a radio report) selected religion as their primary identity – a figure in keeping with other survey results from Ghana and Côte d'Ivoire[17] – 50 percent of those who received the Religion treatment did so. Similarly, 24 percent of the control group, compared with 43 percent of those who received the Ethnic treatment, selected ethnicity as their

[16] The Afrobarometer question begins, "Besides being [national identity] ...," thus excluding nationality as a response. Here, I did not exclude it.

[17] The question closely resembles one asked on the first two rounds of the Afrobarometer survey, in which 33 percent of Ghanaians listed religion as their primary identity in the question on self-identity. No nationally representative surveys have addressed self-identity in Côte d'Ivoire, but a recent study conducted in Northern Côte d'Ivoire found that 28 percent of selected respondents listed religion first and foremost there (see McCauley and Posner 2017).

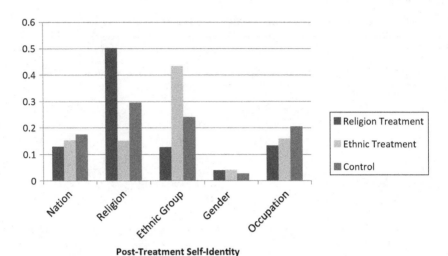

Post-Treatment Self-Identity

FIGURE 3.2. Participants' self-reported primary identities after receiving treatment.
Note: The *y*-axis indicates the proportion of participants citing selected identity types as the group to which they belong "first and foremost." Not shown are responses categorized as "Other." Results from the control group, which received no treatment, can be taken as a baseline.

primary identity.[18] Both differences are significant at the 99-percent confidence level in two-tailed tests. Furthermore, in post-survey debriefing sessions, 94 percent of those polled stated that they referenced the appropriate group (ethnic or religious) "with no confusion" when responding to the survey questions.[19]

Outcome Measures

After receiving treatment (or no treatment, in the case of the control group), subjects were asked a battery of background questions and

---

[18] Whether or not a respondent has been made to think in the context of a particular identity and whether or not she lists that identity as her primary one are distinct questions, so the fact that the treatment failed to transform the primary identity of all participants should not be troubling.

[19] I cannot rule out the possibility that respondents altered the group with which they identify foremost based on a desire to meet enumerator expectations. However, to the extent that respondents thought they were telling interviewers what they wanted to hear, that tendency itself would suggest effective priming of the key identity types. Furthermore, the outcome measures do not reference the identity types of interest in any way, thus reducing concerns that respondents might surmise the purpose of both the primes and the outcome measures.

several questions regarding sociopolitical preferences. The trials, which lasted approximately forty minutes from beginning to end, took place in either the official language (French in Côte d'Ivoire, English in Ghana), a frequently used regional language (Dioula in Côte d'Ivoire, Twi in Ghana), or the predominant local language (Senoufo in Korhogo, Dida in Divo, Dagbani in Tamale, Fante in Cape Coast).

Unlike the observational data mentioned at the beginning of this chapter, the outcome measures for this micro-level experiment could be tailored more precisely to the research question. To evaluate the extent to which ethnicity equates with preferences for local material development and religion equates with moral probity, I used three key measures based around hypothetical vignettes. First, respondents were asked to evaluate candidates for political office:

• Imagine two identical candidates for parliament who have only one difference: Candidate A promises to improve local development, and Candidate B promises to fight moral decay in society. Which would you prefer as your representative?

Subjects could choose Candidate A (development), Candidate B (morals), or neither. Respondents were informed that fighting moral decay could mean working to prevent substance abuse, adultery, promiscuous dress, and disrespect between community members. Improving local development could mean fixing roads, improving health and education services, and building a technology infrastructure.[20] The goal was to assess priorities regarding club goods versus moral behaviors. The order was reversed for a random subset of participants.

Second, participants were asked to select a hypothetical community in which to live:

• If the world were divided into three, in which community would you prefer to live: the community where everyone is wealthy, the community that is peaceful, or the community where everyone has strong moral values?

Subjects could choose any of the three or none; in addition, subjects were asked to rank their preferences from first to third. "Morality" was defined using the same examples as above. The purpose was to again gauge attachments to local club goods versus less geographically constrained moral goods.

---

[20] These examples were developed in the pre-experiment focus groups.

The third measure builds on the survey questions regarding corruption used at the outset of this chapter. While it does not address preferences over local development per se, it squarely pits the priority of moral probity against material interests at the individual level. Subjects were asked about their willingness to pay a bribe in the specific context of educational attainment:

- Here is a scenario: your child just missed the grade necessary to advance to the next class at school. The headmaster informs you that the child can advance if you give him a small sum as a token of appreciation. Would you accept the request so that your child can advance?

Responses were coded on a five-point scale from "definitely not" (indicating a refusal to engage in corruption of this sort) to "definitely" (a strong indication of a willingness to place material advancement over integrity). The vignette focuses most explicitly on the moral dimension, insofar as bribes are typically viewed through the lens of a "moral economy" in the region (Olivier de Sardan 1999) and family educational opportunities relate only tangentially to local development. The measure uses the education context since independent analyses (Reinikka 2006) and focus groups conducted for this study suggest that small-scale corruption of this sort is widespread in the region. Furthermore, educational opportunities may be considered a local club good, since consumption does not deplete the resource but not all communities or individuals have equal access. Thus, this third measure aims primarily to distinguish the priority that respondents in a religious versus an ethnic context place on moral probity – proxied by aversion to a specific form of corruption – though it also helps to adjudicate between the priorities of moral living and material advancement.

To summarize, the framing experiment was designed to randomly force otherwise identical subjects to prioritize either their ethnic or their religious identity (or neither, in the control group). Radio reports that differed only in their reference to ethnic or religious groups primed listeners to those respective contexts, after which the subjects responded to a set of hypothetical vignettes aimed at pitting concerns for local development against concerns for moral probity. The theory advanced in this part of the book suggests that the exogenous status of (narrow) ethnicity as a geographically bounded identity type generates norms in support of local club goods, whereas the unbounded, largely voluntary nature of the religious identity, rooted in sacred texts rather than geographic territory, evokes a relative concern for behavioral and lifestyle choices, or moral living.

I first present results from the pooled, two-country sample for each of the outcomes of interest; I then consider potential covariates and provide evidence to support a causal mechanism related to the mobilizational differences in ethnicity and religion. Concerns of bias due to the self-reported nature of the outcomes are mitigated in three ways. First, the surveys were conducted confidentially in private settings (the respondents' homes), by enumerators with no affiliation to a government or political party and with no clear indication of ethnic or religious group membership. These data collection protocols help to insulate the study from concerns that respondents felt pressured to answer questions in any particular way. Second, there is no clear expectation regarding socially desirable responses, since no obvious stigmas are attached to either local club goods or social behavior policies. Finally, even a systematic bias toward socially desirable responses could not explain the variation in outcomes across ethnic and religious contexts; by virtue of the process of random assignment, there is no reason to suspect that bias in self-reported outcomes would be correlated with assignment to treatment.

Regarding preferences for a "moral" candidate versus a "development" candidate, 64 percent of all survey respondents selected the former and 34 percent the latter. Disaggregating by treatment, however, 70 percent of those receiving the Religion treatment preferred the moral candidate, whereas only 59 percent of those receiving the Ethnic treatment did so, a difference that is significant at $p < .001$ in a two-tailed test and robust to disaggregation by specific religious and ethnic affiliation. Conversely, just 29 percent of those treated with Religion, versus 40 percent of those treated with Ethnic, favored the development candidate ($p < .001$). The top cluster in Figure 3.3, which illustrates treatment effects with mean control group outcomes set at zero, indicates a four-percentage-point boost in support for the moral candidate in a religious context and a seven-percentage-point drop in support for the moral candidate in the ethnic context. These results lend support to the notion that ethnicity fosters a relatively stronger emphasis on the improvement of local land and territory, while religion fosters an emphasis on good behavior. In a post-trial focus group, one respondent tellingly revealed

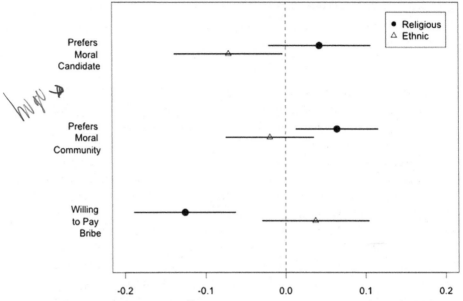

FIGURE 3.3. Treatment effects.

Notes: The *x*-axis depicts differences in the proportion of affirmative responses among treated groups, compared with the control category (control means set at zero). In Question 1, the moral candidate is pitted against a development candidate (control group mean = 0.662). In Question 2, the figure indicates the proportion selecting a community in which everyone has strong morals over one in which everyone is wealthy (control group mean = 0.798). In Question 3, the figure indicates the proportion stating a willingness to pay a small bribe for schooling (control group mean = 0.378). Bars indicate 95-percent confidence intervals.

that he would have to prefer the moral candidate because "I'm not in my home region, so why bother with the development?"

With respect to preferences among hypothetically wealthy, peaceful, and moral communities, the majority of respondents (68 percent) listed their first priority as a peaceful community; just 3 percent mentioned a wealthy community first and 29 percent prioritized the moral community. To distinguish between the interests in a manner that would be fruitful to this study, I took advantage of the rankings that respondents provided, generating a dummy variable coded 1 if the respondent listed the moral community ahead of the wealthy community and 0 otherwise. Again, the results conform to a theory suggesting that religion cultivates an emphasis on good behavior over wealth accumulation: the second cluster in Figure 3.3 illustrates a six-percentage-point boost in the proportion favoring the moral community among those exposed to the Religion treatment (86 percent vs. 80 percent in the control category) and a two-percentage-point decline among those exposed to the Ethnic treatment. The difference between Religion and Ethnic is again significant at $p = .001$; though the outcome is not large in substantive terms, it is notable given the tendency not to prioritize wealth in explicit responses.

Regarding corruption, 34 percent of all participants stated that they would probably or definitely be willing to pay the small bribe to enable their child to advance in school. As the bottom cluster in Figure 3.3 illustrates, however, the inclination to do so depends on which identity context was primed: just 25 percent of respondents receiving the Religion treatment, versus 42.5 percent of those who received the Ethnic treatment, expressed a willingness to pay the bribe ($p < .001$), generating treatment effects against the control category of −12 and +4 percentage points, respectively. Again, the finding suggests that in religious contexts, individuals are relatively more inclined toward the choice that implies moral integrity, whereas their otherwise identical counterparts placed in an ethnic context tend toward the choice that prioritizes material outcomes. An interesting implication of this particular outcome is that actors interested in combating corruption, or at least in generating expressed rejection of corrupt practices, may do best to channel their efforts through religious leadership and organizations rather than relying on political or ethnic actors. The rationale for doing so, according to the argument advanced here, would have nothing to do with any perceived rectitude of religious leaders versus their ethnic or political counterparts, but would instead turn on the exogenous norms that religion evokes.

Given the experimental nature of the data, in which subjects were randomly assigned to treatment and control categories, regression analysis imposes unnecessary parametric assumptions, so these simple comparisons of means are analytically sufficient. I take note of the outcomes in a multivariate regression framework, however, to gain insight into the possibility that other covariates have a substantive effect on the preferences I measure, beyond the effects of the framing treatments. The table is included in Appendix D. Column 1 reveals that, even when controlling for demographic factors and religious group membership, ethnicity and religion foster different preferences regarding material development and morals: subjects receiving the Ethnic treatment are 8 percent less likely than the control group to support the moral issues candidate over the development candidate ($p < .05$), whereas those receiving the Religion treatment are more likely than the control group to do so ($p < .05$). Males are also significantly more likely than females to favor a development candidate over a moral candidate. In Column 2, those primed to religion are 8 percent more likely to prefer the moral community over the wealthy community. Older and more educated respondents similarly favor the moral community. Turning to Column 3, receiving the Religion treatment makes subjects 14 percent less likely than the control group to express a willingness to pay a bribe to support a family member's educational advancement; those receiving the Ethnic treatment express a greater likelihood of engaging in corruption, though the effect does not reach conventional levels of statistical significance. Females and more educated respondents also express a systematic aversion to the bribe, as do Ivoirian residents.

To reiterate, the full experiment was replicated across multiple sites in two countries, producing similar results across research contexts. As Table 3.3 shows, the outcomes hold across both Muslim- and Christian-predominant areas, mitigating concerns that they are a function of one side of the religious fault line or one particular ethnic group.[21] The patterns are also apparent in both Ghana and Cote d'Ivoire but stronger in the latter, suggesting that respondents there were influenced both by the experimental treatments and by the sharper identity-related mobilization efforts that political elites have undertaken since the late 1990s. I discuss this in greater detail in Chapter 6. At any rate, the consistency across sites in this region of Africa adds an important degree of generalizability to the finding that priming ethnicity evokes concerns for local material well-being, while the religious identity is associated with a relative concern for moral issues.

TESTING THE CAUSAL MECHANISM

In addition to demonstrating a treatment (radio reports that isolate ethnic and religious identities) and an effect from that treatment (in terms of differential preferences), the experimental data can also be exploited to elucidate the mechanism that accounts for that effect. In other words, *why* do people who (metaphorically) put on their ethnic hats have different preferences compared with those who wear their religious hats?

I have argued that preferences among individuals in ethnic versus religious contexts vary simply as a result of the characteristics underlying these social identities in contemporary Africa. If the rule-based,

---

[21] Religious and ethnic affiliations at the individual level are accounted for in the regression model's fixed effects.

TABLE 3.3 *Data by Research Site*

	Treatment	Prefers Moral Candidate	Prefers Moral Community	Willing to Pay Bribe
Côte d'Ivoire				
Korhogo (N)	Religion	0.66	0.83	0.20
	Ethnic	0.52	0.81	0.40
	Control	0.60	0.72	0.32
Divo (S)	Religion	0.72	0.86	0.15
	Ethnic	0.55	0.77	0.42
	Control	0.70	0.78	0.36
Ghana				
Tamale (N)	Religion	0.78	0.84	0.33
	Ethnic	0.78	0.72	0.43
	Control	0.76	0.83	0.39
Cape Coast (S)	Religion	0.64	0.91	0.29
	Ethnic	0.57	0.88	0.42
	Control	0.60	0.90	0.45
Kumasi (C)	Religion	0.74	0.88	0.32
	Ethnic	0.48	0.62	0.39
	Control	0.61	0.71	0.38

Notes: N = northern enumeration area, S = southern enumeration area, C = central enumeration area. Figures represent the proportion responding affirmatively to hypothetical scenarios.

geographically expansive nature of religion and the local, land-oriented nature of ethnicity are indeed the mechanisms driving preferences when these identities are prioritized, it should be the case that a religion without formal behavioral codes and with greater attachments to the local land actually inspires preferences similar to ethnic groups. Traditional religions in Africa are exactly this; as I described earlier, the belief system is typically not adoptable by outsiders, and natural, land-based icons such as hills, springs, and notable trees feature prominently (Onaiyekan 1983).

Thus, as a test of the mechanism, I exploit the multivariate regression analyses to evaluate the preferences of participants in the study who self-reported as being practitioners of traditional African religions. The direction of influence of traditional religion on measured outcomes, even when controlling for the experimental treatments those subjects received, is

TABLE 3.4 *Comparison of Treatment Effects and Traditional Religion on Dependent Variables*

	Prefers Moral Candidate	Prefers Moral Community	Willing to Pay Bribe
Religion treatment	+0.04 (0.015)	+0.08 (0.022)	−0.14 (0.030)
Ethnic treatment	−0.08 (0.027)	−0.01 (0.033)	+0.04 (0.029)
Traditional religionists	−0.12 (0.045)	−0.21 (0.128)	+0.05 (0.057)

Notes: Positive and negative signs represent the direction of effects of the Religion and Ethnic treatments and the dummy variable for traditional religionists, drawn from the multivariate logistic regressions. Standard errors are shown in parentheses.

illuminating. Table 3.4 shows a comparison of the signs and magnitude of impact for the Ethnic treatment, the Religion treatment, and membership in traditional African religions, extracted from the regressions. For each outcome, the sign on the coefficient for traditional religion matches the sign on the Ethnic coefficient and is opposite the sign on the Religion coefficient. If this pattern can be taken as suggestive of the fact that local religions with land-based worship sites but missing doctrinal codes and voluntary entry equate more closely with ethnicity, then traditional religion in Africa is the exception that proves the rule: world religions and African ethnic groups are substantively different types of identity for contemporary Africans, and they elicit different political priorities.

One concern that bears mention is that membership in a traditional African religion may act as little more than an ethnic prime: those who label themselves traditional religionists may do so to reaffirm the importance of their ethnic status. In that case, the fact that the regression coefficients on traditional religious membership and the experimental Ethnic treatment share the same signs would reveal little about the distinction between religion and ethnicity, since both are just priming ethnicity. One way to address this concern is to note the correlation between respondents' stated membership in a traditional religion and their tendency to prioritize their ethnic identity first and foremost. Because the correlation coefficient is just −0.002 ($p = .954$), it is safe to argue that those who identify themselves as traditional religionists are not generally among the most ardent supporters of the ethnic identity. Furthermore, in separate data collected for the analysis in Chapter 4, just 3.5 percent of Ashanti ethnic group association members – a committed group of ethnic loyalists – listed their religion as traditional African. If traditional religion were only a synonym for ethnicity or "tribe," we would expect to see stronger relationships between active membership in an ethnic association and traditional religious practice.

CONCLUSION

The strategy I employed to test the hypotheses presented in Chapter 2, and to improve on the shortcomings of observational data, was ambitious – I provided information treatments not with the goal of generating one bias or another, but rather with the intention of altering the identity lens through which participants view sociopolitical questions. Metaphorically, I forced them to temporarily wear either an ethnic hat or a religious hat and then measured their individual-level preferences. That strategy produced moderate but clear effects: when individuals in the study area are assigned to a religious context as opposed to an ethnic context, they express a relative preference for candidates focused on moral policy, for communities that prioritize moral living, and for rejecting small-scale corruption. I attribute this to the rule-based, voluntary nature of world religions, which inspires a preference for geographically unbounded, behavioral outcomes. In an ethnic context, otherwise identical respondents demonstrate a relative preference for candidates who focus on local development, for wealthy communities, and for individual advancement over transparency, which I attribute to their pursuit of local club goods.

The bigger picture contribution of this empirical chapter is an insight into the baselines from which ethnicity and religion are politicized. By allowing only the identity context to vary, I have shown that political entrepreneurs in the region can expect different preferences from their followers when they mobilize those supporters along ethnic or religious lines. Thus, political entrepreneurs might leverage distinct policy promises to ensure the support of an optimal identity coalition, or they might mobilize a particular identity type in order to generate enthusiasm for particular policies. As I detail later in the book, for example, restrictions on non-native access to land in Côte d'Ivoire in the 1990s propelled former presidents Henri Konan Bedié and Laurent Ghagbo to victory while ushering in a period in which politics were viewed in "ethnonational" terms (Bassett 2003; Dozon 2000). When a different set of mobilization tactics was used, the lens through which contestation was viewed switched to a religious one. Similarly, the use of Shari'a law in northern Nigeria (Falola and Heaton 2008) and laws against homosexuality in Uganda (Kaoma 2009) to mobilize supporters along religious lines, or appeals to indigenous Hutu rights to land in Rwanda (Prunier 1995) and Igbo control of oil fields in southern Nigeria (Badru 1998) to elicit support along ethnic lines, can be viewed as mobilization efforts that exploit the differential preferences associated with ethnicity and religion at the individual level.

One objection to the premise underlying this component of the study is that, in keeping with the ambiguous nature of religion as an identity,[22] some individuals may treat their religion *as* their ethnicity. This is largely true of Arab Muslims in Chad, for example, and other predominantly Muslim countries in the region show comparatively low levels of ethnic favoritism, which might suggest that the religious identity is used in place of an ethnic one (see Franck and Rainer 2012). If this were broadly true, there would be little need to explain heterogeneity in identity types. One response to that objection is simply to assert that, in fact, the vast majority of sub-Saharan Africans view these identity types as distinct. Instead, the research design accounted for this complication by allowing respondents themselves to self-categorize: the treatments did not delineate the groups to which respondents belonged, they simply primed ethnicity or religion. Respondents then answered the battery of questions on social and political preferences according to whatever sentiment had been primed in the context of the experiment. Thus, while this study uses blunt divisions to address an exceedingly complex issue, the empirical results demonstrate that doing so can teach us new things about the mobilizational differences between ethnicity and religion.

The research should not suggest that ethnic and religious identities inspire fixed or orthogonal outcomes – group norms change and are redefined; they may generate unique responses in different places; and types of identity can be intertwined. Rather, what this chapter does is to highlight distinctions in the broad priorities that ethnicity and world religions elicit in one particular study region of contemporary Africa, and it suggests important effects regarding the strategic mobilization of identities for political purposes: when elites contemplate mobilizing populations along either ethnic or religious lines, they begin that process of politicization from different baselines. We might imagine related questions that follow from the findings presented here: what strategies can

---

[22] As noted, Chandra (2006) argues that religion is in some cases "ethnic" and in some not, depending on whether the identity is passed down through family or adopted via conversion.

elites employ to overcome coalitional disadvantages based on one of these identity types? How might political leaders inspire collective action through appeals to ethnicity or religion? What outcomes might we expect in other parts of the world, perhaps where the religious identity may be taken as more geographically bounded? These and related questions receive attention in subsequent chapters, but treating ethnicity and religion as distinct in the political context will serve as an important starting point for the analysis that follows in Part II.

4

Observable Implications

In the previous chapter, I showed evidence for the existence of mobilizational differences between (narrow) ethnicity and religion using an original field experiment that manipulated the salience of these identity types
at the individual level. In this chapter, I consider some observable implications of those findings; I hope they will help to further distinguish ethnic
from religious preferences in contemporary Africa and to add a measure
of external validity to the experimental results presented thus far.

The chapter comprises three sections. First, if an experimental manipulation of identities generates different preferences among otherwise identical subjects placed in ethnic and religious contexts, the same trends
should be evident, and perhaps even stronger, among subjects with strong
real-world attachments to their ethnic and religious groups (who came
to the experiment with those particular life experiences). Thus,
I disaggregate the outcomes from the experiment based on level of commitment to the group, comparing the results from experimental participants who are deeply committed ethnic and religious group members to
those with very weak attachments to their ethnic and religious groups.
Second, I compare the experimental findings with responses from active
members of "strong" ethnic and religious organizations outside the data
sample, whose preferences we could also expect to be similarly patterned
after, and even stronger than, the findings from experimental manipulation of random subjects. Third, I consider an observable implication from
the subset of experimental subjects with divided ethnic identities: if the
mechanism underpinning the link between ethnicity and local material
goods is the geographic boundedness of ethnicity that inspires personal
attachments to local lands, it should be the case that individuals with a

mixed ethnic identity – and thus with at least part of their ethnic loyalties located outside the region in which they reside – show evidence of weaker ethnic-based preferences than their counterparts with only one ethnic claim. Together, these analyses should strengthen my claim that ethnic and religious identities evoke fundamentally different preferences that political entrepreneurs can exploit.

The evidence suggests that mobilizational differences between ethnicity and religion are not simply a function of experimental manipulation: for all three outcome variables evaluated in Chapter 3, the differences between ethnicity and religion among experimental subjects are present and substantively greater when I compare uncommitted group members with committed group members. The same is true of differences between members of "strong" ethnic and religious groups, vis-à-vis their randomly selected experimental counterparts. Finally, though the differences are minor, bi-ethnic respondents demonstrate a weaker affinity for local material development than do their counterparts with one single ethnic identity. The evidence follows.

COMMITTED VERSUS UNCOMMITTED RELIGIOUS AND ETHNIC GROUP MEMBERS

To return to the metaphor I came upon during field research, committed adherents to ethnicity and religion are most likely to consistently wear just one identity hat. They devote more time to ethnic- or religious-related activities, and the odds are greater that they view policies, events, and interpersonal relations through their respective ethnic or religious lens. As a result, we might expect that the same trends observed in randomly assigning individuals to one context or the other would be evident (and even stronger) among committed members of ethnic and religious groups as opposed to individuals who simply do not care very much about their ethnic and religious attachments. Personal involvement in ethnic or religious life can thus moderate the effects of the experimental treatments.

Earlier, I explained why relying on committed versus uncommitted ethnic and religious group members would not have been an appropriate primary test of distinctions between ethnicity and religion – we could not be sure whether personal commitments to their ethnic or religious identities lead them to hold certain preferences (which would be consistent with a story of mobilizational differences) or whether their prior preferences lead them to participate actively in one of those groups (which would introduce bias due to selection effects). Having established in

Chapter 3 a causal path from identity type to preferred outcomes,[1] a comparison of committed and uncommitted ethnic and religious group members can now reaffirm the experimental findings in an observational manner.

For the purposes of this analysis, I measure commitment to ethnicity or religion using attendance at ethnic or religious group meetings. Attendance represents a somewhat imprecise measure of commitment in the sense that it can capture a desire for belonging or accumulating social capital in addition to measuring the importance of the identity in individuals' lives; I nevertheless rely on this measure for three reasons. First and foremost, no easily understood parallels for prayer or divine influence – common measures of religiosity – exist in the ethnic context, and I wished to maintain consistency in measures across treatment types. Second, in the religious context, attendance is positively correlated with other measures of religiosity (Mueller 1980), suggesting that the crude measure still allows for reasonable inferences regarding identity attachments. Third, individuals interested in community activism can choose any type of voluntary group to express that interest; the choice to be an everyday member of an ethnic or a religious organization suggests that something related to the identity type is likely at work. As a result, I take attendance as an imprecise but reasonable means of distinguishing those committed to their ethnic identity from those with weak ethnic group attachments and those committed to their religious identity from the religiously uncommitted or unobservant.[2]

Participants were asked, as part of the survey that accompanied the experiment, how often they attended meetings or ceremonies exclusively with members of their ethnic/religious group, the purpose of which was to consider ethnic/religious matters.[3] The idea was that participants

---

[1] I cannot assume the absence of causality running in the opposite direction, whereby preferences lead people to prioritize their ethnic or their religious identities. This undoubtedly occurs. To demonstrate that political entrepreneurs stand to gain different things from mobilizing along religious or ethnic lines, I need only demonstrate that identity contexts can shape preferred actions.

[2] I cannot rule out the possibility that some participants desire meeting more often but are constrained by the unavailability of a religious or ethnic organization. This would be a problem for the fairly small number of subjects who practice an "other" religion or who immigrated to an area where few ethnic group members live.

[3] Participants were asked about either ethnic or religious attendance, the selection of which depended on the treatment they received. Recall that questions were identical across treatments, asking only about "your group." Asking about both ethnic and religious behaviors among the same respondents may have introduced cues during questioning that could elicit biased responses.

TABLE 4.1 *Committed and Uncommitted Identity Group Members as Proportions of the Dataset*

	N	Proportion of Treatment Group
Religion Treatment		
Never attends religious meetings	77	0.171
Attends religious meetings every day	76	0.168
Ethnic Treatment		
Never attends ethnic group meetings	123	0.270
Attends ethnic meetings > once per week	75	0.164

Note: The religious subsets are drawn from the 456 participants who received the religion treatment. The ethnic subsets are drawn from the distinct set of 456 participants who received the ethnic treatment. The control group is not included in this analysis.

responding to the question in a religious context would consider their attendance at church or mosque and that those responding in an ethnic group context would reference their attendance at ethnic group organization meetings, tribal councils, and other similar ethnic-based reunions. Responses were coded on a six-point scale, where 1 indicates never attending such meetings and 6 corresponds to participants who stated that they attend such meetings every day. To compare the committed and the uncommitted, I disaggregated the experimental dataset by attendance frequency and compared responses regarding preferred candidates, preferred communities, and corruption (my key measures capturing mobilizational differences) among those who never attend (coded 1) and those who attend every day (coded 6). However, because few respondents in the ethnic context reported attending ethnic-oriented meetings daily, I expanded the category of frequent ethnic attendees to include those who attend more than once per week (coded 5 or 6). The sizes of the committed and uncommitted subgroups, relative to the ethnic and religious treatment groups from which they were drawn, are listed in Table 4.1.

The rationale for a comparison of committed and uncommitted group members is as follows. Manipulating the salience of ethnicity and religion has some effect on the average preferred outcomes among randomly selected individuals. At the same time, individual life experiences condition those outcomes. For example, whereas the Religion treatment I administered moved subjects closer (on average) to preferences for morality-based policies without geographic bounds, highly religious individuals would have come to the experiment with stronger preferences for morality-based policies to begin with. Therefore, frequent attendance at religious group meetings should be correlated with a relative preference for these religious outcomes, above and beyond the treatment effect. A corresponding preference for ethnic-oriented outcomes should be evident among those who frequently attend ethnic group meetings, relative to those who never attend such meetings. We know from Chapter 3 that statistically significant differences exist across the ethnic-treated and the religious-treated for all three outcome variables.

Now, what we should expect to see as an observable implication is that those differences are at least as important substantively as we evaluate the uncommitted versus the committed. Much smaller sample sizes reduce the likelihood of statistical significance, but a trend toward greater differences among the ethnically and religiously committed would constitute an appropriate confirmation of the findings from Chapter 3.

Figure 4.1 provides visual evidence supporting this expectation: for all three outcome variables, the difference between committed ethnic- and religious-treated subjects is greater than the distance between uncommitted individuals assigned to those same contexts.[4] First, with respect to ideal candidate types, the ethnically uncommitted and committed are equally likely to support a candidate who prioritizes a moral platform over local development: about 37 percent of both those who never attend ethnic meetings and those who frequently attend such meetings favor this candidate. However, 68 percent of the religiously uncommitted versus 78 percent of the religiously committed prefer a moral platform candidate over a development-oriented one. The ethnic-religious differences are thus notably wider among more committed individuals. Concerning preferences over community type, 78 percent of the religiously uncommitted versus 84 percent of the religiously committed prefer a strong moral community over a wealthy one. The ethnically uncommitted actually prefer the moral community at a slightly higher rate (81 percent) than the religiously uncommitted, but among the subjects who frequently attend ethnic group meetings, that figure drops to 76 percent. Again, the gap between ethnic and religious preferences widens among the committed group members, from −3 percentage points to 8 percentage points. Finally, concerning corruption, willingness to pay the bribe does not change from the ethnic uncommitted to those who attend ethnic

---

[4] I do not present control group results or results from participants with middling levels of attendance, for purposes of visual clarity.

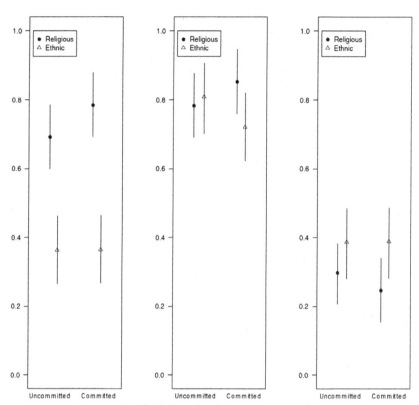

FIGURE 4.1. Uncommitted ethnic and religious group members versus committed members.

Notes: Uncommitted refers to experimental subjects who never attend ethnic or religious group meetings. Committed members are those who attend at least once per week (in the case of ethnic meetings) or every day (in the case of religion).

meetings frequently, remaining at 39 percent. Conversely, 31 percent of the religiously uncommitted are willing to pay a bribe for education, but only 25 percent of those who attend religious meetings every day state that they would do so, a finding in keeping with the expectation that religious attachments inspire preferences for moral probity. As a result, the differences in ethnic and religious preferences again increase when we compare uncommitted group members with very committed ones.

These subset analyses reduce sample sizes significantly, so the difference-in-differences in probability scales are not statistically significant at standard levels. Nevertheless, the trends are as expected for each of the measured outcomes: those most committed to their ethnic and religious identities exemplify the distinctions between ethnicity and religion documented among a wider population of experimental subjects, reaffirming the findings that ethnicity generates preferences for local land and development, whereas religion cultivates stronger preferences for geographically unbounded outcomes rooted in morality.

"STRONG" ETHNIC AND RELIGIOUS GROUP ADHERENTS

A similar observable implication may be made with respect to members of "strong" identity group organizations outside the experimental sample. Almond et al. (2003) use the term "strong religion" to describe those religious organizations and denominations with high expectations governing attendance, loyalty, exclusivity, and conformity to the group's mission; one might also call them extremist or fundamentalist. I adopt the notion of strong groups here in reference to both religious and ethnic organizations that inspire or demand deep commitments from their members. If the experimental findings from Chapter 3 are to be believed, what might they tell us about the attitudes and behaviors of strong ethnic and religious group members in the real-world context of West Africa? We could expect that those individuals, who again consistently wear just one identity hat (either ethnic or religious), epitomize the distinct preferences of ethnic and religious contexts. Furthermore, they would be especially likely to espouse views consistent with ethnicity/religion when primed by a natural setting – a church or mosque in the religious context, for example, or a tribal council meeting in the ethnic context. Inasmuch as strong group members epitomize the distinctions between ethnicity and religion, we could anticipate that patterns in their preferences would be similar to the patterns in the experimental results and that the distance between strong ethnics and strong religionists would be at least as great as the distance between ethnic-treated and religious-treated individuals in the experimental study, whose identities were briefly manipulated but who otherwise brought a wide variety of complex identity attachments to the experiment. Incorporating subjects not exposed to the experimental conditions renews concerns over selection bias, but, coupled with the experimental findings, they add important external validity to the analysis.

To compare results from the experiment with strong group adherents in the real world (free of experimental manipulation), I interviewed a total of 194 individuals from strong identity groups in Kumasi, Ghana. To ensure that the findings are not driven by something unique about the Kumasi area, I also included 118 randomly selected Kumasians in the experimental sample (as noted in Chapter 3). The strong group members belonged to either an Ashanti ethnic group association or to a Charismatic Pentecostal Christian Church or the Ahlu Sunnah wal Jama'aah Muslim organization.

To add some context to the inclusion of these particular groups, Charismatic Pentecostalism is the driving force behind the recent, overwhelming wave of Christian renewal in Africa, and the movement has enjoyed particularly widespread expansion in Ghana. Today, over a quarter of Ghanaians label themselves members of Pentecostal-Charismatic churches (Anderson 2013). Modeled after American evangelical churches with superstar preachers and in some cases megachurch facilities, they emphasize the role of the spirit in Christian worship, often manifested through glossolalia (speaking in tongues), dance, prophesy, and miracle healing (Anderson 2013). Observers attribute the success of Charismatic Pentecostalism in the region to relative gender and age equality, minimal hierarchy, compatibility with traditional beliefs, and an emphasis on being saved now rather than waiting for the afterlife (Gifford 2004). I drew the sample of strong Christian adherents from Charismatic Pentecostal churches due to the relatively encompassing nature of this particular brand of Christianity; public opinion data suggest that Pentecostals in the region are more likely than other Christians to prioritize religion in their lives and to attend religious services.[5] In total, sixty respondents were drawn from two churches, the In Him Is Life Christian Church and the Ebenezer Miracle Church. Interviews were conducted after religious services or church-related meetings.

The Ahlu Sunnah wal Jama'aah (ASWAJ) Muslim group represents what is commonly referred to as Wahhabism, a branch of Islam devoted to strict compliance with the words and practices of the Prophet Mohammed. Originating in 1700s Saudi Arabia under the leadership of Mohammed bin Abdul al-Wahhab, some followers in 1979 officially eschewed a named association with Wahhab – whom they view not as a prophet but as a leader who stressed returning primacy to the Prophet – and adopted the name meaning "followers of the Sunnah" to characterize themselves as most authentic among Sunni Muslims.[6] In the study region, ASWAJ

---

[5] See Round 5 data from the Afrobarometer surveys at http://afrobarometer.org/data/merged-round-5-data-34-countries-2011-2013-last-update-july-2015.

[6] Interview with Al-Hajj Haziz Al-Hussein Zakaria, Chairman of the Maryam Centre for Interreligious Dialogue, Tamale, Ghana. January 28, 2009.

represents only a fraction (approximately 10 to 15 percent) of Muslims; they are noteworthy for their dress and appearance (robes and beards for the men, burkhas for the women), exclusivity in lifestyle, scriptural literalism, a resistance to accommodating traditional practices, and a commitment to the ideal that no boundaries should exist between the religious and the sociopolitical.[6] Like Charismatic Pentecostals, ASWAJ members in the region demonstrate higher levels of religious commitment than their orthodox and Sufi Muslim counterparts.[8] The research team interviewed seventy-six ASWAJ members during the Ahlu Sunnah Wal Jama'aah National Conference held in the spring of 2009. Respondents were primarily residents of the Kumasi area but also came from across Ghana and in some cases from neighboring countries, having gathered as part of a group of approximately 5,000 for prayer and speeches. Four male research assistants interviewed the sixty male participants; a female research assistant interviewed the sixteen female participants.

Members of three Ashanti ethnic group associations were chosen to represent the strong ethnic adherents. Those groups include the Asante Old Students' Association (membership of approximately 300), the Asante Kroye Kuo (membership of 140), and the Asanteman Nkosoo Kuo (125 active members). Mission statements for each suggest a desire to preserve the historical legacy of the Ashanti and to advance the contemporary interests of the Ashanti people. That mandate is significant: the Ashanti Kingdom was the most dominant in present-day Ghana from the late seventeenth century until its eventual defeat and submission under English Colonial rule (Edgerton 1995). The paramount chief, the Ashantehene, maintains informal authority over matters of land, education, language, and development in the region (Boafo-Arthur 2003). A subgroup of the broader Akan, the Ashanti comprise the largest ethno-linguistic group in Ghana, and the language of the Ashanti (Twi) is the most commonly spoken (CIA World Factbook 2015). Ashanti association members span age categories of both genders; they meet independently from one another and from the traditional cabinet of the Ashantehene, but they are in frequent consultation with the traditional

[7] Personal communication with Sheikh Mohammed Kamil Mohammed, Regional Imam of the Ahlu Sunnah wal Jama'aah, Kumasi, Ghana, February 22, 2009.
[8] Too few Muslim respondents in the Afrobarometer surveys list their subgroup to make statistical analysis worthwhile. Nevertheless, Wahhabi/ASWAJ respondents outpace other Muslims in the measures of religiosity cited above. See Round 5 data from the Afrobarometer surveys at http://afrobarometer.org/data/merged-round-5-data-34-countries-2011-2013-last-update-july-2015.

hierarchy.[9] For the sample of strong ethnic group adherents, the research team interviewed fifty-eight Ashanti association members in the spring of 2009; interviews were conducted just after their weekly association meetings.

Kumasi was the most appropriate place to base this component of the research for several reasons. First, the Ashanti are widely viewed as having the strongest historical legacy in the region and as being particularly proud of their ethnic identity; nationally representative public opinion data indicate that the Ashanti are more likely than any other major ethnic group in Ghana to list their ethnicity as the most important of their individual identities.[10] Furthermore, the period of research corresponded with the national conference of the Ahlu Sunnah Wal Jama'aah in Kumasi, providing a rare opportunity to collect data from a large sample of group members in an informal yet very religious setting. Finally, the Pentecostal-Charismatic movement is an integral part of the fabric of modern Kumasi culture (Gifford 2004).

Participants were solicited via a convenience sampling procedure. Survey questions were identical to those posed to experimental subjects in the randomized component of the study presented in Chapter 3; the only difference was that strong group adherents were not exposed to an experimental treatment prior to the survey. The intention was that their active participation in strong identity group organizations, along with the context in which the surveys were conducted, would serve as more intense, real world "treatments." As a reminder, my interest was in distinguishing the preferences of strong ethnics from strong religionists. Thus, whereas differences may exist between the strong Christians and Muslims, for example, I focus my analysis on the comparison of strong ethnic and religious group members, vis-à-vis a similar comparison of treated experimental subjects. The expectation is that differences noted between ethnic-treated and religious-treated subjects in the randomized experiment in Chapter 3 would be exacerbated among strong ethnics and strong religionists.

The evidence supports this claim. As Figure 4.2 illustrates, the differences that were apparent among experimental subjects in ethnic versus

---

[9] Interview with Simon Marfo, President of the Asante Old Students' Association, Kumasi, Ghana, February 10, 2009.

[10] Based on responses to the question, "In addition to being Ghanaian, how do you identify yourself first and foremost?" As noted, this particular survey question was dropped from the Afrobarometer survey after Round 2. See Round 2 data from the Afrobarometer surveys at http://afrobarometer.org/data/ghana-round-2-data-2002.

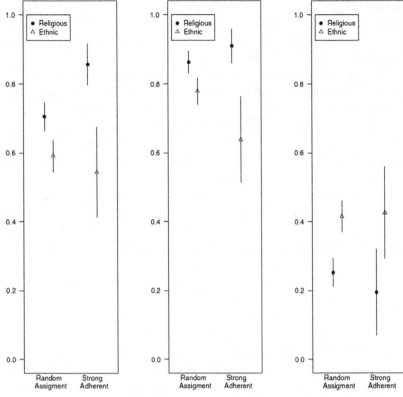

FIGURE 4.2. Experimental subjects compared with strong ethnic and religious group members.

Notes: The y-axis represents proportions who responded affirmatively. Random assignment refers to experimental subjects who received either the religious or the ethnic prime. Strong adherent refers to members of the Charismatic churches, the Ahlu Sunnah Wal Jama'aah Muslim group, or the Ashanti associations.

religious contexts are all apparent, and in fact stronger, when comparing strong ethnics versus strong religionists. First, strong ethnic group adherents are significantly less likely than their religious group counterparts to prefer a moral issues candidate over a development candidate (54 vs. 83 percent), a ratio greater than the comparison of ethnic- and religious-treated subjects in the randomized experiment (59 vs. 70 percent). Second, strong religious group members are more likely than the religious-treated experimental subjects to prefer living in a moral community over a wealthy community (90 percent vs. 86 percent), whereas strong ethnic group members demonstrate less interest in the moral community compared with the ethnic-treated subjects (64 percent vs. 78

percent). This finding, too, is in keeping with the expectation that the stronger the ethnic attachment, the stronger the priority on local material development. Third, members of strong ethnic groups are significantly more willing than their strong religious counterparts to pay a bribe (48 percent vs. 17 percent), a ratio that is again greater than the ratio of ethnic-treated versus religious-treated experimental subjects (43 percent vs. 25 percent).

These observed data among strong group adherents complement the experimental data from Chapter 3, and they suggest two important lessons that will serve the second part of the book. First, constitutive differences between ethnicity and religion exist in contemporary Africa, and they contribute to distinct preferences. Second, individuals who dedicate themselves to demanding ethnic and religious organizations, and who presumably identify with their respective identity types in a deep and consistent manner, are even more likely than the experimental subjects to follow the patterns of mobilizational differences in ethnicity and religion that I have described. This out-of-sample test thus illustrates the possibility that some ethnic and religious adherents may be particularly prone to mobilization efforts by political leaders, especially when institutions break down and contentious politics take over. That the participants in this component of the study were not exposed to any artificial treatments but instead brought their own life choices to bear on their survey responses also adds a measure of external validity to the experimental findings.

A shortcoming in this analysis is that almost all strong adherents are also residents of Kumasi, Ghana. It is possible, therefore, that the results from strong ethnic and religious group adherents are reflective not of mobilizational differences between identity types, but instead of something peculiar about Kumasi. To address this concern, I included in the experimental dataset 118 observations from randomly selected residents of Kumasi.[11] Table 4.2 presents the rates of affirmative responses to key outcome questions among this subset from Kumasi and among the pooled subset from the other research sites in the north (Tamale) and south (Cape Coast) of Ghana,[12] disaggregated by treatment type.

[11] Observations were included in the findings reported in Chapter 3. See Chapter 3 for a discussion of participant selection processes.
[12] I did not include subjects in Côte d'Ivoire, as I anticipate country-level differences attributable to the politicization of religion during the recent conflict (see Chapter 6).

TABLE 4.2 *Responses among Residents of Kumasi and the Rest of Ghana*

	Mean, Kumasi	Mean, Rest of Ghana	p-value
Religion Treatment			
Prefers "moral" candidate	0.74	0.71	0.682
Prefers "moral" community	0.88	0.87	0.907
Willing to pay bribe	0.31	0.32	0.921
Ethnic Treatment			
Prefers "moral" candidate	0.48	0.67	0.021 *
Prefers "moral" community	0.62	0.80	0.015 *
Willing to pay bribe	0.39	0.42	0.935
Control Group			
Prefers "moral" candidate	0.61	0.68	0.372
Prefers "moral" community	0.71	0.87	0.024 *
Willing to pay bribe	0.38	0.42	0.318

* $p < .05$.

When exposed to the Religion treatment, randomly selected Kumasi residents are statistically no different from participants in the north and south with respect to the three outcome measures. Among those who received the Ethnic treatment, conversely, residents of Kumasi are less likely than their counterparts in the north and south to favor a moral issues candidate over a development-focused candidate and less likely to prefer a moral community over a wealthy community. Otherwise stated, their concerns about local development and wealth are stronger. However, if these outcomes are generally reflective of the cosmopolitan environment in Kumasi – Ghana's second largest city, whose population exceeds one million – we would expect the same trends to be evident among respondents who received the Religion treatment, but they are not. Thus, the uniqueness of Kumasi alone is likely an incomplete explanation for the choices of strong ethnic group adherents who reside in the city (and who tend to favor local development and wealth to a greater degree than others).

Among the control group, residents of Kumasi are again fairly similar to participants from other areas, though they place relatively less emphasis on living in a moral community as opposed to a wealthy community. Thus, despite some idiosyncratic differences, residents of Kumasi are not so different from their counterparts in the north and south of Ghana as to explain the stark contrasts in preferences among the strong ethnic group adherents and strong religious group adherents that the research team uncovered through interviews in their identity group settings in Kumasi. These observational data add further confidence to the claim that ethnicity and religion have constitutively different effects on otherwise similar individuals in this West African study region.

PREFERENCES AMONG BI-ETHNICS

The evidence for mobilizational differences between religion and ethnicity that I have presented thus far suggests that when ethnicity is mobilized, individuals are more interested in local land and development that serves their kin. It also suggests that when religion is mobilized, those same individuals show a relative tendency to prioritize moral and rule-based matters over local, material ones. Underlying these and other findings is the fact that most individuals in the study region have undivided, "pure" ethnic and religious identities – that is, they identify with just one ethnic group and with just one religious group. These consistent identities give meaning to "us versus them" distinctions, such that when one or the other identity type is mobilized, individuals can see themselves with little difficulty as an in-group member to some and an out-group member to others. Some individuals, however, do not have such undivided identities; they report belonging to two groups within the same identity type, typically as a result of inter-marriage. A third observable implication in this study is that these individuals – bi-religionists and bi-ethnics – should have conflicting or unclear loyalties and preferences when subjected to identity mobilization. Thus, among participants in the experiment with mixed ethnic or religious identity, we should expect an attenuation of the results, relative to the sampled population of subjects with "pure" identities.

Membership in ethnic and religious groups was self-reported. Thus, categorization as a Malinké, Senoufo, Christian, Muslim, or any other ethnic or religious group member is a function not of biology or history but of a personal choice regarding self-identity. In that sense, many more subjects are likely to be of mixed ethnic and religious lineage than the numbers who reported being so; others have adopted one or the other of their parents' identities (or perhaps a third, unrelated identity) as their own, such that, when asked, they report having only one ethnic or religious identity. This is particularly true of religious identity: 2.5 percent of sampled individuals reported being a member of no religious group, but, consistent with David Laitin's (2000) claim that one cannot be "bi-religious," not a single participant reported having a dual or mixed religious identity.[13]

Self-identification as bi-ethnic, conversely, was more common: 8.7 percent of the total surveyed population, and 10.7 percent of the subset who received the Ethnic treatment, reported being of two ethnic groups. That there is a slight difference in reported bi-ethnicity among the total sample and the ethnic-treated subset should not be surprising; having received the ethnic prime would have made experimental subjects more attuned to their personal ethnic identity, whereas subjects who received the religion prime or who were placed in the control group would have assigned less importance (and therefore less nuance) to the question regarding ethnic identity. To be clear, the figures do not suggest that only a tenth of respondents are of mixed ethnic parentage. This would be a minimum, capturing only those who reported being so, a choice that rested entirely with the respondents themselves. If they provided this information to enumerators, they were also asked if they considered themselves to be primarily of one or the other ethnic group. Recording ethnic identity in this manner averted the risk of double-counting or dropping subjects but also afforded the advantage of insight into heterogeneous treatment effects among a distinct (bi-ethnic) subset of respondents. Ivoirians were somewhat more likely than Ghanaians to label themselves bi-ethnic, owing both to the greater number of ethnic groups in Côte d'Ivoire and to migration patterns there.

Because no subjects in the sample labeled themselves bi-religious, I restrict this analysis to the bi-ethnics. We should expect that, relative to subjects who reported having only a single ethnic identity, bi-ethnic subjects would have preferences less like the thoroughly mobilized ethnic ideal and more like those primed to religion. Otherwise stated, they should be relatively less committed to local land and development, which would presumably favor just one of their ethnic identities – the one in whose territory they reside.[14] The expectation regarding bi-ethnics' willingness to pay a bribe for education is theoretically unclear, as this

---

[13] Enumerators did not probe the religious and ethnic backgrounds of participants' parents.

[14] Alternatively, bi-ethnics could have relatively stronger preferences for material policy, owing to their ability to essentially draw from two possible ethnic pots. However, local development implies an advantage only to the group in whose geographic domain it occurs. Thus, supporting local development is akin to supporting material progress for only one of a bi-ethnic's two groups.

TABLE 4.3 *Responses among Bi-ethnic and Single-Ethnicity Participants*

	Hypothesized Relative Effect of Bi-ethnicity	Mean, Single Ethnicity	Mean, Bi-ethnicity	Difference of Means	Relative Effect of Bi-ethnicity
Prefer "moral" over development candidate	+	0.59	0.61	+0.02	*nss*
Prefer "moral" over wealthy community	+	0.77	0.80	+0.03	*nss*
Willing to pay bribe	?	0.425	0.428	+0.003	*nss*

Notes: Means represent proportions of single ethnicity respondents and bi-ethnic respondents answering affirmatively. + relative increase; − relative decrease; ? ambiguous expectation; *nss*, not statistically significant.

represents a materialist commitment to the family more than to the ethnic community.

Table 4.3 suggests that bi-ethnicity does attenuate the effects of the ethnic treatment. Bi-ethnics in the study are slightly less committed to a development-first candidate and are somewhat less interested in living in a wealthy community over a moral community, compared with single-ethnicity respondents (though these findings do not reach conventional levels of statistical significance). If mobilization along ethnic lines causes individuals in the study region to sink more deeply into their ethnic identity and to make choices to defend and prioritize their ethnic land and territory, these results are precisely what we should expect to see among bi-ethnics. The mobilization of ethnicity evokes for them mixed and conflicting loyalties rather than undivided ones with clear ethnic homelands, so the impact of mobilization along ethnic lines is, for these individuals, attenuated.

CONCLUSION

In Chapter 3, an experiment demonstrated that groups identical in expectation have different preferences when assigned to an ethnic context, a religious context, or a control group. In this chapter, by paying particular attention to experimental subjects who regularly attend identity group meetings versus those who do not, I provided further evidence that ethnicity and religion evoke different preferences regarding geographically local material goods versus geographically unbounded moral goods. Replicating these findings among members of strong ethnic and religious groups in Kumasi, Ghana, I also demonstrated that the causal inferences I made in the experimental component of the study can be observed in the real world. Finally, a closer examination of bi-ethnics in the experimental dataset, who by virtue of self-identifying with the mixed ethnic lineage of their two parents may not behave as quintessentially "ethnically" as single-ethnics do, provided yet another means of confirming the unique, mobilizational characteristics of ethnicity and religion. Having established systematic individual-level differences in ethnic versus religious contexts, the question now becomes: under what conditions are political entrepreneurs likely to mobilize followers according to one identity type or the other?

PART II

In this part of the book, I switch levels of analysis. Having built an explanation for variation in individual-level preferences across identity contexts, I now explore how political leaders exploit those preferences to their advantage in conflict settings. Some questions in the study of conflict demand analysis from only one level or the other. Weinstein (2007), for example, asks why rebel insurgents either adhere to the rebellion's mission or digress to indiscriminate killing and crime; the answer turns on the distinction between ideological and resource-based rebellions, so the role of political leaders in shaping the behavior of their supporters can be treated as a constant. Working from a different perspective, Rothchild (1997) asks why ethnic conflicts occur and how they can be managed. He finds that colonial manipulation of ethnic identities created an incentive for African political leaders to mobilize support along those lines, so the answer comes at the elite level; he focuses less, as a result, on the impact of ethnic identity manipulation on the individuals themselves. Here, in seeking to understand why African conflicts sometimes become ethnic and sometimes become religious, both levels of analysis are critical. Conflict frames – from the actors who engage in violence to the targets of violence to the rhetoric leaders use to the reporting that ensues – clearly implicate both the elite and mass levels. Thus, I take Kalyvas's (2006) advice to evaluate individual- and elite-level motivations in tandem, to understand how one informs and influences the other in the course of conflict.

To accomplish that task, I build on the general pattern of individual-level preferences outlined in Part I to explain the mobilization tactics that leaders employ and the identity frames that are ultimately assigned to

93

African conflicts.[1] Either ethnicity or religion may serve political ends, depending on the context, as the cases that follow will show. The objective of this part of the book is not to impugn a particular identity type or side in conflict as more violence prone. Instead, I elucidate the role of ethnic and religious preferences in the calculations that elites make during conflict, a particularly charged setting of institutional breakdown and open space.

Much as Part I was organized, I begin with a theoretical model – this time of elite choice in conflict settings – and then follow the theoretical chapter with empirical evidence. The empirical data at this stage comprise three conflict case studies from recent history: Côte d'Ivoire from the 1990s through the 2000s, Sudan's civil wars that covered most of the period from 1955 to 2005, and Nigeria's Biafran War in the late 1960s and early 1970s. I selected these cases for a variety of reasons. The Ivoirian case allows readers a sense of the political factors underpinning the data presented in Part I. The civil wars in Sudan and the Biafran War in Nigeria constitute arguably the deadliest civil conflicts in modern African history; as such, they have long attracted the attention of scholars and continue to do so. Nevertheless, the frames of these well-known examples of conflict have not been treated in the manner that I do here, recognizing ethnicity and religion as alternate resources exploited within changing political landscapes. Furthermore, I found great evidentiary value in taking advantage of the relative richness of descriptive data available for these cases from modern history, as opposed to more ancient or ongoing cases.

Most important, each of these three cases entails a change in the predominant conflict frame (from ethnicity to religion). Within-case variation of this sort allows me to focus on the choices of political leaders based on the effects of ethnicity and religion; it controls for potential differences in group size and for institutional and national-level factors, because those variables remained largely unchanged even as the identity frame shifted. This constitutes the cleanest test of the exploitation of mobilizational differences in ethnicity and religion, in an otherwise exceedingly complex area of study.

Relying on three cases with similar outcomes runs the risk of inviting objections based on selection bias: the explanation I develop in the book,

---

[1] Those preferences say nothing of actual proclivities toward violence in ethnic or religious contexts. I treat the emergence of violence as exogenous but largely attributable to diverse political economic causes distinct from the constitutive elements of identities such as ethnicity and religion.

one might argue, may appear valid only because I have selected on the dependent variable and ignored counterfactual cases or cases with outcomes that do not conform to the theory. In fact, concerns of selection bias should be mitigated by the fact that the only two outcomes of interest in this study – ethnic versus religious conflict frames – differ within each case. At periods, ethnicity emerges as the principal lens through which the conflicts are viewed, and the theory of mobilizational differences explains why; at other times, religion constitutes the central frame, and again the theory offers a reason why. Cases with no identity frame do not represent the counterfactual; they simply do not appear in the model, since the objective is to explain why an ethnic or religious frame emerges once conflict has begun. As I noted at the outset, I work from the premise that ethnicity and religion are powerful shapers of individual preferences but that they are also tools that leaders exploit in the course of conflict, not the causes of conflict themselves.

Still interesting to the reader may be the fact that in all three cases, conflicts initially framed in ethnic terms later became religious. In this sense, the selection of cases does not follow the typical comparative method of varying a key input for one case and demonstrating how that case differs from the others. Instead, I have chosen to examine the plausibility of the argument using some of the most noteworthy conflicts in recent African history. That each conflict's frame changes from "tribal" to "Muslim-Christian," however, is telling: because a key part of the geographically unbounded nature of religious rules is the ties that they create with co-religionists elsewhere, religious frames frequently afford a strategic advantage that ethnic frames do not as conflict drags on. I cite examples with different trajectories in the concluding chapter, but I note here that this pattern is in keeping with data showing a pronounced rise in the proportion of conflicts viewed in religious terms since the end of the Cold War (see Fox 2004). The transnational connections that accompany largely landless, rule-based religious identities in Africa help to explain why.

Each case study stands as a separate chapter. In each, I trace the histories of ethnic and religious identities in the country to demonstrate that both constitute plausible options for leaders seeking to mobilize supporters. I then outline the incentives that political leaders in each case faced and how those incentives changed at key turning points as the circumstances of conflict and political tension around them changed. Finally, I consider the elements of identity frames – the actors, targets, rhetoric, and reporting – to document the changes in conflict frames that follow from changes in elite incentives.

5

A Theory of Identities, Political Choice, and Conflict

The goal of this book is to distinguish the political use of ethnicity from religion in African conflicts, but I begin this chapter with a well-known example of identity mobilization from outside the region. Saddam Hussein by all accounts ruled in Iraq with little commitment to ideology, making use of ideological appeals only in service of his political survival (Karsh and Rautsi 2002). To the extent that any consistent ideology underpinned his regime, Saddam had two favorites: a Ba'athist party platform, which blended pan-Arabism with a secular socialism opposed to Islamic law, and a national Iraqi identity based on the country's Mesopotamian past (Podeh 1994). In January 1991, however, faced with the impending Gulf War, his political calculus changed. The famously secular Saddam called a People's Islamic Conference early in the month, and just a day prior to the January 15 American-imposed deadline for an Iraqi withdrawal from Kuwait, decreed that the Muslim *takbir* – *Allahu Akbar*, or "God is great" – be inscribed, in his own handwriting, on the national flag of Iraq (Head and Tilford 1996). Two days later, in a defiant letter to American President George H. W. Bush, Saddam made frequent use of Islamic verses and expressed the readiness of the Iraqi people to fight the "atheist" enemy (Podeh 1994: 11).

What Saddam sought, with little efficacy, was a swift change in the salience of identities in Iraq, by playing the religion card. But why the religion card, rather than the Ba'athist card, the national Iraqi card, or some other social identity card? Ba'athism, though privately decried as a tool of the authoritarian regime, meant access to university and to teaching and civil service jobs; membership in the party was in the millions and its influence was equated with a strong Iraq (Podeh 1994). Mobilizing an

Iraqi nationalist identity (much as ethnicity functions at the local level in sub-Saharan Africa, I argue) may have provided the support Saddam wanted for a defense of borders and land. What is more, mobilizing Iraqis around the religious identity ran the risk of underscoring the Sunni–Shi'a fissure rather than broadening Saddam's support base.

Key parallels are missing – the Gulf War represented an inter-state conflict rather than a communal dispute within borders, so the audiences and desired coalitions did shift – but the exploitation of religion in this instance is still telling. Importantly, from the onset of Iraq's tensions with the West, the size of the parties in actual conflict remained static; only the labels that Saddam employed to describe his own side and the opponent changed. According to John Simpson of the BBC, if the Iraqis had shared Saddam's apparent disgust in the ways of the Western infidels, "they would have made Iraq a formidable opponent" (Simpson 1991), and Mueller (1994) notes that Saddam, facing low troop morale, needed his army to recognize a moral imperative to "fight well enough to cause American casualties to rise." Both analyses suggest a leader intent on cultivating inter-group resentment in moral terms. In addition, however, Saddam also stood to benefit from transnational popular support in Muslim countries by appealing to religion. He met only minimal success on both fronts, but to the extent that he made a moral play for support and attempted to reshape transnational ties and opinion, his efforts mirror those of political entrepreneurs elsewhere. I argue that leaders in many African conflicts follow a similar logic, which frequently recasts our view of those conflicts as ethnic or religious, irrespective of their underlying causes.

In this chapter, I outline a political logic that explains when – given the mobilizational differences between ethnicity and religion that affect mass preferences – political entrepreneurs are likely to play one of those cards rather than the other. This theoretical account problematizes the relationship between elites and masses. Supporters can provide innumerable local resources to a leader, for example, while leaders can provide the military strength that protects individuals and communities (Kalyvas 2006: 14). A large literature also demonstrates that political leaders frequently draw on the cultural repertoires of the masses in order to achieve instrumental political goals (Martin 1998; Richards 1996; Zulaika 1988). Other scholars have made reasoned claims that politics involve strategic political leaders engaging with expressive, impassioned masses (Coleman 1990; May 1991) or that elites act instrumentally while masses follow out of emotional fear (Hardin 1995; Posen 1993). My argument from Part I differs slightly from that latter perspective; I argued that individuals indeed seek to maximize their utility in instrumental fashion, only in an identity context that is constrained by the salient frames around them. Nevertheless, theorizing from both the bottom up and the top down paints a more complete picture of the manner in which identities such as ethnicity and religion matter in our understanding of political outcomes.

The chapter comprises four sections. First, I evaluate the contributions and shortcomings of the commonplace argument explaining political choice as a function of group size. While not incompatible with a theory of mobilizational differences in identity types, I argue that calculations of group size leave a critical set of cases unexplained, making it all the more important to also weigh the consequences of distinct identities. Second, I offer a set of assumptions about elite behavior in the face of conflict. Third, I describe the process of political choice over conflict strategies and identity frames, emphasizing three proximate sources of political power – land, moral authority, and international support. The final section summarizes central points and concerns. The basic argument is that political entrepreneurs in settings of conflict have complex proximate interests, all of which serve the broader aim of gaining and maintaining power but which in instances of overlapping cleavages can transcend numerical advantages. Sometimes that may mean mobilizing an identity group in support of a key outcome (e.g., land control). At other times, it may mean pushing a key outcome in order to mobilize the optimal identity group. In either case, the framing of African conflicts as either "tribal" or "Muslim–Christian" turns on the relationship between identities, their associated preferences among the masses, and the strategic calculations of elites.

GROUP SIZE ARGUMENTS

Analyses of political competition typically prioritize relative group size as a determinant of winners and losers and of important political outcomes. Horowitz (1985) lists large group domination over a significant minority group as a critical determinant of ethnic conflict. Others cite the existence of many (therefore relatively small) groups within a country's borders – referred to as ethnic diversity or fractionalization – as causally related to economic growth and the quality of government (Alesina et al. 2003; Easterly and Levine 1997; Habyarimana et al. 2007). Muller (2008) claims that societies comprises several cultural groups face an inevitable path to conflict, as ethnic nationalism galvanizes those groups to seek control of territory. Montalvo and Reynal-Queral (2005) argue that polarization – the presence of a limited number of relatively equal sized groups in competition – is a better predictor of civil conflict than fractionalization, and Esteban and Ray (2008) suggest that polarization minimizes the incidence but intensifies the severity of conflict. These arguments are all for good reason, as group size stands as the first consideration in political competition.

To the extent that political entrepreneurs have agency in these arguments, then, it comes in manipulating the size of groups to their advantage. Leaders, of course, cannot easily transfer individuals from one group to another *within* an identity type, such as from Muslim to Christian, or Akan to Ewe. Yet as the experimental results in Chapter 3 show, moving individuals *across* identity types – encouraging them to prioritize religion instead of ethnicity, or language instead of region – is quite a different matter. Posner (2005) thus explains why politicians play the particular identity card that they do: they seek to define contestation in terms of the identity type that generates a minimum winning coalition. Otherwise stated, political entrepreneurs faced with constraints from political institutions (e.g., voting rules) mobilize supporters along the identity lines that provide just enough support for victory while minimizing the division of spoils. In this sense, manipulating the size of groups does not suggest changing the groups to which individuals belong; only the salience of their identity types is varied, thereby altering the frame of competition.

Arguments that explain political competition and conflict solely in terms of group size leave important questions unanswered regarding the role that political entrepreneurs play, and Posner's contribution addresses that concern. It also raises new ones. First, what consequences might political leaders expect when they mobilize supporters according to one identity type as opposed to another? Second, how are we to understand the choice among conflict frames when, regardless of the identity card played, the coalition of supporters (and hence group size) remains unchanged?

The first of these concerns is addressed by the findings in Part I of this book: in ethnic versus religious contexts, individuals regard matters such as land, moral commitments, and transnational relationships in different ways. These findings suggest the need to problematize identity outcomes and to build them into explanations of political choice, rather than treating identity types as important only in terms of coalition size. For some political issues, such as voting, the distinction may be trivial insofar as the umbrella definition of ethnicity generates outcomes indistinguishable from a more nuanced approach: voters align behind the leadership of their mobilized identity type and cast ballots, irrespective of what the mobilized identity means to them as individuals. Head counts, in the context of voting, are typically the only outcome that matters. Stripping identity types of distinct mobilizational advantages and treating labels such as ethnicity, religion, caste, race, and region as synonymous, however, undermines our ability to understand involvement in conflict. We would ideally like to know what motivates some rebels to pick up arms and fight to overthrow a government, even if those individuals represent only a small portion of supporters (see Lichbach 1998). We should also seek to understand why partisans extend infrastructural and logistic support to combatants during the course of conflict. And our understanding of conflict is improved still further to the extent that we recognize when and why transnational support is forthcoming. To explain the choice that political entrepreneurs make regarding the frame of conflict, we must therefore give consideration to the relationship between the political leader's own proximate interests and the expected behavior of supporters.

   The second concern – that group size may remain unchanged even across different identity contexts – underscores the challenge of overlapping, or reinforcing, identity cleavages. In contexts of overlapping identity, two or more identity types are highly correlated. A society is divided into roughly the same sets of opposing group members even when identity labels differ, so Religion A is synonymous with membership in Ethnic Group X and Religion B is synonymous with membership in Ethnic Group Y (if religion and ethnicity are the two salient identity types). Figure 5.1a depicts stylized proportions of overlapping cleavages in a society with two ethnic groups and two religious groups. Nigeria, whose civil war is explored in Chapter 8, is commonly cited as an example of overlapping identities: approximately 40 percent of the population is Muslim and of the Hausa-Fulani northern ethnic groups (the upper-left quadrant in Figure 5.1a), whereas just 5 percent are Christian and also of those northern ethnic groups (the upper-right quadrant).[1] Some 35 to 40 percent of Nigerians are Christian and members of southern ethnic groups such as the Igbo and Yoruba (bottom-right quadrant), while just 10 percent are Muslim and also members of the southern ethnic groups

---

[1] Proportions are drawn from the CIA World Factbook (2015). www.cia.gov/library/publications/the-world-factbook/.

(a) Stylized Proportions

	Ethnicity X	Ethnicity Y
Religion A	High %	Low %
Religion B	Low %	High %

(b) Stylized Geographic Distribution

Ethnicity X/Religion A
- -
Ethnicity Y/Religion B

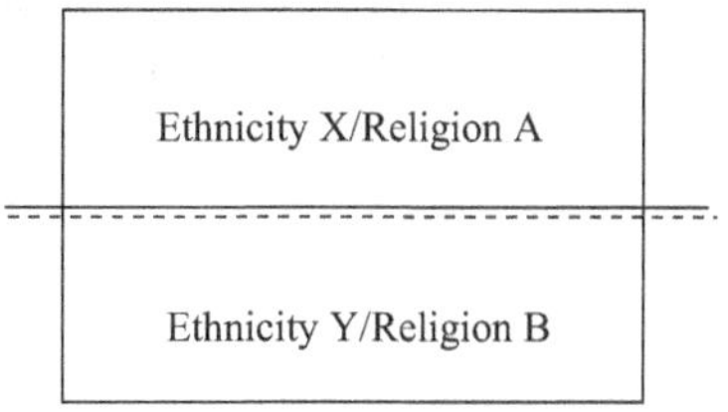

FIGURE 5.1. Overlapping identities.
Note: % refers to proportion of individuals belonging to each respective category.

(bottom left). Geographically, a society with overlapping identities might look similar to the stylized graphic in Figure 5.1b: northerners share one religion and one ethno-linguistic identity, whereas southerners are of a different religion and also a different ethno-linguistic identity.[2] This scenario is common to the ten to fifteen African countries situated along the northern band of sub-Saharan Africa where savannah meets Sahel and a natural demarcation between Muslim- and Christian-dominated areas emerged, overlapping with local ethnic identities. Belgium, Sri Lanka, Quebec, and the former Yugoslavia constitute other examples of states or areas with overlapping social cleavages.

Standing in contrast to overlapping cleavages are cross-cutting cleavages, where only a weak correlation between two major identity types persists. The salient identity types cross-cut one another, ensuring that each religious group has representation from different ethnic groups and that each ethnic group comprises members of different religions (see Figure 5.2a for stylized proportions of one possible cross-cutting identity cleavage). Rwanda, whose 1994 genocide is addressed in the concluding chapter, offers an example of cross-cutting identity cleavages: Muslims are equally likely to be Hutu or Tutsi (with each quadrant comprising 5 to 7 percent of the Rwandan population), and Christianity is also prominent among both major ethnic groups (though the Hutus comprise a substantially larger share of the overall population; approximately 70 percent of the Rwandan population are Hutus and Christians, whereas 10 to 15 percent are Tutsis and Christian). Figure 5.2b offers a stylized example of geographic distributions of cross-cutting identities.

[2] Frequently, these are broader ethnic identities that encompass multiple smaller ethnic groups by way of shared language, location, and cultural norms.

(a) Stylized Proportions   (b) Stylized Geographic Composition

	Ethnicity X	Ethnicity Y
Religion A	High %	Low %
Religion B	High %	Low %

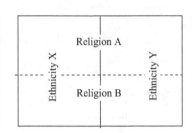

FIGURE 5.2. Cross-cutting identities.
Note: A depiction of equally distributed cross-cutting cleavages would put proportions of 25 percent in each quadrant.

In terms of political outcomes, scholars for more than a century have recognized overlapping cleavages as posing the greater problem, for the reason that they generate mutually reinforcing divisions: the same people lose regardless of the issue dimension or identity that is politicized, which tempers incentives to compromise (Bentley 1908). Competing institutional solutions thus aim to address the challenges posed by overlapping cleavages (Horowitz 1985; Lijphart 1975).[3] The aim of this project, however, is somewhat different; it is to understand why identity types such as ethnicity and religion are exploited or made salient in the course of conflict, even when the cleavages overlap and the size of support coalitions does not vary across identity contexts.

A theory that takes into account the mobilizational differences between ethnicity and religion at an individual level can explain political choice under either social cleavage structure; I will demonstrate this in the following chapters. Theories that do not – and which focus instead only on relative group sizes – are still terribly important; they explain the first consideration in political competition. Yet those theories are best suited to explain the frame of political competition where identities cross-cut, or, at a minimum, where cleavages generate variation in the size of a political leader's support coalition. Absent recognition of the impact on individual passions that stem from politicizing ethnicity, religion, or any other social identity, however, they offer no means of systematically explaining the choice of conflict frames where identity types overlap or are of similar sizes. This is a shortcoming in "ethnic politics" arguments that treat all

---

[3] To the extent that overlapping cleavages generate geographic segregation, Dowd (2015) argues that policies might aim not just to accommodate differences but also to create more diverse neighborhoods, since integration can fortify support for liberal democracy.

forms of identity alike: when the groups to which a political leader might appeal are of equal size and populated by the same individuals, which card can we expect that leader to play? To extend the research on conflict and ethnic politics, I combine the findings from Part I with some commonplace and otherwise plausible assumptions about elite incentives to add insight into these complex cases of conflict, where group labels matter critically even as group sizes remain unchanged.

ELITE BEHAVIOR

What drives the choice that political entrepreneurs make over conflict frames? I develop an explanation rooted in four key assumptions. First, I assume that political entrepreneurs have options to choose from in their calculus over which identity type to politicize. Conditional on the historical, social, and political patterns that make identity types at least potentially salient, the assumption puts multiple identity cards in the hands of elites, who then select one to play. Absent this assumption, conflicts in the region would occur *only* along ethnic lines, or *only* along religious lines; we would fail to see cases of conflict in the same environment defined along different cleavage lines in different periods. Yet we do. The assumption is plausible for many of the reasons developed in Part I: political entrepreneurs themselves belong to multiple identity groups, they share those identities with supporters (either the same set of individuals in the case of overlapping cleavages or sets of individuals that vary as the cleavage changes), and identity types that are not salient in time $t = 1$ can become so in time $t = 2$. I have alluded to several plausible choices in addition to ethnicity and religion; to explain the elite choice over frames as political strategy requires only a minimum of two. In the study region of Africa, at least that many have potential political salience, but I treat ethnicity and religion as most prominent.

Second, I make the assumption that political entrepreneurs are knowledgeable about the individual-level effects of identities – ethnicity and religion, in particular – outlined in Part I. That is, they understand the associations between identities and preferences over policies and strategies. That knowledge can be assigned in either of two ways. One is to make the assumption, common in rationalist theories of political choice, that political leaders have perfect information; doing so minimizes extraneous or stochastic explanations for outcomes and prioritizes strategy over informational variation. Alternatively, elite knowledge about the effects of identity manipulation on individual priorities can accumulate over time through a process akin to natural selection: those leaders who understand identity effects and exploit them appropriately remain leaders, whereas those who misinterpret the effects of mobilizing along identity lines, or who fail in their strategic exploitation of those effects, lose status as leaders and thus fall out of the model.

Third, political entrepreneurs in this model have the ability to manipulate the priority of identities among their followers, and hence to shape the broad identity context in conflict settings. This assumption is critical to any explanation providing agency to the political entrepreneur, rather than letting the size of groups alone do the work of shaping conflict frames. Evidence of just how easily the manipulation of individual-level identities can be was presented in Chapter 3 – recall that simply by receiving either the Ethnic or the Religion treatment, subjects became approximately twice as likely to list the targeted identity as their most important (relative to the control group, for whom no particular identity was targeted). If brief experimental treatments produce such notable effects, it should be uncontroversial to assign the same ability to political entrepreneurs in the real world. Evidence from other contexts supports this claim: voters develop stronger attachments to their ethnic groups when politicians prioritize these identities in the lead up to elections (Eifert, Miguel, and Posner 2010); colonial administrative strategies in Nigeria led to identification with city-states where the religious identity would otherwise have been expected to dominate (Laitin 1986); and attachments to nationality, ethnicity, and religion vary across borders where social features are held constant and where only national political factors vary (Miles and Rochefort 1991). Returning to the argument from Part I, this is not to suggest that individuals do not pursue their own preferred outcomes within any particular identity context; it implies only that the identity context in which they find themselves, and thus the identity type they are most likely to prioritize, is a function of elite political choice.

Finally, I assume that the central goal of political entrepreneurs is to gain and maintain power. Their tactics for doing so, however, are not monolithic. Generating adequate turnout to ensure a plurality of voter support, for instance, may constitute a sound political strategy to acquire power in consolidated democracies with free and fair elections. Where political institutions break down totally and give way to civil or communal conflict, conversely, political entrepreneurs may face entrenched exclusion and defeat to the extent that they are unable to generate other forms of collective action among supporters. Furthermore, the accumulation of power may result through many strategic approaches. I assume that political entrepreneurs target whatever proximate concerns ultimately put them in position to control resources and power, either manipulating policy and strategies to shape identity salience or manipulating identity salience in the service of particular policies and interests. I develop these concerns and the associated strategies for addressing them in the following section.

In Africa, the capacity for manipulating ethnic and religious identities is high. Both are prominent social markers with historical links to political outcomes in many African countries (see Chapter 2), and they represent the two most common social modes of self-identification among African citizens. Along the band of countries in the north of sub-Saharan Africa, as well as elsewhere, ethnic and religious identities tend to overlap, generating the conditions under which political entrepreneurs must choose labels for political contestation without the ability to significantly alter the composition of their support bases. Finally, community networks are important sources of political power in Africa, stemming from low-income socioeconomic conditions and less institutional guidance (Fafchamps 2001). The upshot for political choice is that whole networks can move across identity types in unison, giving effective political entrepreneurs swift access to alternative identity frames.

THE PROCESS OF POLITICAL CHOICE

Equipped with these assumptions, we can view the political decision-making process of identity manipulation in the following manner. To gain or maintain power, elites seek to address their most pressing proximate or short-term needs: inter alia, votes, material resources and wealth, land and territory, inclusion in the political process, perceived moral legitimacy or authority, and international support.[4] Still, they cannot do so alone; success in competition for political power requires a support coalition, willing to mobilize collectively in the interest of the leader. Thus, we would expect the political entrepreneur to weigh the effects of playing any one of multiple identity cards on his supporters and constituents (who either provide critical support or shirk in their commitment to the group and its leader). The lesson from Part I was that evoking distinct identities is associated with different priorities regarding some of the very issues central to the accumulation of elite power: religion, for instance,

---

[4] The determination of proximate political needs is exogenous to the model. It is taken as given.

prioritizes transnational ties and moral probity over materials, whereas ethnicity evokes commitments to land and resources. The goal, then, is for the political entrepreneur to manipulate either the identity frame or the policies such as to match constituent priorities with his or her own proximate needs, and to articulate that political choice as the centerpiece of inter-group tensions.

In the institutional open space of civil conflict, political elites may thus take either of two strategies. First, they might publicly articulate perceived aggression against the in-group in terms of one identity or another. In short, they play an identity card – *We are Christian,* or *We are Igbo* – in order to frame the conflict in particular identity terms. Doing so evokes the same associations developed in Part I – ethnicity eliciting collective action in defense of local land and material resources, and religion inducing concerns over rule-based moral authority as well as transnational community ties – thus generating support around an advantageous outcome (e.g., land seizures or transnational networks).

Suppose, by way of example, that an African political entrepreneur's proximate concern is control over local gold mines, which would ensure the resources to secure a military victory and gain the presidency. He is aware that in contemporary Africa, religion evokes strong popular concerns over rule-based moral authority, ethnicity elicits collective action over local land and resources, and race causes individuals to prioritize some other set of policy concerns (not developed here). A strategy of framing inter-group tensions in terms of ethnicity would thus provide a means of suggesting to supporters that, in an already contentious setting, the lands and resources that those gold mines represent constitute an issue worth fighting for. He plays the ethnic card, thereby manipulating the policy preferences of supporters so that they mobilize collectively in defense of the gold mines above all else.

Second, the order might be reversed: leaders may publicly push particular policies or strategies with identity-related consequences that they as leaders understand, so that *We are Christian* or *We are Igbo* emerges as a cry from their support coalitions following the policy play. On one hand, that might be done to create salience along a politically optimal identity line, for example, if identity cleavages cross-cut and the leader stands to reap advantages in terms of coalition size by triggering either ethnic or religious concerns. On the other hand, the strategy of manipulating policies may be a political end in itself but may, by the happenstance of associations between policy preferences and identity types, generate divisions along associated identity lines. In this latter scenario, the goal of the political leader is not the construction of particular identity divisions; instead, those divisions follow naturally (if inadvertently) from the policies and strategies that the leader pushes to gain or maintain power in the course of conflict.

The following are two examples of policy plays generating identity frames in the course of conflict. An African political entrepreneur who is both Hausa and Muslim perceives a potential wartime advantage by mobilizing the Muslim community; perhaps his calculations suggest that his religious coalition is bigger in size, or perhaps he sees the religious-inspired as less likely to negotiate and thus more willing to fight.[5] He thus makes a public push for the incorporation of Shari'a law, thereby mobilizing supporters to cry *We are Muslim* rather than *We are Hausa*. Religion becomes the salient social identity, and the political entrepreneur gains the advantage he had sought in the course of conflict. Alternatively, the African political entrepreneur's proximate concern may be acquiring resources and support internationally that could propel him to a military victory and the presidency. He sets about cultivating alliances with networks outside the country, more likely to be religious than ethnic. Though his goal may only be to obtain support transnationally and not to alter the salience of identities at home, the mobilizational differences in ethnicity and religion ensure that, in making a play for transnational alliances, a religious frame to the conflict at home emerges. Note that the model accounts for differences in group size but also explains political choice in contexts where group size is constant but where discrete ethnic or religious frames to conflict nevertheless emerge.

In either case, political entrepreneurs follow a calculus that suggests altering popular priorities – either on identities directly or on policies that correlate with identities – in order to create strategic avenues to power when political institutions break down. The argument does not constitute a general theory of identity in conflict for two reasons: first, precise elite interests (as means to gaining and maintaining power) are variable, and second, each salient identity type must be unpacked before its exploitation can be understood. The former concern may be mitigated by viewing

---

[5] I do not include propensity to violence as a difference between ethnic and religious contexts; theory and data suggest that mobilization in conflict can occur along both lines and that neither ethnicity nor religion is peaceful or violent in a constitutive sense (see McCauley 2016). There is evidence to suggest, however, that religious conflicts tend to be more intense than non-religious ones (Pearce 2005). These findings speak to the consequences of conflicts framed as either ethnic or religious, an important concern that comes after the objective of this book and that I comment on in the Conclusion.

power as an end, the means to which are equally interesting to consider, and by noting that the strategic process elites undertake to match their own avenues to power with the effects of identity at the individual level can improve understanding of identity politics in conflict settings. Regarding the latter concern, I acknowledge a distance between this argument and more general ones that account for the politics of all identity types with a unified theory. Instead, I limit the analysis to the two most prominent identity types in Africa – an approach that amounts to providing examples of exploitable identities rather than a general theory of identity. Nevertheless, the argument can offer insights into the complex, strategic decision-making of elites while underscoring the importance of disaggregating the umbrella concept of "ethnic politics." Furthermore, by addressing the most prominent forms of African social identity in the context of elite behavior, this logic expands understanding of African politics in a more practical and nuanced direction.

To partially account for the first of those shortcomings – the under-specification of elite avenues to power – I develop explanations for three important sources of power that correspond to the social priorities evoked by ethnicity and religion.

Land

Control of land and territory is one proximate means to power. Power can be conferred via control of land in at least two ways. First, political entrepreneurs who gain de facto control over territory develop relationships with constituents, either directly or through local traditional leadership. Through patronage networks, the entrepreneur with land control can promise valuable local goods and use rights in exchange for loyalty. Second, control of territory equates with access to resources and wealth located therein. Non-lootable resources such as oil, timber, and difficult-to-extract minerals are particularly attractive to political entrepreneurs seeking to gain control over territory; the ability to generate resources through local taxation (formally or informally) provides a further advantage to controlling lands and territory. From the perspective of the masses, in-group control over local lands, resources, and development ensures a pathway to security in terms of having a viable homeland. At the sub-national level, institutional tactics for exploiting land and territory include extracting formal access to land use, achieving recognized regional autonomy, or, as a last resort where power within borders in unachievable, altering borders through secession.

Keep in mind that I have restricted the argument to settings of conflict, where institutions have typically broken down. Even under the most normal of political conditions, land and local resources are not easily ceded or made available as a negotiable commodity. When institutions break down and conflict emerges, formal transfers of land and territory become even less likely; contentious environments and periods of chaotic political transition correlate with opportunities to claim land and local resources through less formal, and more violent, means. Thus, in settings of inter-group tension, successfully gaining control of land serves as one proximate means for accumulating or maintaining power.

Recall from Part I that popular concern for local land and resources is relatively higher in ethnic contexts – ethnicity, I stated, can be described in shorthand as a land-based identity. The process of identity mobilization as a strategy for land control (and power) is thus straightforward to understand: opportunities to control new territory, to protect existing land, or to gain access to valuable local resources and material wealth generate an incentive for political entrepreneurs in Africa to play the ethnic card. Altering the identity context in this way – just as I did in randomized field experiments – causes ethnic group membership to come to the fore and land concerns to take on greater affective relevance at the individual level. Under these conditions, a conflict having nothing to do with ethnicity at its outset may come to be viewed in ethnic terms, pitting "tribal" enemies against one another.

Moral Legitimacy

In other contexts, control of land and local resources may not be an efficient or feasible avenue to power. An alternative approach to gaining an upper hand in settings of conflict is to control perceptions of moral legitimacy.

Moral legitimacy can support the accumulation of power in two respects. First, leaders of good moral standing are most likely to attract the trust of their constituents (Maccoby 1981). Trust in leadership facilitates acceptance of intra-group inequalities and subordination – in short, allowing political entrepreneurs to minimize dissent in their quest for power (Alagappa 1995: 4). Second, moral authority constitutes an avenue to power via a perceived license to construct and define legal statutes (Hall 1997). In feudal Europe, moral authorities in the Church exploited opacity between divine law and legal statute for the purposes of placing material resources at the service of Rome (Hall 1997); in the contemporary African context, administrative structures that give formal or quasi-formal administrative roles to moral leaders, an artifact of the colonial era, similarly confer a degree of statutory legitimacy on those with moral authority (Vanderlinden 2007). The implication for political entrepreneurs is that, to the extent that in-group members perceive their leaders as promoting a proper moral path, an opportunity exists for elites in settings of political tension to consolidate support for an instrumental agenda – be it extending political tenure, overcoming political exclusion, or limiting inter-group challenges – and thus to accumulate power.

The task of the political entrepreneur interested in accumulating power via moral legitimacy is to ask which social identity generates the strongest relative concern for matters of morality in the face of inter-group dispute. The answer, as I demonstrated in Part I, is religion. Placed in a context of world religion, irrespective of the tradition, group members have a relative preference for moral and lifestyle issues over resource-based ones. They condemn corruption in relatively greater numbers, stating, as one focus group participant did, that "even if it will help my child in the short run, I know God will remember what I did."[6] They also place a high priority on moral imperatives, due to codified guidelines of right and wrong. These outcomes – though unexplained in models emphasizing only group size – are not only plausible on an individual level; they are also understood by the political entrepreneur. The aim of the entrepreneur, then, is to exploit the collective religious identity of supporters in order to make concerns over morality and lifestyle a matter worth defending collectively, even to the extent of violent conflict.

Just as the hypothetical examples above made clear, moral probity and mobilized religion can be associated in either direction. One might imagine political elites promoting behavior-related statutes, condemning the opposition as dangerously corrupt, or otherwise prioritizing moral and lifestyle policies, with the aim of mobilizing supporters along religious lines. Conversely, political leaders might call attention to their own piety, make public displays of attending religious ceremonies, or otherwise prioritize the religious identity, all with the aim of generating support for particular policies or strategies – say, for example, the imposition of Shari'a law – as the proximate political goal. Supporters in either of these (manipulated) contexts would both prioritize outcomes of moral probity and identify more strongly with their religious identity. Thus, just as land

---

[6] Focus group FG-4-b.

and local resources are associated with the politicization of ethnicity, moral authority serves religious coalitions, generating collective concern about lifestyle issues and again positioning the entrepreneur to maximize power. Importantly, the benefits of politicized religion come not because the political entrepreneur's moral standing or probity is itself any different in the religious context than in an ethnic, racial, or other context. Rather, by playing the religious card, he simply makes moral divisions the foremost concern of constituents, thus matching their interest in collective action with his own proximate pathway to power and victory. In this manner, contentious politics having nothing to do with religion at their outset can become for supporters and participants a matter of Muslim–Christian differences.

International Support

A third avenue to political power in unstable or contentious settings is to expand international support. Doing so can pay dividends in several respects. First, favorable international public opinion may reshape the contours of conflict to one's advantage, lending pressure to either cut short imminent defeat or legitimize ongoing conflict. Transnational networks may also generate much needed resources for communal groups facing conflict; this is particularly true of potential ties between communal groups in Africa and co-group networks in the West or in oil-wealthy states in the Middle East. Finally, in-group members locally, who may view relationships between their own leaders and foreign elites as a signal of efficacy, are likely to confer an added measure of legitimacy on political entrepreneurs with international support. Thus, in contentious political settings where the balance tilts toward conflict, one strategy for African political entrepreneurs to increase their odds for success would be to cultivate support beyond their borders.

They would be unlikely to do so by playing the ethnic card. In fact, with historical exceptions where African elites have generated transnational support via political ideology (during the Cold War) and race (during the apartheid era in South Africa), contemporary identity options that African leaders can exploit internationally are limited. The exception is religion: political entrepreneurs in Africa, of Christian or Muslim stripes, can appeal to expansive religious networks with ongoing interest in the religio-political affairs at the geographic periphery of their traditions. Especially where identities overlap, a simple reframing of local tensions as religious can thus pay important dividends from beyond national borders. Nigerian Hausa, for instance, have no ostensible co-identity with Saudi Arabian Arabs, and thus no apparent access to in-group support from that source. Nigerian Muslims and Saudi Arabian Muslims, conversely – subsets that, at the risk of belaboring the point, could represent the same individuals otherwise labeled Hausa and Arabs – are united by belief in shared doctrine, generating a source of pressure, resources, and international legitimacy that can aid in the accumulation of power even as the size of the group in conflict does not change per se.

Framing conflict in terms of religious differences can thus serve multiple avenues to power, each turning on individual-level preferences that arise from the features of a geographically unbounded, rule-based identity. Insofar as religion is a relatively landless identity in contemporary Africa, coalitions mobilized along religious lines are more inclined to free-ride on decisions regarding local land and development, viewing those issues as the purview of other, perhaps more parochial-minded community members. Their attention would instead be drawn to the rules that govern their religious world – in Part I, I documented how this association leads to greater rejection of corruption, for example. This focus on rules shared across religious networks also inspires stronger attachments beyond borders. In this way, policies and strategies that focus on trans-national alliances serve to prime supporters' religious identity and impart a context of religious politics on the conflict at home. Or, in the other direction, leaders may prime religious identity to generate support for transnational alliances that ultimately serve the instrumental goals of political leadership. If the framing of tensions as religious allows political entrepreneurs to match popular concerns with their own best strategies to gain or maintain power in the course of conflict, we can expect otherwise secular conflicts in the region to be framed as Christian–Muslim ones.

SUMMARY AND DISCUSSION

The depiction of African conflicts as ethnic or religious turns on a process of elites matching their own political exigencies with the preferences of supporters under different identity contexts. I have not explained how all identity types can be exploited or how avenues to power outside land, moral legitimacy, and international support can be achieved. What this argument does, however, is to explain the relation-ship between individual identities and strategic approaches to power. In terms of both focal strategy and identity mobilization during conflict, political entrepreneurs have choices to make – choices that are often constrained by the fact that available identity types may provide no relative advantage in group size. Leaders must instead base that choice on matching identity salience to their own plausible avenues to power. This logic of choice is consistent with the case evidence I present in the following chapters. It makes sense, however, only if we take seriously the findings from Part I – that different identity contexts are associated with discrete individual-level preferences.

Matching popular concerns with political needs constitutes a systematic approach to identity mobilization in settings of African conflict, but it does not guarantee success. Successful identity manipulation (with success defined modestly in terms of collective participation, rather than victory) hinges on an important caveat: mobilized identities should correspond to latent popular concerns in order to generate collective action in the name of the group. For example, I have demonstrated that mobilizing along ethnic lines evokes concern for land, resources, and kin. If popular experience includes no perceived threat to land and resources, however, mobilization in the name of ethnicity is likely to fall flat. For the political entrepreneur, power must in those cases be achieved through alternative means. Similarly, mobilization of religion evokes concerns for lifestyle rules; if historical, social, and political patterns suggest that those rules could come under threat with a change in political control, playing the religion card can effectively activate those concerns. Absent underlying threats to norms built on religious rules, however, there is little reason to suspect that religious mobilization would pay dividends politically, or even that prioritizing moral legitimacy would mobilize a religious coalition. During the Gulf War in the early 1990s, Saddam Hussein sought to activate a collective defense of Iraq by emphasizing the transnational networks and the distinctions of right and wrong synonymous with religion, but he did so in a context in which other regional geopolitical concerns trumped anxieties over the perceived lifestyle threat that the enemy may have posed. In sub-Saharan Africa, the same is true: mobilizing identities evokes distinct preferences, but whether or not those preferences are sufficient to elicit collective defense of the group hinges on sensibilities to latent, historically based inter-group threats. Race, for example, is in some southern African states and many other political contexts a salient cleavage, yet in other African countries it is not. Absent latent concerns over the issue dimensions related to a social identity, that identity is unlikely to foster sufficient emotion and affective pull to generate collective action. An explanation lies in the fact that the latent salience of social identities still matters.

One final consideration: political competition of any sort involves (at least) two opposing sides, the leaders of which should be assumed to have equally strong commitments to gaining and maintaining power. In determining why conflicts become either ethnic or religious, then, we are left to answer the question of who, exactly, determines the predominant frame. When one side's leadership manipulates identity or manipulates policies to mobilize an optimal identity, what should we expect of the opposing side? The cases described in the following chapters serve as telling illustrations that multiple frames can emerge to describe a single conflict setting at different times: political entrepreneurs use the identity that presents the best opportunity for political gain, but the conditions under which conflicts occur frequently change, and with them change the incentives for identity mobilization. The exploitation of mobilizational differences across identity types can thus emerge in a variety of ways. Political entrepreneurs from each side may share strategic goals and see an opportunity for political gain through mobilization of the same identity type. Or, in settings of cross-cutting cleavages, advantages in coalition size may suggest the straightforward politicization of a majority identity type, leaving the opposing side the challenging task of redefining conflict in other, non-numerical terms. Third, group leaders may play a game of proactive mobilization that demands a response from the same identity frame, thus undermining opponents' abilities to pursue their own preferred frames. In short, the frames that emerge to describe African conflicts as ethnic or religious are determined in part by the interactions and responses of political elites, as those leaders also interact with and respond to their supporters (see Kalyvas 2006). The evidence of a dominant frame then comes in the actors, the targets, the rhetoric, and the reporting integral to the conflict itself.

This argument does not preclude the salience of multiple identity types in conflict, but it does suggest that one tends to predominate at a given time. In this way, it clarifies why conflicts whose causes have little to do with identity differences are sometimes fought in the name of labels like ethnicity and religion. Since Tilly (1964), it has been a matter of the political science literature, if not of popular understanding, that the identity descriptions of conflict – as "tribal," "faith-based," and so on – serve as poor predictors of the actual internal motivations of those who engage in or otherwise support collective violence. The best answer to why such labels emerge, therefore, is not that certain identity groups experience primordial hatred or that conflict frames are always determined by the relative size of groups. Instead, political leaders make strategic choices based on the social preferences elicited by religion, ethnicity, or other identity types.

In Part I, I provided evidence of mobilizational differences in identity types in Africa: norms associated with ethnicity and religion that evolve in particular time periods and geographic areas generate unique individual-level preferences. In this chapter, I described what happens when political entrepreneurs exploit these differences in order to frame conflict in a manner most advantageous for cultivating support. The following chapters offer case study evidence consistent with these claims, in an effort to untangle the complex dynamics of identity, choice, and conflict.

6

Ethnic and Religious Identity in Côte d'Ivoire's Conflict

For much of its post-1960 existence as an independent state, Côte d'Ivoire[1] enjoyed recognition as the region's "miracle": annual economic growth rates averaged 7 percent for a twenty-year period; a plantation economy benefited from external factors of production and heavy foreign investment to make the country the world's primary producer of cocoa and a major coffee exporter; education opportunities expanded even in the poorest areas; relations between social identity groups were harmonious; and political institutions and leadership remained stable as neighboring countries in West Africa suffered through coups and civil wars. The reversal of fortune was thus as surprising as it was abrupt. By the end of the 1990s, Côte d'Ivoire was marred in violent political conflict that divided the country in half along social identity lines. Elections meant to redress political grievances between groups did not materialize until 2010, a transition did not occur until 2011, and only recently have political institutions regained a sense of normalcy. During the course of violence, one opposition spokesperson equated ongoing tensions to "[genocide-era] Rwanda in the making" (Afrik News 2010).

In this chapter, I explore why the conflict in Côte d'Ivoire first implicated ethnicity and then came to be viewed by many participants and observers in religious terms, pitting Christians against Muslims. Why was Bakary Kaba, the sixty-year-old victim described in the opening chapter,

---

[1] Prior to October 1985, the country's name was officially translatable to the English-language version "Ivory Coast." Since that time, by presidential decree, the name is non-translatable, and the official English-language version is "Republic of Côte d'Ivoire" (see N'Diaye 2005).

killed for praying and wearing Muslim robes? Why were priests and imams assassinated, and churches and mosques burned? Why did prominent Muslim leaders come to fear a "hunt for Muslims," while some Christian organizations contested perceived efforts to "Islamize" the country? (see Miran-Guyon 2012).

The case is interesting given that religion had nothing to do with the origins of conflict in Côte d'Ivoire. Though the population is closely divided between Christianity and Islam,[2] no religious grievances were raised during the contentious period prior to an outbreak of violence. Religious law was never a topic of political debate in Côte d'Ivoire, and religious groups and associations played little organized role in issuing demands or fomenting discord. Instead, a religious cleavage, along with ethnic and immigrant-national cleavages, happened to coincide with political-economic motivations for conflict, largely along north–south lines. Identity differences, as is frequently the case, were thus introduced as a tool of conflict rather than a cause. In this chapter, I aim to explain the conditions under which ethnicity and religion served usefully as such tools – in short, why ethno-national tensions developed, and then why religious identity mattered at all when ostensibly it should not have. I will demonstrate that political entrepreneurs had a choice regarding the frame of conflict and that, when the established political system broke down, elite efforts to achieve important political advantages culminated in framing the Ivoirian conflict first along ethnic and then along religious lines.

Though little to nothing suggested either ethnic or religious grounds for war, the case is illustrative of the role that identity types can play in conflicts along the stretch of Africa where both ethnic and religious divisions meet and often bisect countries. While other studies describe identity struggles that have been shaped by elements of religious law (Laitin 1982) or driven by numerical advantages (Chandra 2004; Posner 2005), I introduce the notion that identity frames are intimately tied to the policies and strategies that elites pursue, owing to the manner in which their followers respond to ethnic and religious cues. I hope that doing so will convey the macro-level importance of the micro-level data drawn from Côte d'Ivoire and described in Part I.

---

[2] As noted earlier, Côte d'Ivoire's population is approximately 40 percent Muslim and 33 percent Christian, though the Christian population is growing quickly and enveloping previous practitioners of traditional religion. See CIA World Factbook (2015).

THE FOUNDATIONS OF ETHNIC AND RELIGIOUS IDENTITY IN CÔTE D'IVOIRE

The identity options available for mobilization during Côte d'Ivoire's recent conflict were established long before the *crise identitaire* itself began.[3] Dating back centuries, ethnicity and religion have been the primary markers of social belonging.

Small stateless societies, rather than centralized ethnic kingdoms, formed the foundation of ethnic identity in Côte d'Ivoire. Yet whereas over sixty distinct ethno-linguistic communities are currently represented, the social norms, politics, and patterns of patronage have long been dominated by only a small number of major ethnicities. In the north, the northern Mandé – including the Malinké, Bambara, and Dioula – and the southern Mandé – including the Yacouba – trace their origins to the ancient trading center of Kangaba in present-day Mali, with earlier links to the Wangara trading communities in Western Sudan (Levtzion and Pouwels 2012). From those trading communities, networks formed along patrilineal lines, and traders who moved south to acquire gold and kola nuts as early as the late eleventh century eventually formed settlements and small chiefdoms in what is now northern Côte d'Ivoire. Voltaic farmers and craftsmen, particularly the Senoufo in the northeast, intermarried with the Mandé but also maintained their own distinct ethnic identity (Chappell 1989). Collectively, these groups are thought of as "northern" ethnicities (Toungara 2001).

In the south, Kru-speaking ethnic groups, including the Bété and Dida among others, are often considered the earliest migrants to Côte d'Ivoire (Chappell 1989). Predominating in the southwest, they have origins in present-day Liberia, though their presence in Côte d'Ivoire predates the influence of Europeans, not to mention the construction of national boundaries. Despite the early presence of Kru in the region, however, their decentralized political structure left them susceptible to influence and control from more centralized Akan groups. The Akan – notably the Anyi in the southeast and the Baoulé in the center – have historical ties to the Ashanti kingdom in Ghana. As the Ashanti kingdom flourished in the seventeenth century, migrants expanded the kingdom's reach and developed a position of strength in what is now Côte d'Ivoire through advantageous marriage arrangements, commercial control, and a royal

---

[3] See Pulinckx (2001), who describes the conflict, fittingly, as a national-scale identity crisis.

hierarchy (Chappell 1989). Engaging principally in farming and gold production, both the Akan and Kru ethnicities fortified their status as southern ethnicities well before the influence of Europeans.

Complicating the north–south ethnic divide in Côte d'Ivoire were policies of administrative favor during the colonial era, coupled with ethnic-based labor migration policies upon independence (Nordås 2014). The French employed a colonial strategy of "direct rule," in which traditional governing structures were dismantled and administration of the colony was placed in the hands of large numbers of French bureaucrats, yet they still leaned heavily on the Akan to facilitate organization and control. Felix Houphouët-Boigny, a large-scale Akan farmer and a legislator, took advantage of that favoritism: originally working in opposition to French rule, he later established Côte d'Ivoire's first independent political party, the Parti Démocratique de Côte d'Ivoire (PDCI), and demonstrated himself to be a moderate statesman sympathetic to colonial interests. In return, French manipulation of Côte d'Ivoire's 1957 municipal elections would ensure that the PDCI won all seats in the Ivoirian legislature (Fauré 1993). Upon independence on August 7, 1960, a fairly smooth transition from French colonial rule to an independent, one-party Ivoirian state took place, with Felix Houphouët-Boigny as its President. He would serve in that capacity until his death in 1993.

Houphouët-Boigny's strategy for political and economic development in Côte d'Ivoire was threefold. First, he instituted a market-driven agricultural economy that mirrored the "plantation economy" model employed by the French since the 1930s: export commodities such as cocoa, coffee, and rubber were prioritized, tax structures attracted foreign investment, and land tenure policies promised ownership to anyone willing to cultivate the land (Alpine and Pickett 1993). Second, Houphouët-Boigny maintained an intentionally weak military to minimize defense expenditures and potential internal power threats: troops never numbered more than 14,000, and a 1961 Defense Pact surrendered Côte d'Ivoire's external security to the French in exchange for economic policy considerations (N'Diaye 2005). Third, Côte d'Ivoire coupled its market economy with excessive government spending: civil salaries accounted for over 60 percent of the state budget during the Houphouët-Boigny era (Bakary 1997), and more than 200 parastatal firms were created (N'Diaye 2005). The education system was a notable beneficiary of state spending, as teachers received lavish salaries and university students were guaranteed living stipends (Bakary 1997).

Critical to the pillar of market-driven agriculture was an invitation extended to migrant laborers from neighboring countries – most of whom shared an ethnic identity with the fledgling Mandé and Senoufo groups that inhabited northern Côte d'Ivoire. Houphouët-Boigny ended the French practice of forced labor and instead attracted foreign workers with promises of land and opportunity, in exchange for their labor in the commercial agriculture sector. In addition to land tenure, migrants were given the right to vote, and those present in the country prior to 1960 received the option to declare themselves Ivoirian citizens (Bouquet 2007).[4] By 1998, the last official census year in Côte d'Ivoire prior to conflict, 26 percent of residents were listed as immigrants; current unofficial estimates range from one-quarter to one-half of the Ivoirian population (Marshall 2010).

The impact on Côte d'Ivoire's ethnic balance was severe. Once dominated by Kru and Akan populations, the northern ethnicities came to represent approximately half of the Ivoirian population, as over 75 percent of economic migrants to Côte d'Ivoire were of the Mandé and Voltaic ethnic groups (Akindès 2003: 14). What is more, many of those migrants settled in the forest zone of the southwest, while others took up commercial activities in Abidjan and Côte d'Ivoire's other southern economic centers (Toungara 2001). Côte d'Ivoire's southern population is thus much more mixed than in other neighboring countries with northern savannahs and southern tropics. However, as I explain below, the mixing did little to attenuate a perceived north–south divide in ethnic terms.

Longstanding faith traditions created a similar identity divide in Côte d'Ivoire along religious lines. Islam followed the pattern described in Chapter 2, spreading first peacefully along trade routes and later through the work of self-proclaimed jihadists. The earliest Muslims – those Dioula traders seeking gold to take back to North Africa – arrived in the eleventh century (Levtzion and Pouwels 2012). Using commercial connections, the Mandé trader Shehu Watara established Muslim rule in the kingdom of Kong in northern Côte d'Ivoire, and soon, Muslim leaders had established administrative control over the lands of the Bobo, Lobi, and Senoufo. There is some indication, however, that the gold producers of the tropical South wanted little to do with conversion, fearing a loss of control over a key component of trans-Saharan trade

---

[4] The matter of citizenship for post-independence economic migrants was never fully settled during the Houphouët-Boigny era. See Bouquet (2007).

(Levtzion and Pouwels 2012) A renowned line of Islamic teachers in the northwest adopted the perspective that true conversion could come only in God's time, so the south remained largely unaffected by the expansion of Islam (Levtzion and Pouwels 2012). Later, in 1885, the Islamic militant Samory Touré launched a violent offensive against moderate Muslims who, in his view, had fallen too heavily under the sway of Europeans and who had lost their commitment to Islam (Roberts et al. 1973). Leading an efficient military machine that aimed to reform social norms, Touré's supporters took control of land across northern Côte d'Ivoire, targeting areas where the presence of Islam was strong but the practice weak. The movement was finally defeated by the French in 1898, but not before becoming nearly synonymous with the Dioula and Mandé ethnicities and transforming the way of life in what is now northern Côte d'Ivoire.

Christianity's presence in Côte d'Ivoire began in fits and starts. Entering what is now Côte d'Ivoire from the southern Gulf Coast, the Portuguese explored the area in the late 1400s and adopted the view that missionary work would both help the Catholic Church to expand and also streamline trade relationships (Law 1991). Yet no lasting impact came of the small number of Portuguese missionaries who accompanied their traders. In the late seventeenth century, the French Order of Dominicans established a mission in Assini in southern Côte d'Ivoire, but, as Law notes, "labored much and achieved nothing" (see Law 1991: 54). Several factors worked against successful Christian expansion at the time: first, high mortality rates from tropical diseases like malaria severely impacted missionary work. Social mistrust from practitioners of traditional religions also played a role on the ground, while jurisdictional disputes between European powers and the Vatican hampered missionary expansion from afar. Finally, local gold producers were equally skeptical of Catholic missionaries as they were of Muslim traders (Lindenfeld 2005). Eventually, however, certain attributes became apparent. Bible teaching increased local literacy rates, and French efforts to suppress the slave trade in the 1840s created a favorable climate for European missionaries to expand their work there (Johnson 1967). By the end of the nineteenth century, Catholic missions had established a strong presence in the south.

A rich competition with Protestants began at the turn of the century, marked particularly by the missionary work of Liberian William Wade Harris from 1913 to 1915. Building an independent prophetic movement, Harris baptized more than 100,000 followers and had established such a presence by the time of his expulsion[5] that the British Wesleyan Methodist Missionary Society retroactively lent its support and took up the mission (Pritchard 1973). French Catholics always maintained an advantage by dint of their association with the colonial power, however, so Catholicism has remained the primary denomination in southern Côte d'Ivoire, despite recent inroads from the new Pentecostal movement. Of course, the same migration policies that brought northern ethnic group members to the south also introduced Muslim minorities to the tropical part of the country, so a largely Christian south is today more religiously mixed than historical perceptions would suggest.

 To summarize, longstanding patterns of trade, settlement, and conversion created a north that was largely Mandé/Senoufo and as well as Muslim. Meanwhile, early migration from kingdoms in Ghana and Liberia, coupled with defense of the gold mining and production industries, similarly established the south as the territory of Kru and Akan ethnic groups with little early influence from Islamic movements. Eventually, European missionaries found success, and the south became about as Christian and Kru-Akan as the north was Muslim and Mandé-Senoufo. Houphouët-Boigny's post-independence development policy then introduced a complication to Côte d'Ivoire's identity context, encouraging northerners – the vast majority Mandé and Muslim – not just to migrate southward but also to claim and use land where the opportunity arose: "*la terre appartient a celui qui la met en valeur*," he was frequently quoted as saying.[6] Rather than attenuating the overlap of ethnic and religious identities, however, the spread of labor migrants seemed instead to reinforce the notion among southerners that the original inhabitants and rightful residents of the south were the Christian Akan and Kru, and northern Muslims would remain foreigners and intruders. The stage was thus set for ethnic and religious identity frames to color Côte d'Ivoire's political economy.

ETHNICITY AND THE EARLY STAGES OF POLITICAL CONFLICT

 Houphouët-Boigny's reign lasted thirty-three years, due in large part to his masterful skill in coopting potential adversaries and spreading patronage across identity group lines. The armed forces were highly paid, and

---

[5] With the start of World War I, the French feared any social disruption in its colonies, so Harris was returned to Liberia. See Pritchard (1973).

[6] "The land belongs to those who make effective use of it." See Collett (2006).

military leaders from all ethnic backgrounds benefited from plush positions in ministries and parastatals (N'Diaye 2005). Ministries multiplied – the Education Ministry became four distinct ministries, and the Agriculture Ministry three – to generate additional posts for potential rivals (Bakary 1997), and the least loyal were often sent abroad as ambassadors (N'Diaye 2005). In regions outside his own Baoulé ethnic group territory, Houphouët-Boigny invested in schools and health clinics and had six sugar processing plants built in the north of the country (Collett 2006). As a Christian, he coopted the Muslim constituency and leadership with the building of mosques, bank notes for imams, state-sponsored *hajj* to Mecca, and the appointment of an advisor of Muslim affairs responsible for doling out patronage (Miran 2006).

All of that was possible because, for the first twenty years of independence, the Ivoirian economy kept pace with Houphouët-Boigny's development vision and satisfied his need for resources. Despite an annual population growth rate of 4 percent (including 10 percent growth in the southwest and in urban centers), the economy continued to grow at an average annual rate of 7 percent from 1960 to 1980 (Hugon 2003: 107), earning it the distinction as West Africa's "Ivoirian Miracle" (Daddieh 2001). In the 1980s, however, growth began to shrink: a decline in the world price of cocoa after massive market oversupply (Alpine and Pickett 1993), a depreciating currency (Chirot 2006), decreasing productivity of land (MacLean 2004), and an ill-advised decision to transform Houphouët-Boigny's natal village of Yamoussoukro into an expansive capital city (Crook 1989) all contributed to the onset of economic crisis. In 1987, when debt servicing reached 50 percent of exports, Côte d'Ivoire defaulted on its debt (Hugon 2003); over the remaining six years of Houphouët-Boigny's rule, the poverty rate more than doubled, from 17.7 to 36.6 percent; students lost their subsidies; and civil servant salaries were halved (Bakary 1997). The 1980s became known as the "lost decade" in Côte d'Ivoire (Adepoju 2002), and in the face of resource scarcity, identity group interests would become a new challenge for Côte d'Ivoire's ruling elite.

Houphouët-Boigny consented in 1990 to the nation's first multi-party election since independence, but with little time for opposition parties to organize, his PDCI party won the plurality rule contest with 82 percent of the vote (African Elections Database 2010). The main opposition party, the Front Populaire Ivoirien (FPI), headed by longtime opposition holdout Laurent Gbagbo, placed second with 18 percent of the vote. To lead the new government, Houphouët-Boigny appointed as Prime Minister

Alassane Ouattara, an American-educated economist who served previously at the International Monetary Fund (IMF) (Konate 2004). The choice of Ouattara, a Muslim Dioula from the north of Côte d'Ivoire, was seen by most observers as a shrewd selection based on both technical competence and the need to appease an important block of out-group Ivoirians in a new era of resource scarcity (Konate 2004). Upon Houphouët-Boigny's death in December 1993, however, the controversial Article 11 of the Ivoirian constitution transferred the presidential mandate not to Ouattara but to the Speaker of the National Assembly, Henri Konan Bedié, a Catholic Baoulé like Houphouët-Boigny.[7] Ouattara left the PDCI, forming a new political party known as the Rassemblement des Républicains (RDR), and Bedié assumed the presidency with less than two years remaining until the scheduled 1995 elections. At this point, the key players were in place for a conflict that would extend over the following two decades.

Henri Konan Bedié, representing southern interests, took office in 1993 with limited resources and a pending election. With expansive patronage and cooptation no longer an option, Bedié instead aligned with the political interests of his base, introducing the policy of *Ivoirité* mentioned in Chapter 1, which gave formal advantage to the southern, "original" ethnic groups of Côte d'Ivoire, particularly in terms of access to land. *Ivoirité* was ostensibly defined as a "*projet culturel*" intended to "forge a common culture for all people living on Ivoirian soil, foreigners as well as citizens" (Le Pape 2003: 34, author's translation). In fact, the policy created explicit political advantages for those born in Côte d'Ivoire of southern ethnic heritage, by distinguishing "pure" Ivoirians from those of foreign descent (Le Pape 2003). The notion of characterizing residents along immigrant-national lines was not new in Côte d'Ivoire,[8] but Bedié escalated what had been a symptom of economic migration into a system of discriminatory, ethno-national laws: Article 35, an amendment to the

---

[7] Article 11 was considered controversial because Houphouët-Boigny had been under pressure at the time of his death to amend the article, and because his failure to do so left the impression that he intended to perpetuate the southern-Christian-Baoulé hold on power (see Cisse 2004).

[8] Houphouët-Boigny's plantation economy depended on compartmentalizing foreign workers and national civil servants, and his distribution of patronage required classification along identity lines (Bakary 1997); Gbagbo, the opposition candidate in 1990, also raised the prospect of reducing immigrant standing for fear that Houphouët-Boigny's system of patronage had generated too strong a hold on the immigrant vote (Banegas and Losch 2002).

Ivoirian constitution, stipulated that candidates for President must be born not only in Côte d'Ivoire but also of parents born on Ivoirian soil; candidates also had to prove five years of continuous residence in Côte d'Ivoire prior to elections and to have never presented themselves as representatives of another country (Bouquet 2007).

The clear target was opposition candidate Alassane Ouattara, who was born in the north of Côte d'Ivoire but to parents of unclear national lineage,[9] but *Ivoirité* had equally profound effects on all residents of northern ethnic heritage: citizenship was restricted, identity cards were confiscated, and lands were seized.[10] In particular, Bedié appealed to the principle of *Ivoirité* to amend the rural land tenure law (Code Foncier Rural de Côte d'Ivoire, No. 98-750)[11] in 1998, thereby proscribing those who failed to meet the revised conditions of citizenship from owning land and sparking an exodus of Mandé workers from the forest zone of the south to the north (Roubaud 2003). In essence, *Ivoirité* served two pro-south goals: it excluded Ouattara, a viable candidate, from running for office – an exclusion that would hold until December 2010, an election that he ultimately won – and it took land from Mandé migrants and placed it in the hands of southerners, especially the Baoulé and Bété, thus giving Bedié renewed support from his base. Ultimately, those political economic choices would frame Ivoirian tensions in ethnic terms as the country entered its period of greatest instability.

From Chapter 1, recall that the frame of political conflict is shaped by four key elements: the actors, their targets, the rhetoric, and the reporting. Outright violence in this early stage of the Ivoirian conflict had been avoided, but the manipulation of political institutions lent an air of urgency to the tensions between Bedié, Ouattara, and their respective supporters; it signaled that war was close to inevitable. In this context, an evaluation of the elements of framing reveals the extent to which Ivoirians had come to see their politics in ethnic terms. First, the principal actors at this stage of the Ivoirian tensions, aside from the presidential contestants themselves, were traditional ethnic chiefs and aspiring southern landholders on one side versus migrant laborers on the other. Chiefs were principal conduits between administrative decrees and individual-level exploitation of Côte

---

[9] Accounts differ as to whether Ouattara's parents were born in Côte d'Ivoire (according to his own statement, in Le Pape 2003) or Burkina Faso (Ivoire Business 2009), or if the matter is inconclusive as a matter of record (Collett 2006).

[10] Interview, Karim Diarra, Forces Nouvelles Liaison to the Government of Côte d'Ivoire. Korhogo, April 10, 2009.

[11] For the text of the law, Loi No. 98-750 du 23 Decembre 1998, see Droit Afrique (2010).

d'Ivoire's fertile lands, both under Houphouët-Boigny's policy of liberal land distribution to migrant laborers and later under Bedié's restrictive policy of *Ivoirité* (Berry 2008). Their involvement in the reassigning of lands conveyed a clear sense of ethnic entitlement for southerners (and disenfranchisement for Mandé northerners) as *Ivoirité* unfolded. Targets were not a critical part of the framing at this stage as violence had not yet begun, but the singling-out of individuals for harassment and discrimination along ethnic lines, principally through identity card seizures, reinforced the ethnic frame (see Reuters 2014). Third, the rhetoric of "pure" and "original" Ivoirian identity accompanied the policy of *Ivoirité* and became commonplace as southerners sought to distinguish their rights from those of labor migrants. Insofar as the same language had been employed by southern ethnic groups, especially the Bété, to describe their own ethnic origins since well before independence, its resurgence further cast an ethnic frame over the deteriorating political context.

Finally, the reporting from observers of Ivoirian politics routinely characterized the tensions during Bedié's regime, prior to full-scale violence but within a setting of democratic breakdown, as ethnic or ethno-national in nature. Roubaud (2003: 77) argues that at this stage, prior to rebellion and violence, "ethnic identity appeared to be an essential criterion in the polarization of public opinion" (translation by author). Dozon (2000) suggests that an ethnocentric reflex took over as a result of *Ivoirité*, and Ford (2003) pointedly notes that Bedié "set the seal on ethnic conflict in the country," again as a result of *Ivoirité*. Bassett (2003) and Vaisse (2003) describe the breakdown in political stability as a period of ethno-national fervor.

Remember that both ethnic and religious identities colored Ivoirian social life for decades, and each divided the population along similar geographic lines. Thus, in the post-Houphouët-Boigny era of limited resources, either could have become a salient source of political division. The logic from Part I helps to explain why, in fact, ethnicity rather than religion emerged as the central fissure by the end of the 1990s: given the association between ethnic identity and land ties, the discriminatory policy of *Ivoirité* not only ended accommodation of migrants in Côte d'Ivoire but also recast the politics of a once inclusive country in purely ethnic terms.

RELIGION AND THE ONSET OF VIOLENCE

More than thirty years of PDCI rule under Houphouët-Boigny and then Bedié came to an abrupt end on December 24, 1999, the result of a bloodless coup. Soldiers who had been demobilized as a result of Bedié's purge of non-southern forces, and others seeking redress for unpaid wages, mutinied to overthrow Bedié (Collett 2006). Lacking leadership experience, they enlisted General Robert Guéï – a former military officer from the West who had been dismissed for failing to deploy troops against Bedié protesters – as the coup's official leader (Banegas and Losch 2002); his loyalists included many northerners and RDR sympathizers, and he received important backing from RDR insiders (Roger 2010).[12] Following the coup, Bedié fled to France, Guéï assumed political leadership in anticipation of the October 2000 elections, and both Ouattara and Gbagbo (former opposition leaders during the 1990s) took part in a government of national unity during the transition period.

In the run-up to the October 2000 elections, General Guéï transformed himself from transitional military leader to aspiring ruler: brutality against northerners, journalists, and political activists increased (Le Pape 2003), and the same discriminatory laws remained in force. Having come to power with support from the targets of *Ivoirité*, Guéï now exploited *Ivoirité* with aims to run in the 2000 election (N'Diaye 2005). He renewed the exclusion of Ouattara based on questionable citizenship grounds; he also purged the civil service of more northerners and ordered the forced removal of more migrant workers from the southwest (Toungara 2001). Former president Bedié was excluded on technical grounds (having allegedly failed to submit the proper paperwork), and Guéï entered the October 22 election confident of success (Kohler 2003: 43). Instead, in an election marked by only 37 percent turnout (African Elections Database 2010), Guéï was defeated by the only remaining viable candidate, Laurent Gbagbo of the FPI. Guéï's efforts to annul the election and declare himself the "President of the People" were rebuffed by a popular uprising that drew comparisons to the anti-Milosevic revolution in Yugoslavia (*New York Times* 2000), and Gbagbo – the longtime opposition candidate of southern, Christian, Bété origins – was declared President.[13]

At that stage, violence began in earnest. Gbagbo rejected a demand to conduct a new election that included the northerner Ouattara – instead joining the two previous leaders in exploiting the ideology of *Ivoirité* for political purposes (Chirot 2006) – and partisans from both sides took to

---

[12] General Abdoulaye Coulibaly and General Lasana Palenfo, both active in the RDR party, were instrumental leaders in the coup (AllAfrica 2009).

[13] See McGovern (2011: 6) for a summary of the 2000 election.

the streets in violence. Northerners were accused of violence against southerners (U.S. Department of State 2003), and southern, Christian military police officers were blamed for the attack against "northern Muslims" that left fifty-seven dead and buried in a mass grave on the outskirts of Abidjan (Le Pape 2003). Within days, several hundred Ivoirians were killed, and violence took on sharp north–south and identity group descriptions.

On September 19, 2002, north–south tensions culminated in a civil war that would last officially into 2007, and unofficially until the end of the decade. Approximately 800 discontented former military troops, demobilized through military purges that continued under Gbagbo in 2001 and 2002, formed the basis of the Mouvement Patriotique de Côte d'Ivoire (MPCI) rebel group, which undertook preparations for a new coup d'état (Bakary 1997). The MPCI forces were bolstered by a mélange of participants: youth volunteers from the north and from neighboring countries, particularly Burkina Faso; local traditional Dozo fighters, believed to have magical powers in combat; and conscripts who were rounded up in northern cities during the early morning of September 19 and throughout the active conflict period (Banegas and Losch 2002). Initial efforts to descend on the capital of Abidjan in the south failed, but rebel troops succeeded in seizing the northern cities of Bouaké and Korhogo, and they quickly controlled the entire north of Côte d'Ivoire (Vaisse 2003). Within weeks, the MPCI was joined by two rebel groups from the northwest, and together they united as the Forces Nouvelles (FN). Their objectives – to remove Gbagbo from office, to achieve redress for socioeconomic and political discrimination against northerners, and to start a transition to free and fair elections – remained political and economic (Banegas and Losch 2002), but important identity divisions remained in play.

The key turning point in the conflict frame, from ethnic to religious, came with the northern, Muslim candidate Ouattara's exclusion from the 2000 presidential race and the ensuing violence in the streets of Abidjan. On both sides, starting with northerners and spreading to the southern incumbent government, that episode marked a shift in the strategic interests of elites, creating incentives for them to cultivate a religious frame.

From the northern perspective, Ouattara and his RDR supporters faced the ongoing challenge of exclusion from the political process, perceived by many as rooted in his status as a northerner, a Dioula, and a Muslim (Daddieh 2001). What is more, the political-economic conditions of the period – resource scarcity, a leadership vacuum in the aftermath of Houphouët-Boigny's death, and weak political institutions for resolving dispute – left little chance to reverse his exclusion by working through legal domestic channels. Instead, he implicitly sanctioned the Forces Nouvelles rebellion, and, with violence under way, offered a consistent description of the conflict that would accomplish the dual goals of awakening sensitivities to justice and fairness at home and generating legitimacy and support from abroad. Those are precisely the mobilizational advantages that religion provides.

From the southern perspective, when the framework of democracy was still in place in the 1990s and vote counts still served as a political entrepreneur's primary resource, little suggested that longtime opposition figure Laurent Gbagbo would exploit a Muslim–Christian divide for political purposes: he actively courted the Muslim vote, and he advocated for Ivoirian membership in the Organization of the Islamic Conference (OIC) and for a Saudi Arabian embassy on Ivoirian soil (Miran 2006). The collapse of the democratic system and the emerging reality of conflict, however, along with the religio-political challenge from Ouattara, altered Gbagbo's calculus. Given the choice to appeal to supporters' identity as southerners, Christians, Bété or Krou, or "pure" Ivoirians, which hat would Gbagbo wear to mobilize his constituency toward a favorable outcome?

Gbagbo's foremost incentive upon gaining power in 2000 was to ignite a defense against the northern Muslim supporters of Ouattara, who contested the legitimacy of Gbagbo's rule and were willing to take to violence as a result. Furthermore, in an environment of increasingly hostile Muslim–Christian international relations,[14] appealing to a transnational, rule-based identity such as religion (and Christianity in particular) was for Gbagbo a strategic means for cultivating international support for the status quo in Côte d'Ivoire (with himself as the elected President). Gbagbo, too, mobilized supporters along religious lines.

Starting with the outbreak of violence in 2000 and lasting into the middle of the decade, the actors, targets, rhetoric, and reporting on the conflict all pointed to a religious frame. Actors supporting the northern rebel movement included Muslim religious leadership in Côte d'Ivoire; Imam Boubacar Fofana, Spokesperson for the Superior Council of Imams, characterized the Gbagbo regime as "built in the blood of the

---

[14] The embassy bombings in Kenya and Tanzania in 1998 drew African leaders and states into a wider Muslim–Christian debate (Lyman and Morrison 2004). The September 11 attacks in the United States would occur during the course of the identity crisis in Côte d'Ivoire.

martyrs of Islam" and presented the council's political position with the statement: "we have no trouble saying that the Muslim community is behind Alassane [Ouattara]" (Konate 2004; author's translation). In the south, Gbagbo formed a wartime team of advisors from outspoken evangelical Christian leaders. A Catholic by birth, Gbagbo converted to a Pentecostal denomination just prior to the 2000 elections, and his wife, an influential member of the Ivoirian Pentecostal community, was viewed as a conduit to militant Christian support (Nordås 2007). The National Council of Protestant Churches, consisting primarily of young, militant Pentecostals, formed in 2001 and became a regular advisory board to Gbagbo (Reforme 2005), and Pastor Moise Koré, who was later linked to the purchase of arms for government loyalists, served as the principal spiritual advisor to the President (AllAfrica 2009). Finally, Gbagbo gave license to armed forces, both military and paramilitary, to forcibly confront opposition supporters in the name of Christianity: gendarmes military police officers were accused of several incidents of anti-Muslim violence, including the massacre of fifty-seven people noted above and the assassination of Bakary Kaba (mentioned in Chapter 1). Capitalizing on the lack of opportunities for youth in Abidjan, Gbagbo lent financial support to the Jeunes Patriotes, who not only engaged in Islamophobic violence against northerners and Muslims in the south (Bouquet 2007; McGovern 2011), but also enforced informal prohibitions against mosque building (Kirwin 2006).

The targets of violence beginning in 2000 were also clearly selected on religious grounds. Several mosques were burned in Abobo and Abidjan, and gendarmes were accused of spraying tear gas in other mosques (*New York Times* 2000); churches were burned in Kong in the north and in Daloa in the southwest (Economist 2000); and Christian groups reportedly came under attack in northern cities (U.S. Department of State 2003). By late 2001, some Muslim and Christian religious leaders were appealing for calm on the grounds that their property and followers were under mortal threat in a conflict with no apparent foundation in religious grievances on either side (Hartill 2002).

The rhetoric took on a religious tone just ahead of the critical election from which Ouattara was excluded. In a public appeal, Ouattara stated that he was excluded from running for President "because I'm a Muslim from the North" (Roger 2010). Roger argues that in religion, Ouattara "found his battle horse"; he complained of the number of Muslim holidays versus Christian ones, of the construction of the Catholic basilica of Notre Dame de la Paix with state funds, and of the general exclusion of

Muslims from opportunities in Côte d'Ivoire (Roger 2010). An RDR party member speaking in unison with Ouattara drew together the themes of religion and violence: "they don't want to hear our calls to prayer at mosque. But if we accept that, we aren't good Muslims ... it is better to have death than shame ... we have arms just as they do" (Roger 2010; author's translation). From the loyalist camp in the south, the religious rhetoric was just as severe: Gbagbo adopted the Christian language of "deliverance" (Banegas 2006: 546) and spoke of the north of Côte d'Ivoire as the "new Jerusalem" (Reforme 2005). In the aftermath of September 11, 2001, Gbagbo characterized the opposition from the north as the "Ivoirian Taliban" (Soudan 2003: 61) and frequently referenced the threat of international Islamic terrorism (Banegas and Losch 2002). Upon his inauguration following the disputed elections, he publicly asked that "God Almighty save us from the evildoers" (Banegas and Losch 2002).

Finally, reporting from scholars and observers shifted from an ethnic or ethno-national frame during the Bedié regime to a Christian–Muslim one following the outbreak of violence. The Agence France Presse labeled Gbagbo and Ouattara according to their religious identities but made no mention of their ethnic ones. Meanwhile, *The New York Times* categorized the violence as evidence of "rising Muslim power," and the Ivoirian journal *Reforme* (2005) noted that President Gbagbo had taken a turn toward "very Christian." Kaplan's (2003) distressing analysis categorized the war as one between the "Muslim-North and the Christian-South," and Le Pape (2003) notes that religious passions were one of the key tools exploited by the conflict's antagonists.

A clear shift had taken place in the framing of Côte d'Ivoire's conflict, from the conflict over land that sparked ethnocentric tensions during the 1990s to the violence described in Muslim–Christian terms beginning around the 2000 election. It is worth reiterating that the war was never a religious one, not in terms of its content, either side's grievances, nor the causes of incompatibility. Numerous scholars are quick to point this out (see Bassett 2003; Marshall 2010; Miran 2006; Toungara 2001). Yet we are still left with explaining why conflicts like this one implicate the actors, targets, rhetoric, and reporting that they do, rather than taking on some other frame. The answer advanced in this book is that the political choices leaders make to protect their own proximate interests, especially when identity types overlap, either build on or exploit the specific mobilizational advantages of identities such as ethnicity and religion at the individual level. In the early stages of political conflict, land-related policies were introduced that cast divisions in ethnic terms. In the latter stages, political leaders explicitly evoked religion to achieve the legitimacy and support they required during wartime. The outcome was a political dispute that became a national-scale identity crisis, at one time ethnic and later religious.

SUPPORTING EVIDENCE

Recall from Chapter 3 that the effects of ethnic and religious manipulation were somewhat greater in Côte d'Ivoire than in Ghana: placed in a religious context, Ivoirians showed a stronger preference for behavior-related, rule-based outcomes than their counterparts in Ghana, despite consistent effects in both places. This can be taken as suggestive evidence that elite mobilization along (especially) religious lines affected Ivoirian respondents above and beyond the experimental treatments. More concretely, if the description of the Ivoirian conflict above is accurate, we should expect to see a change in the salience of religion among Ivoirians by the middle of the 2000s. Did Ivoirian residents actually draw on their religious identities to a greater degree than they might have otherwise, had the conflict never occurred? In this section, I introduce original data to demonstrate that the salience of religion was indeed magnified with the onset of a religious conflict frame.

The best approach would have compared attachments to identity types prior to and after each stage of the conflict in Côte d'Ivoire; an increase in religious attachments could then have been taken as evidence that the conflict intensified the salience of religion. That research design, however, would have called for measurements in service of an event yet to occur. Alternatively, researchers can gain traction on the effects of national political contexts by comparing responses from the residents in question to responses from otherwise identical individuals exposed to a different political context. This is a particularly fruitful strategy if the political contexts were exogenously imposed on individuals and independent of the social and historical factors on the ground, thus allowing one's political environment to be treated "as if" random (Dunning 2008).

For this reason, a number of scholars (Cogneau and Moradi 2014; Laitin 1986; Michalopoulos and Papaioanno 2014; Miguel 2004; Miles and Rochefort 1991; Posner 2004) have exploited African borders as sources of causal leverage.[15] Since those borders were typically drawn

---

[15] See McCauley and Posner (2015) for a listing of cross-border studies and an explanation of the benefits and challenges that the method invites.

along rectilinear lines or watersheds with little thought to the peoples they divided (Alesina, Easterly, and Matuszeski 2011; Englebert et al. 2002), I might rely on measurements of identity attachments in Côte d'Ivoire and compare them with identity attachments, among otherwise identical individuals, at the same time, who happen to live across a border in a different political context.

I turn to results from an analysis conducted in 2005 on either side of the border between Côte d'Ivoire and its northern neighbor, Burkina Faso. Situating the analysis astride this border, rather than the Côte d'Ivoire–Ghana border, provides a control for French colonial effects, and the relatively free flow of individuals across this particular boundary makes the test a harder one. Furthermore, by choosing locations very close to the border, I maximize control over unobservable factors that might otherwise affect attachments to ethnicity, religion, or other identity types.

To document the differences in religious identification on either side of the border, a research team and I administered a survey to approximately 200 respondents distributed across four research sites, two on either side of the border.[16] The sites were selected to be as similar as possible and as close to the border as possible; in fact, the two rural, predominantly Lobi villages of Boussoukoula, in Burkina Faso, and Kalamou, in Côte d'Ivoire, are situated only seven kilometers apart (the two urban market towns – Niangoloko, in Burkina Faso, and Ouangolodougou, in Côte d'Ivoire – lie approximately fifty kilometers apart). After selecting participants via a random sampling procedure with stratification by age and gender, we asked the participants a number of demographic questions and four key survey items to probe the salience of their identities:[17]

1. Each person has several ways of identifying him/herself: nationality, religion, ethnic group, occupation, gender, personality, point of view, etc. For you, which identity is most important?
2. After that, which identity would you place in second position?
3. Could you marry a person of a different religion?
4. To whom do you feel closer: a person of your country who is not of your religion, or a person of your religion who is not of your country?

---

[16] The results of this study are part of a separate paper written with Dan Posner (McCauley and Posner 2017). This account draws on that paper.
[17] Neither Burkina Faso nor Côte d'Ivoire was included in the early rounds of Afrobarometer surveys, when a similar question on self-identity was asked. This eliminates a potential source of comparison data.

TABLE 6.1 *The Salience of Religious Identity in Burkina Faso and Côte d'Ivoire*

	Full Sample %	Burkina Faso (%)	Côte d'Ivoire (%)	CI – BF difference
Lists religion as most important identity	18.8	10.0	27.8	17.8 * (0.04)
Lists religion among top two identities	36.0	23.0	49.7	26.7 (0.14)
Willing to marry across religious lines	66.3	75.0	57.1	−17.9 (0.08)
Feels closer to co-nationals than co-religionists	59.7	77.3	40.3	−37.0 * (0.02)

Notes: Differences reported in column 4 are from two-sample t-tests with unequal variances; standard errors are shown in parentheses, calculated by cluster mean as in Dunning (2012: 181). N = 4 combined cluster observations; two per country.

* $p < .10$ in two-tailed tests. I highlight this level of statistical significance given the relatively small sample size.

In most demographic respects, respondents from the two sides of the border were quite similar (see Appendix E); that is to be anticipated given the sampling protocols, and the characteristics on which they do differ – likelihood of being Muslim and likelihood of having migrated, both of which are greater in Côte d'Ivoire – can be explained by the patterns of labor migration described above. When it comes to the key measures of identity salience, however, the cross-border differences were striking. As Table 6.1 illustrates, respondents living on the Côte d'Ivoire side of the border were almost three times more likely than those living on the Burkina Faso side to identify themselves primarily according to their religion (27.8 percent vs. 10 percent) and far less likely to mention nationality (25 percent vs. 42 percent).[18] Respondents living in Côte d'Ivoire also ranked religion among their top two identities at a much higher rate (49.7 percent vs. 23 percent) than did individuals in Burkina Faso; they expressed less willingness to marry across religious lines (57.1 percent vs. 75 percent); and they were less likely to favor co-nationals over co-religionists (40.3 percent vs. 77.3 percent). Together, these findings serve as a fairly robust indication that, among otherwise similar respondents, those who happened to live on the Ivoirian side of the

[18] Below, I address the issue that the two findings are not independent of one another.

border – and thus to have been exposed to the mobilization along religious lines that took place during conflict in the early 2000s – were significantly more attached to their religious identities.[19]

The cross-border environments differ in ways other than just exposure to the politicization of religion, so I took a number of steps to address alternative explanations for the stronger attachments to religion in Côte d'Ivoire. First, I noted above that respondents in Côte d'Ivoire were more likely to be Muslim; see the descriptive statistics in Appendix E. If Muslims are more likely to self-identify in religion terms – and they are; 25.7 percent of Muslims do so, compared with 10.6 percent of Catholics – this group-level difference could explain the apparent cross-border difference in religion's salience. According to the regression analysis presented in Appendix F, however, when an interaction between country of residence and religious group membership (Muslim or Catholic) is included in the individual-level analysis of the likelihood of ranking religion first, religious group membership remains insignificant, while the country in which the respondent resides maintains close to statistical significance and is substantively important. Furthermore, the cross-border difference in religious salience is significant even among the subset of Muslims in the sample, so the Ivoirian political context seems to trump the effects of Islam.

It could also be the case, as classic secularization theorists would argue, that religion is more important in Côte d'Ivoire because those respondents are poorer (see Berger 1967). The problem with this argument is that, if anything, the opposite is true: average per capita incomes have historically been (and continued to be) higher than in Burkina Faso, and within the sample, living standards among Ivoirian respondents are slightly (though not significantly) higher than among Burkinabé respondents (refer to Appendix E).

Third, supply-side economists might argue that the difference in religion's salience is explained by the quantity and quality of religious institutions on each side of the border: if a greater supply exists in the Ivoirian research sites, the competition between them could stimulate religious

---

[19] Two important robustness checks were performed. First, I calculated the results by cluster mean to account for the fact that respondents were not individually randomized to one side of the border or the other. Those results are presented in Table 6.1. Second, the analysis was performed using country of origin rather than country of residence, to account for potential endogenous sorting that may have occurred when identity-related tensions began. Doing so attenuates the differences as expected, but they remain statistically significant.

practice, and thus its importance (see Stark and Iannaccone 1994). To address that potential explanation, I gathered information from local religious leaders on places of worship at the research sites. It turns out that the two rural villages of Boussoukoula and Kalamou have the same number of mosques (two) and the same number of churches (two), and those places of worship were founded during the same decades on each side of the border. The urban market towns also have very similar aggregate attendance space and numbers, and their places of worship have been in existence for nearly identical periods of time.[20] These findings suggest that the supply of religion on each side of the border was held constant, so the explanation must lie elsewhere. Finally, it may be the case not that religious attachments are noteworthy in Côte d'Ivoire but rather that attachments to nationality are particularly strong in Burkina Faso, thus deflating the relative importance of religion there through the compositional measure I used. Yet there is little reason to suspect that the residents of Burkina Faso are particularly nationalistic. Instead, to the extent that the salience of national identity is high in Burkina Faso, some consider this a secondary effect of the civil strife in Côte d'Ivoire, accentuating the national pride of Burkinabé who were spared such conflict (Loada 2006).

In sum, living on the Côte d'Ivoire side of an arbitrary border is associated with stronger attachments to religion, and not because of Muslim tendencies, secularization, the supply of religious institutions, or particular circumstances in Burkina Faso. Having ruled out those alternatives, the most likely explanation is a political one rooted in the greater exposure of Ivoirian respondents to the politicization of religion during the period of political upheaval described above.

CONCLUSION

Scholars of Ivoirian politics are in some cases quick to reject the description of Côte d'Ivoire's conflict as a war between the north and south. They note that, notwithstanding the general contours of the religious fault line across this part of Africa, the description of the conflict as one between a Muslim north and a Christian south makes little spatial sense, since migration patterns resulted in a religiously and ethnically mixed

---

[20] Catholic and Protestant churches were established in urban locations in the 1930s; mosques had been there since the 1880s, when Samory Touré expanded his self-proclaimed jihad (Roberts et al. 1973). Mosques were established in the rural locations in the 1980s, and churches followed in the 1990s.

country (Bassett 2003; Le Pape and Vidal 2002; Miran 2006; Touré 2000). They point out that many Muslims live in the south of Côte d'Ivoire and that the so-called Muslim north has a large minority of non-Muslims (Miran 2006). Descriptions of the conflict as a religious war, a north–south war, or a war based on ethnic hatreds are thus attributed to an uninformed international press (Bassett 2003) and are said to mislead rather than inform (Vaïsse 2003).

Indeed, the outbreak of violent communal conflict in Côte d'Ivoire had its roots in political and economic disenfranchisement rather than identity differences, and international news sources frequently mischaracterized the events as rooted in religious, ethnic, or regional hatreds.[21] Yet dismissing the importance of the north–south divide that also separates Ivoirians by religion and ethnicity would be shortsighted for several reasons. First, political party cleavages that initially had few regional ties developed strong regional identities in the aftermath of *Ivoirité*. Southern ethnic groups entrenched themselves behind their respective political leaders in the FPI and the PDCI, while Muslims and those of northern ethnicity found common identity with the RDR's Ouattara (Toungara 2001). Second, ethnic and religious identities in Côte d'Ivoire do overlap: an independent field study conducted by L'Observatoire Économique et Statistique d'Afrique Subsaharienne (AFRISTAT) and Développement, Institutions et Mondialisation (DIAL) reveal that less than 5 percent of the Akan and Kru southern ethnic groups are Muslim and that less than 5 percent of northern Mandé are Christian (see Roubaud 2003). Only 14 percent of northern residents were described in the 1998 census data as Christian, and although 30 percent are listed as practicing traditional religions, that figure is disputed by the Muslim community and does not correspond with data from the World Christian Database (2006). Finally, it is precisely the presence of perceived "foreigners" in the southern region of Côte d'Ivoire that gave purchase to the ideology of *Ivoirité* at the communal level. Southerners in the southwest farming region referred to immigrants, Muslims, and those of northern ethnicities as *"la communauté nordiste"* (Ford 2003), and Toungara (2001: 65) has argued that northerners and "affiliated clans living in the South" share the same political interests. Despite, or perhaps because of, economic migration that complicated patterns of ethnic and religious settlement, the political conflict of the 1990s and 2000s was easily understood in north–south,

---

[21] See, e.g., Agence France Press (2003), *New York Times* (2001), *Washington Post* (2000).

ethnic, then religious terms. When the incentives of political elites changed, so too did the identity lens through which that conflict was seen.

A second objection could be that political leaders played the identity cards that they did simply as part of a numbers game, to amass an optimal coalition of supporters during the political conflict. While coalition size is one of the most important calculations that political elites make, and is not inconsistent with an argument rooted in mobilizational differences between identity types, the Ivoirian case highlights the need to look beyond the numbers. In a context of overlapping ethnic and religious identities, little numerical traction could be gained from mobilizing one or the other. Instead, Henri Konan Bedié opted for a strategy of mobilizing his base with preferential land policies in the 1990s, and instability framed in ethnic and ethno-national terms followed. Later, with the critical election of 2000 and the outbreak of violence that followed, Alassane Ouattara and Laurent Gbagbo each sought to cultivate legitimacy and transnational support, the result of which was the awakening of religious divisions.

7

Ethnicity and Religion in Sudan's Civil Wars

That civil conflict in Sudan could have begun prior to its independence in 1956 and continued almost unabated to the present – enveloping note-worthy Sudanese events such as a genocide in Darfur, the emergence of Osama bin Laden and Al Qaeda, and the creation of a new, sovereign state in the south – testifies to the entrenched nature of violence in Sudan's politics. Figures suggest that more than 2 million Sudanese died and nearly 5 million were displaced preceding the 2005 Peace Agreement (Toft 2007); more than 300,000 others lost their lives in the Darfur violence; and a new civil war in South Sudan has killed thousands more. It is also a testament to the enduring power of ethnic and religious identities in the region, which have colored Sudanese conflict, in one way or another, from the beginning.

In this chapter, I explain how the mobilizational differences in ethnicity and religion outlined in Part I help to explain the frames of conflict in Sudan from 1955 to 2005.[1] A first civil war raged for seventeen years, ending with the Addis Ababa Agreement in 1972; that war, I demonstrate, is largely treated as a secessionist conflict between black Africans in the south and the Arab government that controlled Sudan from the north. A tenuous respite held until 1983, when a second civil conflict began, this time implicating religious differences and ending only with a Comprehensive Peace Agreement in 2005. Why, in conflicts whose northern and southern adversaries remained unchanged, was religion absent from the first but central to the second? Why did ethnic

[1] References to Sudan in this chapter thus refer to Sudan as it was constituted prior to the creation of an independent, sovereign South Sudan in 2011.

tensions describe the early conflict but take a back seat to religious differences later on?

Unlike the Ivoirian conflict, I evaluate the Sudan case from afar. By exploring its recent history – and, just as important, its historiography – I show that elite incentives hinged on resources, land, and development during the first conflict and that participants as well as scholars have tended to view this period as one of ethnic or racial strife in Sudan. I then trace the incentives of actors in the subsequent conflict to rules and international ties, and I demonstrate that that conflict was, and continues to be, viewed as a war between Muslims and their non-Muslim or Christian counterparts.

Note that in this chapter, I treat ethnicity somewhat more broadly than I have to this point in the book; in fact, the distinction might more appropriately be viewed as an ethno-racial one that encompasses a variety of distinct ethnic groups in both the south and the north. Since one's Arabness or status as black African follows the social norms in this particular place much as ethno-linguistic differences govern preferences in fully sub-Saharan countries,[2] as I explain below, I treat this categorization as the principal, ethnic alternative to religion in Sudan. From there, I can evaluate the strong and enduring social salience of both ethno-racial and religious identities in Sudan, but also the puzzling fact that their political salience waxed and waned in a systematic manner from one conflict to the next.

THE FOUNDATIONS OF ETHNIC AND RELIGIOUS IDENTITY IN SUDAN

As elsewhere in the region, individual attachments and patterns in social life in the period before and during conflict were largely described in either ethno-racial or religious terms. The foundations for both categories are deep and well-established in Sudan.

 Though Arabs had lived and traded in the region since the mid-600s, traveling first to Egypt and then further south in search of grazing lands, the establishment of an Arab ethno-racial identity in the northern part of Sudan emerged in earnest with the Arab invasion from the north in the sixteenth century (Poggo 2009; Toft 2007). Arab traders opened lines of communication from this new outpost to the rest of the Arab world, and

---

[2] Race might also be considered an element of otherwise narrow ethnic identity in Chad and Niger, similarly situated at the southern cusp of the Sahara.

their complex system of trade and exchange quickly provided advantages in terms of settlements, protection, and power (Deng 1973). As Yusuf Hassan (1973: 90) describes it, the expansion flourished largely through trade, intermarriage and patrimony, and offspring, such that social identity in the region prior to 1500 "was not so much overthrown as turned inside out."[3]

That the Arab expansion – and, hence, Arab identity in Sudan – petered out geographically around the tenth parallel and remained confined primarily to the northern portion of the country was a function not of politics or choice, but of nature. As Poggo (2009: 11) describes, the vast swamp called the Sudd coupled with flat plains and a humid climate brought hardship and disease for which northern Arabs, and the camels that served as their transportation, were ill-suited. As a result, a natural barrier formed, preventing all but a few Arab adventurers and slave raiders from venturing further south (Deng 1973). That natural barrier would be reified by political arrangements, and eventually violent conflict, later on.

Black Africans in Sudan accounted for approximately 59 percent of the population of 40 million at the time of the Peace Agreement in 2005. Sudan's population of 10 million in 1956 was similarly categorized, though a larger share of non-Arabs – nearly a third – lived in the northern provinces (Poggo 2009: 15). A noteworthy Arab "other" in the north contributes to the simplistic notion of an ethno-racial cleavage, yet Sudan is in fact one of the most ethnically diverse places south of the Sahara: close to 600 distinct ethno-linguistic groups comprising 58 principal ethnicities across three major language groupings (Sudanic, Western Nilotic, and Eastern Nilotic) have been identified in the region; ethnic identities include the Dinka (and the Ngok Dinka in the north), Nuer, Anuak, Bor, and Shilluk (Eprile 1974: 24–28). The best organized had established a foothold in the territory by the start of the eleventh century, and competition for lands and grazing territory for cattle quickly followed. Nevertheless, owing to both longstanding patterns of "cultural borrowing" among Sudanic and Nilotic groups and a tendency to perceive the Arab as stranger, the ethnic groups of the south are frequently treated in the scholarship and discourse of Sudan's political conflicts as an ethno-racial union of non-Arab, black Africans (see Daly and Sikainga 1993; Deng 1973; Poggo 2009).

The outcome was a setting in which, by the start of hostilities in the 1950s, Sudanese in the south collectively referred to northern residents as

---

[3] As cited first in Deng (1973).

Arabs (Poggo 2009: 14), while northerners lumped residents of the south together with the pejorative label of 'abd, or "slave" (Collins 2008: 8). The historiography confirms this emphasis on ethnicity: scholars note that, when the British colonizers later turned to a system of "indirect rule" to preclude northern Arab elites from governing non-Arab southerners, politics in Sudan became "tribal" (see Collins 2008: 37; Deng 1973: 23). Those broad ethno-racial distinctions between Arabs and black Africans in Sudan of course belie excessive racial and ethnic intermixing – far more than is typically assumed – that had resulted from decades of labor migration, inter-marriage, and slave trading (Collins 2008; Daly and Sikainga 1993; Eprile 1974; Toft 2007). Yet the perception was that northerners "looked, spoke, and acted like Arabs" (Eprile 1974: 13) and that non-Arab southerners shared habits of lifestyle, economic practices, and appearance, which together merited broad ethno-racial labeling across the tenth parallel divide. A consciousness of ethnic dualism was thus one important aspect of identity in Sudan (Deng 1993).

A similarly salient north–south divide emerged along religious lines. Islam spread through the northern parts of what later became Sudan just as the Arab identity did, first in the seventh century as traders and travelers sought land, goods, and slaves (Insoll 2003). The Arab invasion of 1504 also consolidated a place for Islam in the political and social structures of the region. Then, in 1821, the Turk Muhammed Ali moved from Egypt into Sudan, conquering the northern territory and establishing Turkish Egyptian rule that lasted for more than sixty years, until its overthrow in 1884 by Muhammad Ahmad bin Abdallah, the self-proclaimed Mahdi, or second prophet and restorer of the Islamic faith (Toft 2007). By the time formal British involvement began with the ouster of the Mahdist regime in 1899, Islamic identity was closely linked to society and politics in the northern territories of Sudan.

Traditionally, Islam in Sudan was dominated by Sufism, a mystical brand of worship and ritual. During the post-Mahdist colonial period, however, both British colonial administrators and northern Arab elites encouraged a transformation to orthodox forms of Muslim worship, thus taking advantage of the more stable and hierarchical organization that orthodox Islam provided (see Collins 2008). Muslims were then able to settle disputes in Islamic Shari'a courts in Khartoum, and norms of Islamic dress, worship, and lifestyle spread widely and in systematic fashion across the region.

As discussed in Chapter 2, Christianity spread into the area of northern Sudan much sooner than elsewhere on the continent, by virtue of the close proximity of present-day Sudan to Egypt and Ethiopia, the cradle of Christianity in Africa. The traditional kingdoms of Nubia, Magarra, and Alwa adopted Christianity in the sixth century; its practice persisted there for 1,000 years, until the Arab invasion transformed the north into Muslim territory (Deng 2001). Christianity was indeed slower to spread south of the tenth parallel, however, and made real inroads only with the arrival of missionaries later in the 1800s. During the British colonial period, two factors served to cultivate a Christian identity in the south, despite the fact that many remained affiliated with traditional African religions.[4] First, Governor Cromer in Egypt and Governor Wingate in Sudan, in an effort to stem the political strength of Islam, took numerous administrative steps to bolster Christianity: the Arabic language was prohibited in official business in the south, Muslim officers from the north were transferred back to their home region, and Christian missionaries were supported with new zeal and flexibility. Second, in the dynamic, open religious space that European missionaries perceived in the south, Protestant and Catholic competition sparked both tensions and concerted efforts to evangelize more quickly than the other, leading to a sphere system that designated operational territory but also to a firm Christian hold on the south.[5] As traditional religionists converted to world religions, this ensured that they would by and large become Christians.

The sociopolitical consequences of these historical trends can be summarized in three points: first, Arab and black African ethno-racial identities resonated with Sudanese at the onset of independence and conflict. Second, religious differences between Muslims and non-Muslims were equally as salient, and the rising tide of Christianity in the south ensured that that would continue. Finally, those ethnic and religious cleavages followed the same natural geographic boundary around the tenth parallel, such that the ethnic and religious fissures overlapped and the same communities who won or lost in certain respects were almost assured of the same outcome in other respects. Indeed, scholars typically refer to the shift in the early 1500s, as well as efforts employed by political leadership in the north at the onset of conflict, as periods of both *Arabization* and *Islamization* (Deng 1973; Sikainga 1993; Yongo-Bure 1993). Simply put, ethno-racial identities and religious identities were both of critical social importance by the time Sudan's civil wars began.

---

[4] Both of these trends are described in Collins (2008: 33–46).
[5] See Finck and Iannaccone (1993) and Iannaccone, Finke, and Stark (1997) for a supply-side explanation of religious competition and change.

The colonial-era political context only reinforced those two social identity options for residents of the north and south of Sudan. To placate both Egyptian concerns over lost influence and domestic British concerns of gratuitous expansion (Collins 2008), Britain settled for an Anglo-Egyptian Condominium regime in Sudan, though the upshot was that the Britain ruled while Egypt paid for infrastructure and development (Daly 1993). In fact, the British maintained an interest in the south only because the Nile flowed through it; few efforts were made to develop or improve the region through the first half of the twentieth century (Yongo-Bure 1993). Northern elites were favored in the administration, and the closing of the south to northern traders reinforced not just the economic inequalities across the north and south, but also the identity divisions (see Eprile 1974). The increasingly contentious division convinced the Brits to cultivate Sudanese participation as a bulwark against Egyptian designs on the territory, and those steps led eventually to Sudanese independence in 1956, more a function of British resignation than of a strong independence movement. Further exacerbating the north–south division, the rapid control of the Sudanese administration by northern Arab Muslims in the post-independence era created the feeling among southerners that their northern counterparts had simply taken the reins from Britain (Poggo 2009). "It appears that our fellow northerners want to colonize us," one southern merchant stated.[6]

A consistent theme in the scholarship on Sudanese politics is the manner in which ethno-racial and religious identities – at least as they were constructed and reified in the Sudanese imagination – overlapped so completely. Collins (2008), Daly and Sikainga (1993), Deng (1995), Khalid (2003), Leach (2013), Toft (2007), and Poggo (2009) all describe a setting in which the spread of Arab language and customs along with Islamic religious practice in the north drove the north and south apart in both ethnic and religious terms, created a "southern problem" for the northern-based government, and – despite well-documented mixing – gave rise to a national consciousness firmly divided in both ethnic and religious terms. Yet precisely because the ethnic and religious identities overlap so thoroughly in Sudan, it makes little sense to view either as the cause of conflict, or even to ask what causes ethnic and religious conflicts more broadly. The ethnic and religious identities in Sudan each have well-established and longstanding histories of social salience, but their

---

[6] Reported in Collins (2008: 65).

applications to conflict in Sudan are episodic. Thus, the context of over-lapping identities should instead imply a choice – a choice in how those identities are used in the course of conflict.

ETHNICITY AND THE FIRST WAR IN SUDAN

The cause of an outbreak in violence in 1955 that launched the first war in Sudan is varied and complex, but what can be stated clearly is that its roots lie in political factors, not simply identity differences. Principally, the northern elites who inherited administrative power from Britain faced few political incentives to compromise, so the same part of the country advantaged during condominium rule continued to benefit thereafter (Daly 1993; de Waal 2007). In 1954, as British officials departed, the sweeping "Sudanization" process instituted by the victorious National Unionist Party left only six of the 800 senior government posts in the hands of southerners (Eprile 1974: 20). Subsequent political infighting among northern elites and those with interests in Khartoum versus the peripheral areas of the north left no space for political bargaining with the south, so a systemic denial of public services to the south continued through the subsequent regimes of Major-General Ibrahim 'Abbud (1958–1964), Ismail al-Azhari and the Democratic Unionist Party (1965–1969), and Jaafar Numeiri (1969–1985) (Collins 2008).

On August 18, 1955, southern soldiers in the Sudanese national army received orders to report to Khartoum in the north. Fearing at worst a trap and at best an effort to further deny rights and services to southerners (Collins 2008), the soldiers attacked a garrison of northern officers in the town of Torit, leading to violence that quickly spread through major towns in the southern region of Equatoria. Some 8,000 northern Sudanese troops were transported to the south to crush the rebellion, but those mutineers not summarily executed fled into the hills near the Sudan–Uganda border,[7] becoming the initial insurgents in what would be a seventeen-year civil war.

Separate from the causes of a conflict like this one are the agendas that political elites pursue to serve their proximate interests. In Sudan's first war, I argue, the quest of those elites to achieve or maintain power led to strategic choices that mobilized ethnic interests and shaped the conflict as an ethno-racial one.

---

[7] See Poggo (2009: 42–47).

In the north, cattle herders faced much drier lands. Routinely, then, they took advantage of northern administrative advantage to push south and control, or at least exploit, the coveted pastures in regions demarcated as southern (Deng 2006). Sharkey (2004) notes a pattern whereby northern elites encouraged the seizing of southern land in order to appease those cattle-grazing constituencies in the north; Collins (2008) similarly describes the forced relocation of 50,000 ethnic Nubians from homelands along the Nile river – an effort to obtain control over critical water resources for northern herders and commercial agriculturalists. These decisions were made as political bargaining broke down and the north asserted its de facto control over the south. Given the broader political power struggle between northern and southern interests, though, it would be simplistic to suggest that those land-related affronts caused the civil conflict in Sudan; instead, in a context of hardened north–south divisions and quickly spreading violence, they helped to shape the lens through which that conflict was seen. And from Part I of this book, we know that land is tightly intertwined with the ethnic identity in Africa, helping to explain why this first Sudanese conflict came to be viewed as an ethnic one.

The response from the south was commensurate with northern efforts to control southern land. Principally, southern rebels were overt separatists who sought to secede from the north and establish an independent, sovereign state with full control over their own land and resources (Daly 1993). Authority in the south had already devolved to traditional ethnic leaders through colonial-era indirect rule, and those leaders typically regulated the very resources under threat from the north (Deng 2006). As the Anya-Nya movement emerged in the early 1960s as a formidable rebel force in the south, those traditional ethnic interests in protecting land assets merged with the goal of secession. Taking its name from a poisonous snake venom, the Anya-Nya under the leadership of Joseph Lagu unified fighting units organized along ethnic lines into a southern fighting force seeking separation from the north (Johnson and Prunier 1993).

The emergence of Anya-Nya from a collection of ethnic units protecting their homelands into a southern force underscores the process by which conflict frames develop. Southerners had not sought an ethnic war or ethnic-related interests. Instead, in seeking redress against administrative discrimination, they confronted a northern strategy that put southern land and resources under threat. That threat not only encouraged the unification of southern regions and ethnic groups, but also inspired southerners to "take up spears, bows, and arrows to fight the enemy ... in defense of their homeland" (Poggo 2009: 68). By this process did a political conflict and rebellion take on language of united black Africans fighting an Arab foe. Elites acted strategically and responded in kind. In the union of macro and micro concerns that this book aims to stress, northern and southern supporters reacted to those elite agendas in ways that placed ethnicity at the center of the conflict.

It is instructive to again return to the elements that contribute to a conflict frame. First, the actors involved in the first Sudanese war either acted explicitly in the name of ethnic identities or were described as such. Northerners embraced a movement of Arabization, while, as Deng (1973: 20) puts it, the southern Sudanese were "molded to identify themselves ultimately according to family, tribal, ethnic, and racial values." Anya-Nya fighters fought explicitly as ethnic units against a common Arab enemy even when their forces were unified, and members joining the Anya-Nya were referred to in ethnic (not religious) terms (Poggo 2009). Finally, much of the fighting was conducted by native administrative police on behalf of their ethnic chiefs, a further indication that the actors in Sudan's first conflict were ethnic ones.

Second, the targets and rhetoric of the first war colored the conflict in clearly ethnic terms. Some Anya-Nya fighters representing different ethnic groups in the south refused to relinquish control of their ethnic homelands even after an agreement ending the war (Eprile 1974), suggesting a sacredness of the ethnic tie to land. Daniel Jumi Tongun, one of the southern soldiers responsible for the mutiny at Torit, further evoked the relationship to ethnic kin: "we cannot forget the atrocities you committed against our ancestors!" he exclaimed to his eventual northern captors.[8] And, when 'Abbud imposed military rule across the country beginning in 1958, southerners explained the move as "forcing the Arab culture on us."[9]

Third, the reporting on Sudan's first war regularly describes the conflict in ethno-racial, not religious, terms. Cecile Eprile (1974: 7), in somewhat outdated language, labeled the conflict a clash between the Arab culture of the north and the "Negroid" culture of the south and explicitly stated that this was an ethnic reference. In outlining key informants, interviews, and players from the first war, Poggo (2009: 3–4) describes all of them in ethnic terms, never mentioning religious identities or attachments: Madut was a Dinka; Tombe, a Bari; Lueth, a Lwo, and Mboro, a Ndogo. He unites all of them under the label of "black Africans" in conflict with Arab northerners. Pointedly, Collins (2008: 92) argues that a key problem for

[8] See Poggo (2009: 51).   [9] Ibid.: 59.

the south at the end of the colonial period was that no southern elite emerged as capable of overcoming his ethnic identity and supporting a national agenda.

When a military stalemate finally inspired Numeiri to engage in negotiations with the south, regional autonomy for southern Sudan within a united Sudan became the most palatable option for the two sides. The Addis Ababa Agreement was adopted in 1972, establishing a basis for socioeconomic development but also cultural and racial tolerance across the north and south (Wakoson 1993).

That the first war in Sudan became an ethnic one is not at all to say that religion took a back seat socially in that period; indeed, Islamization complemented 'Abbud's Arabization program, and the divide between southern Christians and traditionalists and northern Muslims intensified. The Sabbath was changed from Sunday to Friday in 1960, reflecting prioritization of the Muslim prayer day; the 1962 Missionary Societies Act strictly limited the role of Christian missionaries in Sudan; and in 1964 Christian missions were expelled altogether (Deng 2001). Yet despite these incendiary religious restrictions, the frame of the conflict hinged on elite choices regarding land and resources, which inspired an ethnoracial perspective rather than a religious one. After the Torit mutiny that launched the war, a commission of inquiry stated with general agreement that the war was not a religious one (Eprile 1974: 82). Summarizing the conflict, Toft (2007: 127) notes that "religion was no more important than any other issue." Instead, a conflict that invited strategic exploitation and defense of land came to be viewed in ethnic terms.

RELIGION AND THE SECOND WAR IN SUDAN

A tenuous, eleven-year period of peace followed the Addis Ababa Agreement, but tensions persisted: political parties were banned, cattle raiding continued along ethnic and racial lines, and the discovery of oil introduced new opportunities for both wealth and dispute (Johnson and Prunier 1993). In a positive shift, Arab and African identities were recognized in the new constitution of 1973, and freedom of religion was guaranteed.

The breakdown in peace and the beginning of a new civil war in Sudan turned largely on internal political tensions in the north. Facing increasing pressure from hardline elements such as the National Islamic Front (NIF) and Sudan's Muslim Brotherhood, Numeiri (President from 1969 to 1985) sought to consolidate his power by further driving a wedge between the north and south. In abrogation of the Addis Agreement, he announced a

plan in June 1983 to divide the southern region into three regions, effectively diluting political power in the south and establishing carte blanche
for northern political interests (Collins 2008: 137). On the heels of recent
oil discoveries in the northern parts of the south, and in response to
continued pressure from northern cattle herders seeking arable land and
pastures, Numeiri also unilaterally altered the established boundary
between north and south, a clear violation of the southern autonomy that
had enabled peace since 1972. Finally, with guidance from the NIF-
affiliated Hassan al-Turabi as Attorney-General, Numeiri implemented
the so-called September Laws, imposing Islamic Shari'a law throughout
Sudan, including the south (Deng 1993). Certainly, this constituted a more
overt role for religious identity in the causes of the second war, though, as
An-Na'im (1993: 113) notes, it was the culmination of violations of the
Addis Ababa Agreement that ultimately ended the brief period of peace in
Sudan, with Shari'a serving as a symbol of southern grievances.

Just as elite efforts to maintain power led to decisions that evoked
ethnic tensions during the first war, elite incentives invited choices that
inspired religious attachments in the second. The real turning point in
conflict frames came in late 1983, when internal political competition in
the north galvanized concerns over lifestyle rules and international ties.
Pressure from al-Turabi and the NIF mounted on Numeiri, leading a once
secular leader with ties to the Communist party to swing thoroughly in
the direction of strict, conservative Islam. He ordered government officials
to refrain from alcohol, performed Friday prayers in public, and began
a series of television lectures lamenting the decadence that came with
secular life (Collins 2008). The motives were political – Numeiri staved
off internal threats from hardline factions within the north – but the
consequence was to put lifestyle and behavioral guidelines at the fore
for both northerners and southerners. Sadiq al-Mahdi replaced Numeiri
in 1985 and ruled until overthrown by current Sudanese President Omar
Hassan al-Bashir in 1989 (Toft 2007). Backed by the NIF, and himself a
devout Muslim, Bashir's rise to power in the course of conflict corresponded with an increasingly strong role for conservative social policies
throughout Sudan.

International ties proved equally important to the northern regime and
equally critical in shaping the second war as a religious one. Since the Six-
Day War in 1967, Israel began supporting the southern rebels in an effort
to establish a second front against Arab interests (Collins 2008). In
response, the post-1983 Sudanese regimes in the north undertook a policy
of engagement with Middle Eastern (and predominantly Muslim)

countries, using religious rhetoric for leverage and inspiring religious perceptions of the new wave of conflict at home. The motive was not so much religious as political; yet, as Deng notes, much of the northern political agenda during the second war can be linked to external resources and sources of support (Deng 1993: 212). These choices in the course of conflict, I argue, help to explain why religion went from being viewed as a peripheral to a central issue in the second Sudanese war (see Toft 2007).

Southern rebels were again faced with responding to a conflict frame generated largely through northern political choices. Whereas southern rebels during the first war were avowed ethno-racial separatists, in the second war southerners answered the imposition of Shari'a law with a secular nationalist platform (Deng 2006). The Sudan People's Liberation Movement/Army (SPLM/A) succeeded the Anya-Nya and, relying on many of the same rebel veterans, became the principal opponent of the north in the fight for a united, secular Sudan (Johnson and Prunier 1993). John Garang possessed less battlefield experience but more education and leadership capacity than his southern rebel counterparts; he would lead the SPLM/A through the Comprehensive Peace Agreement in 2005. The fight he led aimed to protect non-Muslims in the south from the consequences of northern political maneuvering by establishing a democratic, secular government (Collins 2008), an aim that reinforced the religious frame in a new conflict between longstanding enemies.

The effect of these political choices on individuals involved in the second Sudanese war are precisely what we would expect from a theory of mobilizational differences in identities. Hutchinson (2001: 328) describes how southerners "began to develop their religious imaginations in novel directions." Thousands converted en masse from traditional African beliefs to Christianity, and religious prophets also saw increases in their influence as religious advisors (Hutchinson 2001). Northerners, for their part, were encouraged to carry the Qur'an in public (Poggo 2009), a gesture that built on earlier Islamization efforts and that symbolized the framing of the conflict as a religious one. As Deng (2001) states, the south during the course of the second civil war became a place that "unequivocally identified itself with Christianity."

Evaluating the elements that contribute to a conflict frame helps to illustrate the sharp contrast between Sudan's first and second wars. Whereas the actors in the first war embraced their ethnic or "tribal" origins, the southern-based SPLM/A instead presented itself as a secular force combating Islamic intrusion. The New Sudan Council of Churches emerged as a key source of financial and logistical support for the south, pushing fighters to further shed their ethnic identities and embrace their Christian one (Hutchinson 2001). In the north, the ascent of Hasan al-Turabi and the National Islamic Front cloaked the motives of the sitting government in a deeply religious guise; even the formerly secular President Numeiri took to wearing Muslim garb (Fearon and Laitin 2000). Beginning with al-Bashir's takeover in 1989, soldiers from the north repositioned themselves as Muslim mujahideen fighting to protect the place of Islam in government. Even internationally, religious actors contributed to the framing of the Sudanese war: American Christian movements latched onto the tragic story of the southern Sudanese "lost boys," leading numerous churches and religious leaders to pressure the U.S. government on its policy toward Sudan (Collins 2008).

Given that the war was fought largely in southern territory and the institutional strength of Christianity was only beginning to emerge with the new waves of converts, religious targets were not a common feature of the Sudanese war as they were of the conflict in Côte d'Ivoire. On the other hand, the rhetoric employed in the course of Sudan's second war clearly contributed to a religious frame. Numeiri implored northerners in the course of conflict to view religion not as an individual matter but rather as the "cornerstone of society" (Famhi 2012). He regularly framed the conflict as one over values, and he attributed the backwardness of the south to their decadent lifestyles and absence of Islamic guidance (Collins 2008). The architect of Sudan's shift to Islamization Hasan al-Turabi himself stated that "a comprehensive programme of [Islamic] action will see its enemies, both locally and internationally, united against it, but this will establish Islam as a real power in the world again" (in Hamdi 1998: 116).

Finally, reports and observations of the second war contribute to its religious frame and distinguish this war from the first one. The BBC described the second conflict as one in which forces loyal to the government were fighting rebels "from the animist and Christian South" (BBC 1998), a sharp change when we recall that descriptions of the first war did not mention religion at all. Increasingly, Toft (2007) notes, the regime in the north itself described the violence as an Islamic jihad, helping to place religion as the central issue in the conflict. Deng (1993) describes the ethnic and "tribal" loyalties that shaped the first war as having been transcended by the Christian and missionary elite who led southern forces after 1983. Elsewhere, he depicts the gospel as a direct source of southern inspiration during a second period of conflict that was fundamentally about "the relationship between religion and the state" (2001: 5).

Just as religion coexisted with ethnicity as a critical social marker during the first conflict, ethno-racial differences remained important during the second. Ethnic hostilities persisted, particularly for groups such as the Ngok Dinkas – ethnically labeled black Africans but historical residents of the north (Deng 2006). The Sudanese government in the north, in fact, sought to exploit ethnic differences by employing *murahalin* tribal militias that might divide and undermine the unity of the SPLM/A (de Waal 1993). It is easy to imagine, then, how a breakdown in peace and a return to twenty-two more years of civil conflict could have reignited old ethnic mistrust and hatred. Instead, because the political context incentivized behavioral rules (in Shari'a) and international ties, the second conflict became a religious affair.

CONCLUSION

The Comprehensive Peace Agreement that officially ended Sudan's second civil war in 2005 provided guidelines for a referendum vote on southern independence. In 2009, southern Sudanese voted overwhelmingly in favor, and in July 2011, South Sudan became the world's newest sovereign, independent state. The euphoria that followed for Southern Sudanese, however, quickly eroded; in the face of personal struggles for control between Southern politicians Salva Kiir and Riek Mashar, a new intra-South civil war – this time coloring violence in Dinka-Nuer ethnic terms – began.

Arab-African ethno-racial differences, as constructed as they might be, and Muslim–Christian religious differences have shaped both social patterns and politics for generations in Sudan. Why, then, were ethnicity and religion employed so distinctly in Sudan's civil wars, despite pitting the same north–south adversaries against one another? This chapter adds further support to a story of mobilizational differences: strategic interests in staving off threats and securing power have the consequence of evoking different identity priorities, following the individual-level logic presented in Part I. In this case, land-related violations contributed to the perception of ethnic differences during the first war, leaving soldiers to fight for their "ethnic homelands." Later, starting in 1983, the strategic use of lifestyle rules, along with efforts to generate international support, contributed to a religious frame during the second war. There is evidence, furthermore, of a recursive process: political leaders were also able to play distinct identity cards to evoke greater passions over the priorities they favored. Jok and Hutchinson (1999) describe a southern soldier's astute interpretation of his leadership's interests during the first conflict: "We don't care about their political careers. They know this and that is why they make it sound as if tribal wealth is under threat ... in order to persuade people to wage war."[10] Not only do policy priorities evoke distinct identities, but identities can be exploited in service of particular political priorities.

Three alternative perspectives may explain the role of identities in the Sudanese wars. The first – that either ethnicity or religion is primordially more important than the other – fails to stand up to the abundance of evidence indicating differential attachments to ethnicity and religion from the first war to the second. The second, more plausible objection suggests that ethnicity and religion in this part of the world cannot be separated so easily. Indeed, northern leaders employed the agendas of Arabization and Islamization in lockstep, and each remained a critical social divider throughout the long period of unrest. The lesson to take away from this chapter, however, is that the social salience of identities such as ethnicity and religion should be viewed as distinct from their political usefulness. Given distinct strategic interests in 1955 and 1983, leaders exploited these two equally important, overlapping social identities in notably different ways, setting the stage for an initial conflict viewed in ethno-racial terms and a subsequent one evoking religion. Finally, scholars have described the second war in Sudan according to a logic of religious outbidding: northern leaders competing for support, in a context reshaped by international pressures, were forced to appeal to popular, hardline elements by escalating their religious credentials during the second conflict (see de Waal 2007; Toft 2007). My argument is not inconsistent with this one; both suggest that political incentives led to policy choices that in turn amplified the role of religion. Religious outbidding arguments, of course, can explain the absence of religion in the first war, but they are not suited to explain why ethnicity was instead the salient frame of conflict then. A story of mobilizational differences does that.

---

[10] See Jok and Hutchinson (1999: 133), as reported in Hutchinson (2001).

8

Ethnicity and Religion in Nigeria's Biafran War

While Sudan endured two protracted, north–south wars that defined its post-independence existence, Nigeria's recent history is instead littered with innumerable, periodic episodes of violence described in ethnic and religious terms: the Maitatsine Muslim riots, and Christian–Muslim mob violence, in the 1980s. Violent clashes between the Ijaw and other ethnic groups over control of the Niger Delta in the 1990s. Hausa-Fulani battles with the Yoruba ethnic group in the late 1990s and early 2000s. The spread of terror by Boko Haram in the name of radical Islam in the 2010s.[1]

Preceding these conflicts, and perhaps setting the stage for the repeated ethnic and religious rivalries that would color Nigerian politics, was one of the deadliest events in African history: the civil war between Nigeria and the declared Republic of Biafra. Beginning with the announced secession of the southeastern part of the country in May 1967, a war initially expected to last only weeks finally ended in January 1970 after the deaths of an estimated one million people, many of them civilians living in the breakaway Biafran republic (Falola 1999).

In this chapter, I demonstrate that the exploitation of ethnic and religious identities during Côte d'Ivoire's decade of violence and Sudan's half-century of conflict also served political leaders in Nigeria's brutal, thirty-month civil war. The cause of war lay largely in regional power struggles and a quest for control of the central government, making this

---

[1] See Falola (1998) for a helpful summary of Nigeria's religious conflicts. See Osaghae and Suberu (2005) for information on ethnic conflicts. See Aghedo and Osumah (2012) on Boko Haram.

no more a conflict *about* ethnicity or religion than were the two preceding cases. The principal opponents, moreover – Nigeria's Federal Military Government (FMG), with important backing from the northern, Hausa-Fulani, predominantly Muslim community, on the one hand, versus the breakaway Biafran Republic, representing southeastern, Igbo, predominantly Christian interests, on the other – never changed. And yet the frame of the war shifted dramatically after just a few months: initially viewed as a "tribal war" rooted in fears over the extermination of the Igbo people (Kirk-Greene 1971a), Biafra's leaders and the international community came to embrace a description of the war in religious terms, with Christians dying at the hands of "hardened Muslims ... marching to the sea" (see Omenka 2010: 370). Ethno-regional competition never vanished, and the quest for Igbo independence persists over forty years later, but political leaders in the Nigeria–Biafra War nevertheless demonstrated that mobilizational differences between ethnicity and religion can be leveraged to meet changing proximate needs. The outcome was a war – at one point "ethnic" and at a later point "religious" – much longer and bloodier than anyone expected.

In what follows, I provide background on the ethnic and religious histories in Nigeria that resulted in overlapping cleavages – Hausa-Fulani Muslims in the north, and Igbo Christians in the southeast. I then describe the events that sparked the war itself. Next, I use historical data to test hypotheses related to the salience of ethnicity and religion during the course of the war. Specifically, if the theory of mobilizational differences in Africa is correct, we should expect to see that land and local resource priorities led to an ethnic frame of war, pitting Igbos against their Hausa-Fulani enemies. We should then observe that, when local geographic resources became less important and transnational relationships became paramount, political leaders altered the frame from an ethnic one to a contest between Christians and Muslims. Evidence of this changing frame should be apparent in the actors, the targets, the rhetoric, and the reporting that surrounded the early and later stages of the war.

ETHNIC AND RELIGIOUS HISTORIES IN NIGERIA

At least 250 distinct ethnic groups comprise the population of Nigeria, Africa's most populous state. Among them, three ethnic groups predominate, making up about half of the Nigerian population: the Hausa-Fulani in the north, the Yoruba in the southwest, and the Igbo in the southeast (Falola 1999). Far from rigid, primordial identities, however, these principal ethnicities and their corresponding regional strongholds have developed through change, time, and colonial influence.

In the north, the Fulani settled over a millennium ago, having migrated from North Africa; some settled permanently, while others remained itinerant pastoralists (Mang 2013). Accessing land for cattle grazing created incentives for the Fulani to push west and southwest, engaging in military conquest and acquiring slave labor from the Oyo Kingdom; the Hausa kingdoms such as Katsina, Kano, and Gobir; and Kanem-Borno, itself a powerful kingdom since the eighth century (Falola 1999). The Hausa, meanwhile, link their own existence in the north of Nigeria to migration from ancient Mesopotamia. While Hausa kingdoms thrived through the fifteenth century, many of those kingdoms began to crumble as Fulani influence spread (Gould 2012). A union eventually emerged: Hausa became the lingua franca of the region, Fulani organizational structures triumphed, and a Hausa-Fulani identity with ties to Arabs in North Africa would ultimately draw in many northern Nigerians and persist as the dominant northern ethnic group (see Kastfelt 1994).

The story of constructed ethnic identity in northern Nigeria cannot be disentangled from the history of religion and Islam in the region. Those Fulani migrants brought Islam to the region in the eleventh century, using its social and organizational tenets to establish influence among the Hausa and an eventual ethnic union. Starting with small communities in Kanem-Borno, Islam made inroads among Hausa kings over the following three centuries, so that by the 1600s, Islam was established in cities throughout the north (Falola 1998: 24–25). The real golden age of Islam in northern Nigeria, however, began in 1804 when the famous Fulani Islamic scholar Usman dan Fodio launched his jihad against Hausa rulers and moderate Fulani. By 1808, Hausaland was firmly under dan Fodio's control, and an Islamic caliphate was established with its capital in Sokoto (Gould 2012). The influence of the Sokoto caliphate spread quickly, as emirs were given important influence over key links in the region's trade routes, often ruling with a heavy hand.

Thus, by the mid-nineteenth century, a constructed Hausa-Fulani ethnic identity dominated the north and overlapped almost completely with a politically powerful Islamic religious identity, setting the stage for the political appeal a century later to "One North, One People" – the notion of a unified Islamic region with Arab influence and ties (Reynolds 1997). Its influence was sweeping, even as British colonial traders built railways and explored new markets in the region. Much like Sudan, however, the northern, Muslim push southward was halted not by opposing political forces but by the tsetse fly: unable to keep cattle and camels free of disease, the Hausa-Fulani and Muslim advance settled to a stop around the tenth parallel (Gould 2012). The political and organizational strength of the caliphate proved especially resilient to colonial takeover but, after much resistance, ultimately fell to the British in 1903 (Falola 1999).

In the south, the Niger River separated the ethnic Yoruba kingdoms of Oyo and Benin to the west from Igboland to the east. While Islamic incursions influenced the Yoruba kingdoms and resulted in a mixed religious population in the southwest, the forest lands of the southeast were particularly impenetrable and remained distinct from northern influence. There, archeological evidence indicates the presence of the Igbo as early as 2500 BCE and widespread influence in the region by the eighth century (Elizabeth 1976). The Igbo emerged as the dominant ethnic group not through kingdoms but instead through hundreds of autonomous village units developed around patrilineal clans, each with a founding ancestor (Falola 1999: 24), forming what some refer to as the Igbo heartland or Igbo nation (de St. Jorre 1972: 108). Land was essential to the Igbo agricultural livelihood; it was sanctified and celebrated as the property of ethnic ancestors. As Falola (1999: 7) notes, ancient festivals celebrating agricultural harvests persist among the Igbo today. Smaller ethnic groups in the region have in some cases remained distinct (in the case of the Ibibios and Ijaws, for example) and in other cases adopted the Igbo language and contribute to a broader Igbo ethnolinguistic identity in the southeast.

The Christian religious identity in southeast Nigeria developed much later. While the Portuguese established contacts in the 1480s, Christian missionary influence in the region met very limited success over the next three centuries. Only in 1842, in the aftermath of the jihad and spread of Islam in the north did Christianity begin to establish foundations of any sort in Nigeria. The most natural opportunities arose in the non-Muslim areas to the south, which mitigated religious tensions but also reinforced the overlapping ethnic and religious cleavages in the region, as Igbos adopted Christianity, and Catholicism in particular, in wide numbers (Kastfelt 1994). Long accustomed to protecting their land interests against southern intruders, the Igbo proved open to Christian missionaries largely by virtue of the missions' explicit lack of territorial interest. Instead, missionaries working in the region expressed a desire to transfer moral status and religious rules to southeastern Nigerians (Kastfelt 1994: 133). In addition, the Christian missions adopted a strategy in the nineteenth century of admitting indigenous Nigerians to the clergy and constructing schools as a means of broadening the southern, Christian network and establishing a new brand of Christian elite (Kastfelt 1994). Indeed, whereas the influence of Islamic structures and Quranic teaching defined the north, only 41 formal schools existed there by the end of the colonial period, compared with 842 in the south (Onu 2001).

In another similarity with Sudan, the colonial era in Nigeria reified those ethnic and religious patterns. Britain's formal entrée into the region began with the private Royal Niger Company (RNC), which established a foothold in Lagos in 1860, expanded into the Niger Delta, and by the end of the nineteenth century formally controlled much of present-day Nigeria for commercial purposes (Falola 1998). In 1900, the British government took control from the RNC, at great profit to the latter,[2] and organized the territory into two distinct and autonomous regions, the North and South, under the control of Sir Frederick Lugard. Perfecting Britain's preferred policy of indirect rule, Lugard changed little in the North: the structure of the caliphate remained intact, emirs continued as administrators now working at the behest of the British, and Shari'a law was employed as a juridical principle (Falola 1998). The Southeast, however, had no history of kings or regional administration, which the system of indirect rule required. Thus, the warrant chiefs appointed by Lugard met great difficulty in establishing authority, and the British were ultimately forced to rely on more direct measures of rule while accommodating the non-centralized social structures of the Igbo (Waugh and Cronjé 1969).

Northern and Southern Nigeria may from that point forward have evolved as two separate, sovereign states, with quite distinct ethnic and religious populations, but for the fact that the North proved entirely insolvent (Uche 2008). So as not to remain reliant on subsidies from British taxpayers to support the North, Lugard in 1914 opted for amalgamation, uniting the North and South into one country of Nigeria, under the control of Britain.

THE FOUNDATIONS AND CAUSES OF CIVIL WAR

Anticipating an eventual shift to independence starting in the 1940s, the British imposed changes that would ultimately create the incentives for civil war. First, in 1947, the South was divided into a Western and an Eastern region, thereby establishing a government with a weak center and

---

[2] Paid £450,000 for its territories, the RNC also obtained royalties on all mineral exports for a period of 99 years. See Gould (2012: 15).

three semi-autonomous regions, among them the dominant North that southerners already perceived as a mouthpiece of British rule (Kirk-Greene 1971a). Next, local governance ordinances and a constitutional change created opportunities for Nigerians to gain legislative control from the British. The upshot was the emergence of political parties along ethno-regional lines, built largely on the foundations of preexisting networks: the Northern People's Congress (NPC), with strong links to the Muslim Sardauna of Sokoto, dominated the North; the Action Group (AG) held sway in the Southwest; and the National Convention of Nigerian Citizens (NCNC), with support from the Igbo State Union, dominated the Southeast (Falola 1998: 52–54). Finally, administrative indigenization, incorporating more Nigerians into the civil service, was viewed by the British as a strategy to begin redressing the administrative advantages of the North that stemmed from indirect rule. Its consequence, however, in light of the educational advantages of the South, was an imbalance favoring southerners, and Igbo in particular, in the military and in administrative capacity more generally. Estimates put the share of Igbo officers in the Nigerian military at the time at 75 percent, and inequalities in literacy were equally as notable (Nafziger 1972: 191).

In describing Nigeria at the onset of independence in 1960, scholars refer to a political setting in which – again, much like Sudan – ethnic and religious identities overlapped almost completely, despite minority ethnic groups nested within the principal ethnolinguistic zones. Omenka (2010: 367) notes the strong social and economic differences between North and South, and that the press of the period began referring to a "Muslim North" and "Christian South." Omeje (2004: 426) argues that religious structures in the North and an upsurge in the importance of ethnic associations in the South created a "recipe for disaster given the overlap of religious and ethnic identities." These ethnic and religious divides were reinforced by geography, leading the North to strengthen ties with Sudan, Egypt, and Saudi Arabia, while the Southeast sought support from Western countries (Williams 1997). Nigeria scholar Niels Kastfelt (1994: 77) notes that being of a southern ethnicity "implicitly came to be defined as not being a Muslim." And Toyin Falola's (1998) rich work on the sociopolitical context in Nigeria stresses that Islam in the North successfully merged with ethnicity just as mass Christianity followed southern ethnic lines. The scholarship on Nigeria thus highlights the (at least perceived) extensive overlap of Hausa-Fulani and Muslim identities in the North along with Igbo and Christian identities in the Southeast. In terms of the salience of those identities, owing to both pre-colonial histories and colonial institutions, religious structures were most influential in the northern, Hausa-Fulani, Muslim region, whereas ethnic ties served as the backbone of the southeastern, Igbo, Christian area.

After independence, the new Nigerian government proved hopelessly beholden to a system of patronage politics that rewarded connections over transparency (Gould 2012). In January 1966, a coup launched by mid-level officers met broad popular support as an indictment of the corrupt regime; by virtue of ethnic disparities in the military, however, five of the six coup leaders happened to be Igbo (de St. Jorre 1972). Installed as the head of a new military government, Aguiyi Ironsi – himself an Igbo – appointed military governors for each of the four regions,[3] and in the critical Eastern Region located in the Southeast, that position would go to Lieutenant Colonel Emeka Odumegwu Ojukwu. Meanwhile, Major General Yacubu "Jack" Gowon was appointed Chief of Staff of the National Military. One of Ironsi's first major pronouncements once calm was restored was the Unification Decree of May 1966: intended to quiet ethno-regional tensions by dissolving the semi-autonomous regions, the move instead resulted in northern fears of Igbo domination of the central government (Uche 2008). Students in the North demonstrated, Igbo shops were looted, and songs of ethnic hatred became commonplace. Communal attacks killed hundreds of Igbo (see Kirk-Greene 1971a).

 By this point, the Eastern Region's educational advantages had already incentivized economic migration of mostly Christian Igbos from the Southeast to the North, to fill civil service and other higher-skilled jobs for which most northerners were not qualified. On the heels of communal rioting, a second counter-coup supported by northern soldiers led to the death of Ironsi and installed Gowon as the new Military Head of State. As a northerner of minority ethnic status who also happened to be Christian, Gowon was viewed by supporters as both sympathetic to northern interests and plausibly tolerable to southern factions (Clendenen 1972). Yet with little peacemaking effort from the national government, attacks on southeasterners in the North continued. Violence swelled in September and October. Labeled by many a pogrom against the Igbo people,[4] approximately 10,000 to 30,000 easterners died in the North, and a mass

---

[3] A fourth, Mid-West Region had been added to accommodate pressure from minority groups in the center.

[4] See, e.g., Badru (1998: 79), Falola (1998: 120), Gould (2012: 34), and Omenka (2010: 369).

exodus sent up to one million more back to their "ethnic homeland" (Nafziger 1972: 189).

Secessionist calls had come at times from each of Nigeria's regions. Now, in late 1966, Lt. Col. Ojukwu capitalized on pressure from the Igbo intelligentsia and the fear of a threatened population to take definitive steps toward independent, sovereign status. Weapons were stockpiled and soldiers recruited (Edmonds 1972). In May 1967, when Gowon – the new head of state and FMG leader – proposed a twelve-state federal system that cut the Eastern Region into three parts and neutered its political-economic strength, the final die was cast. On May 30, Ojukwu declared the Republic of Biafra – representing the original Eastern Region and named for the bight along which it rested – an independent state, and civil war was shortly under way.

As causes of civil conflict go, northern democratic advantages coupled with eastern, Igbo advantages in military and civil service representation created stiff competition for control of the central government, and a sentiment in both regions that potential subjugation loomed. A personal power struggle – between Gowon and Ojukwu – also undoubtedly influenced the decision to pursue secession (Vickers 1970). Yet as the war began, descriptions turned on a third, difficult-to-ignore set of factors: land, resources, and oil.

ETHNICITY AND THE EARLY STAGES OF CIVIL WAR

In Chapter 5, I argued that conflicts become ethnic or religious because particular frames suit the proximate interests of political elites. Earlier, in Chapter 2, I suggested that those distinct options exist for leaders because ethnicity and religion are associated with different preferences among supporters: land and local resources constitute ethnic concerns, whereas behavioral rules and transnational ties call to mind religious affiliations. Leaders can thus pursue strategies that make ethnicity or religion salient, or they might evoke ethnic or religious identities in order to generate collective action in support of favored strategies.

At the onset of civil war between the Federal Military Government of Nigeria and the breakaway Republic of Biafra, two factors lowered the opportunity costs that Lt. Col. Ojukwu faced in leading a secession. First, in the aftermath of the pogrom, securing land and property free from discrimination and violence – in short, being able to lay claim to a respected "homeland" – became a central concern for easterners and those who fled the North in particular (Mang 2013: 276). Original inhabitance came to mean much to the supporters of Biafra, enough so that FMG soldiers of eastern origin switched sides and Biafran civilians took part in makeshift military training to fight for the cause, aimed primarily at securing the material and land-related interests of the community (Kastfelt 1994: 77, 159). Second, the elephant in the room of the secessionist movement was the wealth of Nigerian oil, two-thirds of which lay in the ground on the Biafran side of the Niger River (Nafziger 1972: 187). Initially discovered in 1956, Shell-BP began commercial exports in 1958; in just the three years prior to civil war, production had increased by 76 percent annually, reaching 415,000 barrels per day and 33 percent of Nigeria's total export value. Nafziger (1972: 185) called this expansion in oil production "a major factor contributing to the civil war," as Ojukwu sought to extract royalties from Shell-BP that otherwise enriched the FMG.[5]

The FMG had equally strong incentives to prevent the secession. In addition to the potential loss of oil-rich territories, the Eastern Region was also home to Port Harcourt, an important oil refinery city and a port city to the Atlantic Ocean. The war thus became, in Gould's (2012: xvi) words, a "commercial war, for control over Nigeria's natural resources." According to the hypotheses developed earlier in the book and outlined above, we should therefore expect the early stages of the Nigeria–Biafra civil war, when land and local resources were critically at stake, to be viewed through an ethnic lens. This should be particularly true from the eastern, Biafran, Igbo perspective, owing to the fact that Ojukwu was the strategic first-mover: to rally support for a secession and the violence that would likely follow, he would need followers motivated enough to act collectively in support of those oil-rich lands. Playing the ethnic card of Igbo persecution and Igboland defense was his strategy to achieve this proximate goal.

Consider how the frame of the conflict originally evolved, beginning with the actors. Ironsi's appointment of Lt. Col. Ojukwu, an outspoken Igbo defender, to lead the military government in the Eastern Region in 1966 was a clear indication – in the midst of anti-Igbo sentiment – that ethnicity would influence political decisions. In the run-up to the secession announcement, Ojukwu then expelled FGM soldiers of non-eastern heritage from the region, further dividing actors according to ethnicity (Kirk-Greene 1971b: 67). In addition, a self-proclaimed group of "Igbo intelligentsia" – many of them university professors and writers, including

---

[5] Shell did agree to a "token" payment to Biafra of £250,000, but stated that it was doing so only under duress. See Uche (2008).

the celebrated author Chinua Achebe – became early advocates for a separate and sovereign Igbo nation (de St. Jorre 1972: 100). Igbo leaders who ascended during the colonial era to positions of warrant chief, a kind of constructed ethnic leadership position, also took active part in fomenting secession as a means to augment control over local lands (Badru 1998: 82). Finally, civilians in the breakaway republic, particularly those forced from the North, displayed contempt for northerners along ethnic, rather than religious, lines. Popular early war songs were drawn from Igbo tradition, including the civilian chant upon the declaration of Biafran independence: "Ojukwu give us guns/To do away with Gowon and await Hausa/Ojukwu give us guns/There is anger, anger in our hearts" (see Uzokwe 2003: 34). That sentiment persisted through the early months of the war, despite the fact that the FGM was hardly an ethnically cohesive Hausa-Fulani opponent (de St. Jorre 1972: 376).

The targets of the early stages of violence and war also reflected an ethnic frame. The centerpiece, of course, was control over oil-rich territory in the Southeast. Additionally, a sticking point for Biafrans was the loss of property, assets, and land during the exodus from the North, leaving them no option but to retreat to and remain in what they considered an ethnic homeland (Gould 2012: 55). In fact, the fear of Igbo ethnic homelands coming under siege constituted an important selling point for the secession itself (see Falola 1997: 9).

The rhetoric underpinning secession left little doubt that Ojukwu and the Biafrans intended to conduct the war as an ethnic affair, despite Gowon's insistence that it was not the Igbo people but only a small group of leaders whom the FMG targeted (Gould 2012: 143). Upon the declaration of Biafran independence, Ojukwu famously announced that Biafrans were "calling into being the first nation-state in Africa carved out by the indigenous people themselves ..." (de St. Jorre 1972: 132), implying a cohesive ethnic, Igbo identity in Biafra. Biafran Ministry of Information posters at the time depicted masses with an "Igbo" sign front and center, and smaller signs for other eastern ethnic minorities, standing up to a menacing "North" (Kirk-Greene 1971a: 83). As hard as FMG leader Gowon worked to keep ethnicity out of the conflict, FMG officers often took the bait from Biafra's ethnic frame; northern Commander Benjamin Adekunle, for example, articulated the following strategy (reported in Chimee 2013: 131):

I want to prevent even one Igbo having even one single piece to eat before their capitulation. We shoot at everything that moves and when our forces march into the center of Igbo territory, we shoot at everything that does not move.

The reference to opponents in ethnic – and only ethnic – terms, coupled with the linking of ethnicity to local territory, indicates quite clearly how the Biafran rhetoric that framed the onset of war as ethnic also influenced the FMG to adopt an anti-Igbo ethnic perspective.

Finally, in keeping with the expectation that land and local resource concerns contribute to an ethnic frame for conflict, the reporting and historiography on the early stages of the Nigeria–Biafra War signal a clear focus on ethnic differences, and an absence of attention to the religious divisions that also persisted. Badru (1998: xii) notes that participants at the time cited ethnicity as a major impediment to unity. Badru himself called the setting in which Biafra declared independence "an ethnic time bomb" (1998: 1). Clendenen (1972: 164) labeled the start of conflict "a civil war ... and at the same time an intertribal war such as Africa has known for hundreds of years." Tellingly, Vickers's (1970: 632) description of the frame of conflict explicitly links ethnic sentiments to the contest for resources: "Certainly, it was between Hausa and Igbo," he writes. "Yet ... it was only in situations of competition for control over available benefits that hostile ethnic stereotypes were invoked." By and large, from the first coup in January 1966 through the initial months of the civil war, Ojukwu and the Biafrans pressed for independent, sovereign control of Nigeria's oil-rich Southeast, and in so doing, widely colored the reports on civil conflict as a battle for "Igboland" or the Igbo's "ethnic homeland."[6]

A CHANGING WAR AND THE RISE OF RELIGION

Recall that religion had been an equally stark source of division between the North and the Southeast through colonialism and early independence: the emirs of the Sokoto caliphate wielded immense power as administrators in the North, and a wave of missionary expansion and conversions in the Southeast created a sharp religious fissure. Yet little was made of the religious divide upon the secession of Biafra. After a few grueling months of civil war, that would change.

The turning point in the frame of the Biafran War came in the autumn of 1967. After several months of violence with little discernible effect, the FMG pushed Biafra into a defensive posture, reclaiming some territory and working to establish a cordon (Nafziger 1972). After a surprise

---

[6] See also Falola (1998), Gould (2012), Kirk-Greene (1971b), Nafziger (1972), Nayar (1975).

counter-attack by the Biafrans in August 1967, the FMG further increased the pressure, implementing a supply blockade and marching on the Biafran capital of Enugu in battles of close contact and small arms.[7] Quickly, Biafra was down to one-third its original geographic size, and casualties mounted. Oil revenues failed to materialize for the Biafrans, and the blockade began to inflict serious food shortages on the residents of Biafra, increasing malnutrition and starvation. By September, Biafran forces had lost all but a quarter of the original declared territory, including its oil-producing regions (de St. Jorre 1972: 208). By the end of 1967, only a small enclave constituting 20 percent of declared Biafra remained under secessionist control (Nafziger 1972: 198).

Facing overwhelming defeat, the strategic incentives of Ojukwu and the Biafran elite shifted. They had originally inspired a collective defense of the Igbo homeland through appeals to ethnicity; now, after supply shortages and the loss of commercial oil opportunities undermined that strategy, Ojukwu sought a moral basis for continuing the struggle and, most important, for international recognition and assistance. According to the hypotheses outlined earlier in the book, the changing context of the war – in which local land and resources became secondary to moral and transnational support – made appeals to religion, rather than ethnicity, the new optimal strategy.

Again consider the frame of the Nigeria–Biafra War, in terms of the actors, targets, rhetoric, and reporting, this time from the period of late 1967 onward. Concerning the actors: Ojukwu hired a public relations firm in New York to help turn the civil war into an international matter, on the logic that participants had to realize the consequences were beyond local in order to sustain the secession (Gould 2012; 76). From that point, the war became one of the world's first televised conflicts, with gruesome images and pictures of starving children plastering the world media. Key new actors aiding Biafra in 1968 included the World Council of Churches (WCC), Caritas (an aid branch of the Catholic Church), and the Joint Churches Association – a group of thirty-three Christian organizations that then disbanded after the war (Williams and Falola 1995); ostensibly their role consisted of providing humanitarian aid, but cargo shipments mixing arms with aid remained a point of contention through the remainder of the conflict. From a diplomatic standpoint, most Western countries,

---

[7] The FMG armed forces of Nigeria numbered approximately 10,000. The Biafran army began with about half that number but recruited civilians to a point that their troop size was comparable, if less well trained.

including the United States, remained neutral, though both Jewish Americans and religious leaders in the United States sought to influence the Johnson administration in favor of Biafra (Clendenen 1972; Doron 2013). A delegation from Pope Paul VI in February 1968 was particularly influential, as churches became a setting for Biafran residents to offer collective messages to the Christian world (Kastfelt 2005: 3). Meanwhile, the Muslim world remained "a steadfast friend" to the FMG of Nigeria (Williams and Falola 1995: 254).

Targets also shifted from the ethnic to the religious. Christian places of worship were destroyed (Omenka 2010: 370). Religious bodies themselves became targets of the propaganda: Ojukwu's government created an official Churches Front in an effort to bring Christian organizations under the Ministry of Information (Omenka 2010: 374). Late in the war, missionary priests were targeted as instigators of Biafran separatism; seventy-five were arrested in 1970 and held even after the conclusion of hostilities, accused by Gowon of continuing anti-Nigeria acts (Williams and Falola 1995: 294). Since fighting took place almost entirely in Biafran territory and forced Ojukwu's troops into a defensive posture, far less damage resulted in federal Nigeria. Yet the relatively few Quranic schools that existed in the Southeast became symbols of northern control and were destroyed by Biafran residents (Uchendu 2010: 72).

Rhetoric also reframed the conflict in religious terms. Ojukwu adopted biblical analogies in 1968, referring to himself as the Moses of Biafra (Walls 1978: 213), Biafra as David fighting Goliath (Kastfelt 2005: 4), and Biafrans as the parallel of Jews suffering from religious persecution (Clendenen 1972: 178). Media seized on the change: Biafran radio announced a Muslim conspiracy against Christians in the East (Afigbo 1978: 176); posters in American and European churches urged congregants to "help your brothers in Christ, help the Biafrans" (Omenka 2010: 377); and the *Biafran Sun* newspaper ran the headline on January 1, 1968, "Islam – Main Cause of War" (Walls 1978: 209). In February, the *Mirror* newspaper, under the headline "Islamism vs. Christianity," accused the FMG of acting "as a tool of the world moslem league ... in a jihad against Biafrans" (Walls 1978: 209). Influential elites in Biafra also picked up on the theme. Lt. Col. S. M. Ojukwu, a Biafran legislator, stated that "Biafra is a Christian country, and we believe in the ability of the Almighty to come to the aid of the oppressed" (Palmer-Fernanez 2004: 329). Francis Ibiam, a noted Biafran statesman, pointedly noted that "if churches (in the West) do not help us, Christianity will die" (Omenka 2010: 369). Cardinal Heenan of Great Britain is reported to have labeled the conflict "a war of unbelievers against Christianity" (Kirk-Greene 1971b: 46). As for the residents of Biafra, the new frame amplified the conflict as one of moral renewal; as one resident noted, "corruption and self-seeking seemed to drop away" as the war progressed (Walls 1978: 208). Northerners were equally affected by the religious propaganda: anti-Catholic demonstrations spread throughout 1969 with calls of "Away with Pope Paul," and Catholic minorities in federal Nigeria called for a separate Catholic Church of Nigeria independent of the Vatican (Williams and Falola 1995: 293). This despite pleas from Gowon, who wished for the FMG's war with Biafra to remain a local affair and said that "you are not fighting a religious war or a jihad" (Omenka 2010: 369).

Finally, the reporting and scholarship on the latter stages of the war paint a decisive portrait of the shift to religious antagonism. Clendenen (1972), who considers the conflict to have been an "intertribal" one, dispels actual religious dispute in the war but notes that religious propaganda effectively generated international sympathies for co-religionists. Omenka (2010: 367) corroborates that perspective, arguing that the war ended up being "unduly cast as a religious war between Christians and Muslims." Williams and Falola (1995: 2), whose scholarship covers ethnic and religious politics in Nigeria and across Africa, suggest that Nigeria became a religious danger zone on par with Sudan, in a way that few could have predicted earlier in the 1960s. In noting the attention of the outside world, de St. Jorre (1972: 264) argues that Biafrans "made a great play of religion in the war."

In the end, reframing the war in religious terms did draw transnational attention, and in some sense engaged the Biafran people in a broader moral narrative, but never enough to counter the long odds they faced in conflict. In January 1970, thirty months after the start of what looked at the outset to be a brief military operation, Biafra finally folded. Ojukwu left the country for safe haven in Côte d'Ivoire, transferring power to Major General Phillip Effiong with instructions to find a peaceful reso-lution (de St. Jorre 1972: 400). On January 12, Effiong called on Biafran troops to lay down their arms, and three days later the civil war came to an official end. In hindsight, the war was never about religion in a substantive sense, but its propaganda value effectively transformed the conflict. Ojukwu listed his major regret as not making early enough use of "the religious proposition" (Omenka 2010: 389), and the WCC acknow-ledged that its intervention in favor of Biafra served only to prolong an unnecessary war (Kirk-Greene 1971b: 448). Yet partisans still found reason in their faith. The Archbishop of Biafra, challenged at the war's conclusion to justify the misuse of religion, asked rhetorically if it followed morally that Biafrans should suffer simply because the war was not in fact about religion (Omenka 2010: 380).

CONCLUSION

In this chapter, I sought to add to the body of evidence in support of the argument that political leaders manipulate conflict frames to address their proximate interests, taking advantage of the mobilizational effects that ethnicity and religion have on their followers. I traced the history and events of the Nigeria–Biafra War to show that oil, land, and local resources were of primary concern to Southeastern Nigerian secessionists during the early stages of conflict. In that context, Biafran leaders persuaded their supporters to engage in collective defense of Igboland through appeals to ethnicity. In the North and in federal Nigeria, leaders saw little advantage to a war fought in ethnic terms, but anti-Igbo sentiments nevertheless spread quickly. Later, as the outlook for Biafran independence waned, the proximate interests of Biafran elites shifted: to prolong their chances for success, they exploited the morality-based, landless nature of religion in Africa to generate transnational support for their cause. The war from that point was seen by many through a Christian–Muslim lens. Ironically, in a conflict that began with control over oil and territory as a centerpiece, the Biafrans were ultimately left offering exclusive rights to their dwindling oil fields to Europeans in exchange for the moral, religious, and financial aid they needed (Edmonds 1972: 208).

Importantly, both ethnicity and religion were socially important identities to Nigerians, in both the North and the South, long before the civil war. Yet political leaders used those identities at distinct times and for distinct purposes in the course of conflict. As Omenka (2010: 370) describes the change, during the early period of coups, pogrom, and declared secession, "religion had not been invoked as a pretext for violence." This simple summary helps to counter the possibility that both ethnicity and religion served as sources of political mobilization throughout the war. Instead, the evidence is very much in keeping with the patterns observed in Côte d'Ivoire and Sudan: ethnicity and religion evoke different passions that leaders understand and can exploit, so the elites of Biafra used those differences to serve their own changing incentives as the war progressed.

That the three conflicts examined here – in Côte d'Ivoire, Sudan, and Nigeria – all began with ethnic frames and later took on religious frames reveals an important pattern in the strategic usefulness of ethnicity and religion at different stages of conflict. First, insofar as contestation over local resources (including land) serves as the underlying cause of many civil and communal disputes in Africa (Collier and Hoeffler 2004), it follows that those disputes would often begin with the application of an ethnic frame. Conflicts that wear on without resolution often require a change in status quo support in order for groups and leaders to achieve success, so it would then follow that at later stages of communal and civil conflict in Africa, the actors, targets, rhetoric, and reporting shift to the religious.

That progression raises the possibility that the role of religion in African conflicts is really an additive one, fused to ethnic disputes as a means of generating international support but hinging little on the preferences that religion might evoke among followers. Certainly in the case of the Biafran War in Nigeria, it appears that the transnational advantages of exploiting a geographically unbounded identity type trumped the concerns for moral legitimacy that religion can also cultivate, and even group members' own priorities regarding membership in a broad brotherhood of co-religionists seems to have mattered less than their leaders' shrewd mobilization of financial assistance from abroad.

While it is true that access to broader networks counts as an institutional advantage of world religions that could hardly be replicated with an ethnic frame, important grounds exist for also recognizing the central role that supporters' passions play in shaping leaders' choices over conflict frames, even when there is additive value to religion. First, the cases presented here illustrate concern among political elites for mobilizing identity-based behaviors at home, not just abroad. In Côte d'Ivoire, young men were inspired to target religious peace makers and to prevent the building of new mosques; in Sudan, southern Christians called on local religious prophets in ways they never had when ethnicity colored the conflict. Second, in each of the three cases, the evidence suggests not just that religion emerged as a new frame, but also that the relevance of an ethnic frame dissipated – recall, for example, how the reporting of all three conflicts omitted mention of previously critical ethnic differences in describing the later clashes between a "Muslim North and Christian South," and how targets of violence were no longer labeled "ancestral" (see Poggo 2009). The shift *away* from ethnic mobilization, and not just *toward* religion, also suggests that the strategic exploitation of an identity frame is significant in its own right – not simply additive – and perhaps that those frames are best exploited in isolation. Finally, we see evidence in each case of leaders appealing to morality and rules when religion constituted their optimal strategy: in Côte d'Ivoire, electoral fairness was associated with religion; in Sudan, the religious frame was closely linked to a push for Shari'a law; and even in the Biafran War, religious appeals were associated with a reduction in corruption and immorality. Religion's institutional characteristics – much like the effects of coalition size, arms caches, and other wartime factors – are certainly relevant to conflict outcomes. However, the cases presented here suggest that the passions and preferences associated with ethnic and religious identities themselves count importantly in shaping the way leaders frame their conflicts.

9

Conclusion

In this book, I have sought to make a contribution to the broad and important topic of ethnic politics. Yet I have done so with the aim of reevaluating what, exactly, we mean by "ethnic politics," in order to improve in some small way our systematic understanding of how different identities matter in the world of conflict. The basic argument is that social identity types – ethnicity, religion, language, caste, region, nationality – evoke different preferences among individuals when they are prioritized. Political entrepreneurs are thus able to frame and reframe conflicts in order to inspire collective action that advances their own strategic goals. The outcome is that conflicts – even those having nothing to do with identity group differences at their roots – come to be seen as fights in the name of God, in the name of ethnic homelands, or as some other form of identity struggle.

In Part I, I made the case that ethnicity and religion in Africa – two critically important social identities in the region – constitute substantively different identities for individuals, evoking distinct preferences: ethnicity draws people closer to their local lands, whereas religion inspires relatively greater interest in rules of moral probity without geographic bounds. In making this argument, I do not want to suggest that identity types inspire any particular beliefs or behaviors on a fixed basis, for they are always subject to interpretation and change and can generate different responses in different places. Rather, the research presented in Part I demonstrates distinctions in the broad priorities that ethnicity and religion elicit in the study region, based on the notion that social norms develop regionally and remain fairly sticky (Chandra 2012: 146). Otherwise stated, while the argument suggests nothing essential about the tenets

or social platforms of particular ethnic or religious groups, it does rely on
the claim that ethnicity and religion are substantively different in the ways
they affect individuals of a given time and place. I have used the term
mobilizational differences to capture the notion that those constitutive
distinctions between ethnicity and religion allow followers to be mobilized in different ways depending on the identity context.

In Part II, I united individual-level preferences with elite interests to
describe how mobilization along ethnic and religious lines can occur in
settings of conflict. Political entrepreneurs seek power but have different
proximate means of attaining that goal: in some cases, electoral victory
may be sufficient; in others, political entrepreneurs might rely on the
accumulation of land and resources, leverage over perceptions of moral
legitimacy, or international support. In conflict settings, winning elections
is rarely a reliable path to the power those leaders covet; instead, their
success depends on mobilizing followers to act collectively in support of
the leaders' extra-institutional interests. Thus, political entrepreneurs seek
to inspire a fervency over their own means to power during and after
conflict, and they do so by manipulating the frame of political dispute. At
times, as in the example of Henri Konan Bedié's land grab in Côte d'Ivoire
during the 1990s, that means pushing particular policies, which happen to
have consequences for identity salience. At other times, as Lt. Col. Emeka
Odumegwu Ojukwu's late effort to mobilize a Christian coalition in the
Biafran region of Nigeria made clear, leaders manipulate identity salience
with the goal of generating support for a particular policy or strategy.

This argument adds nuance to our understanding of conflict settings in
which cleavages cross-cut or in which one side enjoys a clear numerical
advantage: political leaders in those circumstances can exploit policies
and identity divisions to mobilize an optimal identity coalition. Perhaps
its greater contribution comes in also explaining the political choice that
leaders in contexts of overlapping identity types face. In those cases, their
ethnic and religious constituencies do not change, but the identity hats
that their constituents wear can be altered fairly easily. This represents a
political resource that strategic leaders are wont to exploit, particularly
when institutions have broken down and the path to power runs through
civil conflict.

In each of the cases presented here — from Côte d'Ivoire, Sudan, and
Nigeria — the support coalitions of political leaders remained largely
constant, but their political goals shifted, and with those changes came
an exploitation of different identity frames. The book thus offers a story
of political mobilization and the power of elites. That story is complete,

however, only when multiple levels of analysis are brought together, uniting elite calculations with the inspired passions of soldiers, community members, and supporters who constitute the masses of support that leaders in contexts of civil conflict require.

For several reasons, the explanation that I have developed is well suited to explain identity conflicts not just in these three cases but across sub-Saharan Africa. First, community networks are an important informal institution in Africa, serving as a complement to more formal, yet often weak and ineffective, government institutions (see Bratton 2007). As a result, membership in and association with local community groups – such as ethnic and religious organizations – has particular appeal to individuals, giving these groups a central role in sociopolitical matters, especially communal disputes. Second, pre-colonial social structures and colonial administrative tactics gave rise to a system of "Big Men" – influential figures who dole out patronage in exchange for loyalty and support – that in many ways continues today (see Arriola 2009; McCauley 2013b).[1] That system aids the ability of political entrepreneurs in Africa to mobilize followers along identity lines and grants powerful status to leaders of ethnic and religious groups who may have a stake in the frame of political outcomes. Third, political parties in Africa in most cases continue to have relatively weak issue platforms, instead relying on patronage and community ties (Bleck and van de Walle 2011). Absent strong, issue-based parties, the social identity groups that have traditionally guided collective choices remain a prominent aspect of political life. For all of these reasons, identity attachments – particularly to ethnic and religious groups – are a fixture of African politics, and the mobilizational differences between those identity types can explain a good deal of the framing behind African conflicts. To demonstrate how the same logic can help to explain cases of African conflict with different patterns of identity framing, I consider in passing two additional illustrations: the Rwandan genocide and the ongoing threat of the Boko Haram Islamic group in Northern Nigeria.

THE RWANDAN GENOCIDE

The genocide in Rwanda, in which approximately 800,000 people were killed in 1994, followed a pattern different from the cases described

---

[1] Papers by Mkandawire (2015) and Francois, Rainer, and Trebbi (2015) suggest that constraints on Big Men are increasing, but the model is still largely viewed as a descriptor of African political networks.

earlier: fomented by majority Hutus as an explicit endeavor to rid the country of minority Tutsis, the violence was from its outset through the aftermath rooted firmly in ethnic group differences. Victims were targeted solely on the basis of ethnic identity, often as characterized on bureau-cratic identification cards. Though religious groups and leaders were drawn into the conflict, sometimes in the name of peace (Alger 2002) and sometimes to perpetuate violence (Longman 2010), the actors, targets, rhetoric, and reporting from the Rwandan genocide were defined almost exclusively in terms of Hutu or Tutsi status, not as Muslim or Christian. Yet along with their identities as Hutus and Tutsis, Rwandans also have religious identities: most, approximately 85 to 90 percent, are Christian (Catholics being the largest subgroup), and approximately 10 percent are Muslim.[2] Violence in Rwanda could thus have been fomented in the name of religion rather than ethnicity, or the frame could have changed during the course of conflict. Why did the genocide begin and remain a tragedy framed in ethnic group terms?

First, Rwanda lies well south of the Muslim–Christian fault line in Africa: Christianity established an early foothold in southern and central Africa through explorers and missionaries, but Islam was a relative new-comer, arriving intermittently via traders and Indian merchants from the coast and establishing a consistent presence only in the late nineteenth and early twentieth centuries. The first mosque in Rwanda was not constructed until 1913 (Klusener 2005). As a result, historical settlement patterns did not shape the Muslim presence in Rwanda, and the Rwandan population is less clearly segregated geographically between the major world religions of the region. Furthermore, ethnic and religious identities do not overlap to the extent that they do in Côte d'Ivoire, Sudan, and Nigeria: as I reported in Chapter 5, Muslims are equally likely to be either Hutu or Tutsi, and Christianity is the predominant religion among both major ethnic groups. In a setting such as this one, where important social identities cross-cut rather than overlap, political entrepreneurs are subject to a different calculus when determining how to frame conflicts: rather than maintaining a static support base and altering only the preferences and passions of their supporters, leaders in cross-cutting societies change their constituencies (and usually the size of their support bases) when they alter identity frames. Thus, we should not have expected the Hutu polit-ical entrepreneurs who fomented violence against Tutsis in Rwanda to

---

[2] Figures for Muslims vary from 2 percent (CIA World Factbook 2016) to 15 percent (*New York Times* 2004).

have made appeals to Christianity (or Islam). On the other hand, the Tutsi population that suffered enormous losses and potential extermination may have benefited from an effective appeal to religious commonalities, with both Hutus and a fairly passive international community; evidence suggests that efforts to do so were undertaken but were too little, too late (Longman 2010).

Second, the political interests of those who fomented the violence in Rwanda were not of the sort to have been served by appeals to rules and moral values or to international in-group members (as mobilization along religious lines would do). Instead, the instigators of the genocide, including Hutu military forces and outspoken Hutu apologists in the Rwandan radio media (Kellow and Steeves 1998), regarded political control over land and territory as a central rationale for eliminating the Tutsi. Long ruled by a Tutsi political elite – who benefited from colonial "race science" policies that codified differences in appearance in an otherwise mixed population and contributed to a myth of Tutsis as superiors from a historically dominant land, all for administrative purposes (Hintjens 2001) – Hutu entrepreneurs turned that logic on its head to proclaim Rwanda the indigenous territory of the Hutu majority (Prunier 1995). Furthermore, scholars have cited a scarcity of farming lands due to overpopulation, as well as a drop in the quality of those lands, as factors underlying the explosion of ethnic tensions during the genocide (André and Platteau 1998; Bigagaza et al 2002; Gasana 2000). As the argument in this book explains, a political desire to assert control over increasingly scarce land-related resources is best served by playing the ethnic card, which evokes passions for collectively defending and accumulating local geographic resources in the name of kin, tradition, and indigenous identity. This case differs from those outlined in the previous chapters in that it does not involve overlapping cleavages or within-case variation in the conflict frame. The logic of mobilizational differences in ethnicity and religion is nevertheless equipped to explain the identity outcome.

BOKO HARAM AND ISLAMIC VIOLENCE IN
NORTHERN NIGERIA

As I noted in Chapter 8, Nigeria since the Biafran War has suffered wave after wave of conflict described in either ethnic or religious terms. Most recently, Nigerian security has been deeply undermined by the persistence of Boko Haram, an Islamic terrorist group based in the northeastern part of the country. Founded in 2002, Boko Haram attained notoriety with attacks on police and its subsequent violent suppression in 2009; after a resurgence, its recent kidnappings, mass murder of students, suicide bombings, and ransacking of villages have left approximately 20,000 Nigerians dead and have made Boko Haram one of the world's deadliest terrorist organizations (Amnesty International 2015). Its motives and identity frame are much in keeping with the logic articulated in this book.

Boko Haram, whose names loosely translates to "Western civilization is forbidden,"[3] was founded by Mohammed Yusuf in the town of Maiduguri in northeastern Nigeria. Its active supporters, numbering in the thousands, originate primarily from the local area, many articulating sentimental attachments to Usman dan Fodio's jihad against modern lifestyle launched in Nigeria in the early nineteenth century, as described earlier. Acting largely with impunity in a context of deteriorated government services and security in the north, the group has established a base in key towns in the states of Yobe and Borno. Owing to both opportunity and increasing pressure, it has also spread across borders into Cameroon, Chad, and Niger (BBC 2015a).

While they fit squarely into the category of "strong" religious group members described in Chapter 4,[4] it is worth keeping in mind that, as Nigerians, Boko Haram supporters also possess ethnic identities common to northern Nigeria – many hail from the smaller Kanuri ethnicity, though the group also exploits broader Hausa-Fulani ties (Adibe 2012). Furthermore, though Nigeria's prosperous oil industry is based in the south, chieftaincy control over lands has long been a matter of political dispute in the north (Alimba 2014). Finally, Boko Haram in its public statements has implicitly acknowledged the overlap of ethnic and religious identities in its jihad, labeling the southern Christian infidels specifically by ethnic origin: the Yoruba, Igbo, and Ijaw (see Vanguard 2009). Given the overlapping identity context and complex set of grievances, it is worth asking: why is Nigeria confronting a sustained religious extremist threat, rather than violence in the name of ethnicity? What strategic interests does the group espouse that contribute to the frame of violence?

---

[3] Boko Haram spokesperson Sani Umar notes that the group stands not simply for a prohibition on Western education, as typically described. "It affirms our belief in Islamic culture, which is broader ... it includes education but not determined by the West." See Vanguard (2009).

[4] This should not be interpreted as an evaluation of Boko Haram members' piety. Reports suggest that many do not live in accordance with the Salafist ideology that the group espouses. See Cook (2011).

Despite its now decentralized configuration, evidence supports a consistent picture of Boko Haram's ideology and priorities. Scholars place its emergence in the failed implementation of Shari'a law for criminal matters in Nigeria's twelve northern states[5] and in subsequent moral and behavioral disputes such as the hosting of the Miss World competition in 2002 and the dispute over a Danish cartoon of the Prophet Mohammed in early 2006 (Cook 2011). In the clearest description of the group's underlying objectives, founder Yusuf stated that Boko Haram does not believe in Darwinism or the value of any education contrary to the teachings of Islam (BBC 2011). Instead, it emphasized the Islamic ideology of "enjoining the good and forbidding the evil" (see Cook 2011). Spokesperson Umar's public statement on policy positions articulates a rejection of corruption, Western lifestyle, and moral indiscretions (Vanguard 2009). All of these priorities are in keeping with the association between religion and rule-based morality described in Part I of this book. In addition, Boko Haram has explicitly made its targets not just Christians and moderate Muslims (Onuoha 2014), but also banks, schools, the World Health Organization, and other entities it deems to promote an immoral lifestyle (Cook 2011). Consistent with the landless nature of religion in the region, Boko Haram spokesperson Musa Tanko added: "Islam does not recognize international boundaries" (Agence France-Presse 2010). Most important, despite reverence for dan Fodio's establishment of a caliphate a century earlier, Boko Haram has not sought the explicit control of territory that might have evoked local concerns for land.[6] Only upon a stated allegiance to the Islamic State terrorist group in 2015 did Boko Haram adopt language supportive of joining a caliphate, though even then its center would be located elsewhere (see BBC 2015b).

A sustained threat to peace in northern Nigeria could have occurred along ethnic lines or inspired ethnic labels. Instead, Nigeria's recent violence has maintained one consistent, religious frame from its onset and, tellingly, one consistent focus on rule-based, moral priorities. Though better classified as a terrorist insurgency than a religious war,

---

[5] Nigeria's northern states adopted Shari'a law for criminal offenses, in addition to common civil matters, in 1999. However, intense international scrutiny over botched punishments for adultery diluted its application by the mid-2000s. See Cook (2011).

[6] To the extent that territory has factored into the conflict at all, it has done so only in terms of Boko Haram establishing bases for military operations to institute its ideological vision across the region, and the Nigerian government targeting particular areas as part of its counterterrorism strategy. See Levan (2013).

the combination of rule-based strategy and religious frame is exactly what we would expect given the mobilizational differences between ethnicity and religion.

EXPANDING THE ARGUMENT

I have focused on the impact of ethnicity and religion in Africa, but a consideration of mobilizational differences in identity types can also inform our understanding of conflict elsewhere. Salient identity types overlap in other parts of the world – religion and nationality sharing constituencies on the Irish Isle, for example, and ethnicity and religion overlapping in Sri Lanka – and wherever they do, political entrepreneurs face a choice over how to frame political contests that does not hinge solely on group size. Important religious fault lines also exist in other parts of the world, notably in the Middle East, Eastern Europe, and South Asia, which add the perception of world religious competition to other social cleavages. Most critically, the ability to mobilize constituents in precise ways by manipulating the salience of identity types is certainly not a feature restricted to African leaders: political entrepreneurs in high- and low-income countries, in democracies and authoritarian regimes, and in every region of the world gain advantages by exploiting identity divisions in the context of potential conflict. Insofar as the instrumental interests of constituents are constrained by political manipulation of identity contexts, a theory of mobilizational differences in identity types can offer insight into conflicts almost anywhere, whether the identity cleavages overlap or not.

This argument parts ways with conventional political science explanations for conflict in three important respects. First, instrumentalist arguments typically grant the assumption of a rational pursuit of material self-interests, with perfect information, not just to political leaders but also to the individuals who make the choice to follow those leaders. What I hope this research has demonstrated is that individuals pursue instrumental, rational preferences primarily within a context defined by the political entrepreneur. Given that individual-level priorities can be easily manipulated by political leaders, this book helps to resolve the tension between the potentially competing interests of leaders and followers by constraining (though certainly not eliminating) the assumption of pure instrumentality among individuals and by allowing their priorities to be broadly shaped by leadership. Second, I have presented the affective pull of identities such as ethnicity and religion as an important political resource. Head counts among supporters are sometimes not the most critical calculation that political entrepreneurs make in conflict settings; the argument I have presented here thus suggests a need to get inside the minds and passions of individuals to understand what drives them to act collectively in support of their group when institutions break down, even to the point of participating in violence. Often, the motivation is something other than material self-interest. The third departure from convention is the claim that a group is not simply a group: I have argued that social identity types produce unique sets of attitudes and preferences, leading to the conclusion that religious politics should be seen as something distinct from ethnic politics, which differ from nationalist politics, gender politics, and other forms of identity-group competition.

Each of these elements suggests new theoretical approaches to the study of ethnic politics and conflict. They also add a level of complexity to otherwise parsimonious descriptions of political competition and, for that reason, may strike some scholars as too individualistic, immeasurable, or outside the realm of political science. Yet the explanation that I have constructed in this book also suggests how, with appropriate use of tools from across social science and with strategies for measuring affective differences in systematic ways, our theories of political behavior and conflict can become closer approximations of real-world outcomes. If that were to be the case, a recognition of mobilizational differences in identity types would constitute a valuable contribution.

To be sure, there are things that the argument as presented in this book does not do. Certain to have been noted by some readers is the fact that I set aside the possibility of political leaders exploiting ethnic and religious divides simultaneously during the course of conflict; this would seem to provide double the advantage when those identity cleavages overlap. I did so for both theoretical and practical reasons. From a theoretical standpoint, discretely evaluating the mobilizational differences between ethnicity and religion – and their consequences – allows for new insights into the black box of ethnic politics. From a practical standpoint, even in contexts of institutional breakdown, political leaders are well served by employing a clear and straightforward message that mobilizes supporters to act collectively. Thus, we should expect elites to focus most intently on the identity frame that serves their proximate goal at any given time, even if opportunistic exploitation of a different identity cleavage also pays some dividends. Indeed, the case evidence indicates that predominate frames do emerge even when multiple options are available.

Additionally, I developed an explanation for mobilizational differences and conflict frames not as a general theory but by evaluating two particular identity types, ethnicity and religion. I elected to focus on the two most prominent social identities in sub-Saharan Africa to illustrate how mobilizational differences in identity types matter, but the output is perhaps less satisfying than a general theory. Future research might explore the unique attitudes and preferences evoked in other identity contexts, such as region, nationality, language, or class, and how those preferences are exploited for political gain. I have also downplayed some of the complex distinctions between particular ethnic and religious groups, a liberty I have taken to maintain a focus on disaggregating the umbrella of ethnic politics to its next logical level, one of identity types. The experimental data collected for the project indicate that, on average, individuals in ethnic versus religious contexts have systematically differ-ent preferences, irrespective of their membership in particular groups, but one might also wish to situate this study in the growing body of literature on African Muslims (Reese 2014; Sanneh 2015), the region's Christian Pentecostal movement (Grossman 2015; Lindhardt 2014; McClendon and Riedl 2015), or studies of ethno-linguistic differences (Franck and Rainer 2012; Lieberman and McClendon 2013). Similarly, this study sets aside the blending that takes place between world religions and trad-itional African religions, so future studies could explore the changes in beliefs, attitudes, and political preferences that accompany varying levels of religious syncretism.

Finally, I have simplified the strategic choices that political entrepre-neurs make in response to both complex political contexts and the iden-tity mobilization tactics of their opponents. In the course of conflict, political leaders must think not only about their own proximate goals, but also about the interests of their competition and of external political players. None operates in a vacuum. I made reference to the ability of a first-mover to shape the response of opponents, but I have not offered a systematic theory for the strategic game. My goals were simpler: to demonstrate that individuals have unique preference sets in each identity context and to explain how political leaders can take advantage of those differences to mobilize their supporters in particular ways. If I have succeeded in doing so, the work should contribute something to a richer understanding of "ethnic politics."

Readers may be left with one final question: why does the frame of conflict in Africa matter? From a theoretical standpoint, understanding why conflicts sometimes come to be viewed as ethnic and at other times are perceived as religious improves our knowledge about how the world works. With better comprehension of complex social and political phenomena like conflict frames, rather minor theoretical insights from one region or one problem can advance work on other social scientific puzzles, such that analyses of conflict become more refined and the role of identities like ethnicity and religion can be given a more prominent, comfortable place in political science research. The study of conflict frames also constitutes an important theoretical exercise in uniting multiple levels of analysis, owing to the fact that both elite interests and mass preferences are central to determining the actors, targets, rhetoric, and reporting that color conflicts as ethnic or religious.

Practically, the frame of conflict can alter outcomes. Bakary Kaba would likely not have been gunned down as he stood before his family in Muslim attire had Côte d'Ivoire's conflict not taken on religious undertones. Ethnic sites, lands, and figures are at greater risk when conflicts are seen through an ethnic lens, whereas churches, mosques, and religious leaders become targets of violence when conflicts are framed as Christian–Muslim. Knowing when perpetrators are likely to pursue certain targets rather than others seems an important first step in curbing violence. Furthermore, as I noted earlier in the book, evidence suggests that the degree and shape of violence may differ based on the conflict frame: Lacina (2006) finds that the ethnic makeup of societies, and presumably the way ethnic group members perceive their coalition, affects the severity of civil wars; Fox (2007) presents nearly fifty years of evidence to argue that conflicts fought in the name of religion are bloodier than secular disputes; and Svensson (2007) finds that conflicts fought with religious identity are less likely to be resolved through negotiated settlements. International relations can also be affected by the frame of conflicts. Viewed as inter-religious disputes, conflicts like the ones I have described in Côte d'Ivoire, Sudan, and Nigeria often draw in outside observers who perceive the violence as part of a transnational dispute. External involvement may advance peace just as it may exacerbate the conflict, but the point is that such involvement is less likely to be forthcoming when disputes are regarded as ethnic. Finally, despite the malleability of identities at the individual level, concerns motivated by ethnicity, religion, or other identity types do not feel strategic to the people involved; those identities can take on a paramount role in individual and collective behavior that endures and that shapes social and political competition well beyond the conflict itself.

Ethnic and religious differences have colored many of Africa's civil conflicts. In rare cases, those frames result from explicit identity-based concerns, but in a great many others, conflicts that begin over political economic matters having nothing to do with identity group differences end as wars defined as either "tribal" or "Christian–Muslim." This book has offered an explanation for why the frames of these conflicts vary. Political entrepreneurs in Africa face a choice over how they mobilize followers in settings of conflict, but that choice is best understood by acknowledging the constitutive differences in ethnicity and religion and the ways in which those identities shape individual-level preferences and passions.

APPENDIXES

Appendix A
Observational Analyses of Afrobarometer Data in
Chapter 3

The analysis is limited to data from Round 2 of the survey, since the key question regarding self-identity was dropped from subsequent rounds. Round 2 data were collected from approximately 1,200 individuals in each of 16 African countries: Botswana, Cape Verde, Ghana, Kenya, Lesotho, Malawi, Mali, Mozambique, Namibia, Nigeria, Senegal, South Africa, Tanzania, Uganda, Zambia, and Zimbabwe. Despite the limited number, national-level variation exists in terms of predominant religion, predominant ethnicities, socioeconomic status, democratic progress, geographic region, and a host of other factors, so we may still take the data as broadly representative of African views.

Key Independent Variable:

We have spoken to many [countrymen] and they have all described themselves in different ways. Some people describe themselves in terms of their language, ethnic group, race, religion, or gender and others describe themselves in economic terms such as working class, middle class, or a farmer. Besides being [national identity], which specific group do you feel you belong to first and foremost?

To compare ethnic identifiers and religious identifiers, I limited the dataset to only those respondents who listed ethnicity or religion as their most important identity. That limitation resulted in a sample size of approximately 8,000.

Dependent Variables
1. Land: Over what sort of problems do violent conflicts most often arise between different groups in this country?

Survey responses were open-ended. I code the responses 1 if respondents listed land disputes as their first response and 0 otherwise. Approximately 12 percent of respondents did so.

2. Community Meetings: Have you, personally, attended a community meeting during the past year? If not, would you do this if you had the chance?

Responses were coded on a five-point scale, where 0 indicates that the respondent would never attend a community meeting and 4 is reserved for respondents who often attend. To generate a simple distinction in involvement, I generated a binary variable coded 1 if the respondent attended any meetings in the past year and 0 otherwise. Two-thirds of respondents in the survey stated that they had done so.

3. Corruption: How well or badly would you say the current government is fighting corruption, or haven't you heard enough about it to say?

Responses were coded on a four-point scale from "very badly" to "very well." I recoded responses of "fairly well" or "very well" as 1 and responses of "fairly badly" or "very badly" as 0. Just under half of respondents in the dataset (46 percent) were coded 1.

Multivariate Results

Effects of Primary Mode of Self-Identification on Politically Relevant Attitudes

	Views Land Disputes as Principal Source of Conflict	Attended a Community Meeting in the Past Year	Views Fighting Corruption as a Priority for Government
Self-identifies with religion (as opposed to ethnicity)	−0.041** (0.014)	−0.031* (0.016)	0.066* (0.034)
Male	0.017* (0.009)	0.084** (0.030)	0.010 (0.010)
Age	0.000 (0.001)	0.003* (0.001)	0.000 (0.001)
Education	0.007* (0.003)	0.014 (0.009)	−0.016† (0.009)
Urban	−0.017 (0.018)	−0.177*** (0.032)	−0.035 (0.047)
Socioeconomic status	−0.000 (0.001)	−0.012 (0.009)	0.035*** (0.010)

(*continued*)

	Views Land Disputes as Principal Source of Conflict	Attended a Community Meeting in the Past Year	Views Fighting Corruption as a Priority for Government
Muslim	−0.007	−0.087	−0.051
	(0.022)	(0.053)	(0.060)
Third religion/	−0.035[†]	−0.006	0.029
no religion	(0.020)	(0.033)	(0.045)
Pseudo R^2	0.01	0.01	0.01
N	7836	8375	7632

Notes: Data from the Afrobarometer Round 2 Public Opinion Survey (2002). Logit estimations with robust standard errors, clustered by country, in parentheses. Coefficients presented as marginal effects. [†] $p < .10$, * $p < .05$, ** $p < .01$, *** $p < .001$. Self-identity based on Afrobarometer question 54, "Which specific group to you feel you belong to first and foremost?" The omitted identity group are those who self-identify according to ethnicity (other observations excluded). Importance of religion is coded on a four-point scale, from 1 (not at all important) to 4 (very important). Age is measured on a scale of 1 to 9, representing five-year increments (1 = 18–24, 9 = 60 and up). Education is measured on a scale of 0 (no formal education) to 9 (post-secondary). Socioeconomic status is a subjective, five-point scale measuring present living conditions (1 = very bad, 5 = very good). Christian is the omitted religious category.

Appendix B

CONSORT Checklist for Reporting a Randomized Trial

Section/ Topic	Checklist Item
Introduction	
1a	Title does not identify study as a randomized trial, consistent with conventions of the field.
1b	The design, randomization process, and results are described throughout the chapter.
Background and Objectives	
2a	Scientific background and explanation of rationale: the purpose of the randomized study is to evaluate policy preferences under distinct identity contexts.
2b	Specific objectives or hypotheses: it is expected that subjects exposed to the Ethnic treatment will demonstrate a relative preference for local development and material wealth, and that subjects exposed to the Religion treatment will demonstrate a relative preference for moral and behavioral policies.
Trial Design	
3a	Description of trial design: 325 subjects were recruited via random selection in each of four research sites, with an additional 150 recruited in a fifth site. For a related robustness check, an additional 200 subjects were recruited via convenience sampling from specific religious and ethnic group associations. Subjects were assigned in equal ratios to the Ethnic treatment, the Religion treatment, and the control group. Treatments consisted of five-minute radio reports focusing on social identity groups (ethnic or religious), intended to prime those identity types. Subjects then responded to questions regarding social and political preferences.
3b	Important changes to methods after trial commencement (e.g., eligibility criteria), with reasons: built into the study was the

(continued)

(continued)

Section/ Topic	Checklist Item
	plan to test two different control primes, one with radio content unrelated to identity types and one with no radio treatment.
Participants	
4a	Eligibility criteria for participants: at least eighteen years old. Capable of comprehending questions in local, regional, or colonial languages.
4b	Settings and locations where the data were collected: Korhogo, in northern Côte d'Ivoire; Divo, in southern Côte d'Ivoire; Tamale, in northern Ghana; Cape Coast, in southern Ghana; and Kumasi, in central Ghana. Subjects were evaluated in their homes. Subjects were drawn from those towns and from four randomly selected villages within fifteen kilometers of each of town.
Interventions	
5	The interventions for each group with sufficient details to allow replication, including how and when they were actually administered: radio reports were recorded by local professional radio personalities; the transcripts are included in the appendix. Subjects were assigned to a treatment or control group. The experimental treatments were administered in their homes. Subjects listened to reports on hand-held digital audio devices, responded to comprehension questions, and then answered demographic and key outcome questions.
Outcomes	
6a	Completely defined pre-specified primary and secondary outcome measures, including how and when they were assessed: primary outcome measures addressed relative preferences over local development versus moral probity, assessed via hypothetical vignettes. Secondary measures addressed transnational associations and inter-group exclusivities, assessed via hypothetical vignettes and a behavioral exchange game. Secondary measures not included.
6b	Any changes to trial outcomes after the trial commenced, with reasons: data were collected on all outcome measures but are reported in this manuscript only for primary measures regarding local development and moral probity, in order to maintain theoretical focus.

(*continued*)

Section/ Topic	Checklist Item
Sample Size	
7a	How sample size was determined: sample size was determined by cost and time constraints, with the aim of successful data collection from 300 subjects in each enumeration area.
7b	When applicable, explanation of any interim analyses and stopping guidelines: not applicable.
Randomization	
8a	Method used to generate the random allocation sequence: subjects were selected via household sampling gaps and random draws within each household, with stratification by gender. Assignment to treatment groups was pre-determined via observation number.
8b	Type of randomization: multi-stage randomization, with stratification by gender, in three neighborhood clusters of each enumeration area.
9	Mechanism used to implement the random allocation sequence: each day, the experimenter assigned a random allocation sequence of treatment and control trials to enumerators, who then administered random selection protocols and conducted trials in assigned order.
10	Who generated the random allocation sequence, who enrolled participants, and who assigned participants to interventions: the experimenter generated the random allocation sequence; enumerators enrolled participants via random selection protocols (and participant consent); and the experimenter assigned subjects to interventions prior to selection, based on observation number.
Blinding	
11a	If done, who was blinded after assignment to interventions: participants were unaware of assignment to treatment types until after the experiment; by virtue of not being present with participants during data collection, the experimenter was blind to responses until the assessment of outcomes.
11b	If relevant, description of the similarity of interventions: the Ethnic and Religion treatments differed only in reference to specific ethnic and religious groups and themes cited in the radio reports. They were otherwise identical in content and delivery.
Statistical Methods	
12a	Statistical methods used to compare groups for primary and secondary outcomes: treatment effects were evaluated using difference-of-means tests and multivariate logit analysis.

(*continued*)

(continued)

Section/ Topic	Checklist Item
12b	Methods for additional analyses, such as subgroup analyses and adjusted analyses: treatment effects from the convenience sample were also evaluated using difference-of-means tests.
Participant Flow	
13a	For each group, the numbers of participants who were randomly assigned, received intended treatment, and were analyzed for the primary outcome: Ethnic treatment: 500 assigned, 456 received treatment. The three primary outcome measures were analyzed for 445, 452, and 443 participants, respectively. Religion treatment: 500 assigned, 456 received treatment. The three primary outcome measures were analyzed for 447, 451, and 448 participants, respectively. Control group: 440 assigned, 399 received treatment. The three primary outcome measures were analyzed for 391, 397, and 389 participants, respectively.
13b	For each group, losses and exclusions after randomization, together with reasons: Ethnic treatment: 8.8 percent; Religion treatment: 8.8 percent; control group: 12.4 percent. Reasons included inability to locate randomly selected individual, time constraints on the part of the subject, and inability to comprehend.
Recruitment	
14a	Dates defining the periods of recruitment and follow-up: trials were administered from January to June 2009. The experimenter spent six weeks in each enumeration area for authorization, planning, training of enumerators, and administration of trials. Recruitment of subjects and administration of trials took place over the last three weeks of each visit.
14b	Why the trial ended or was stopped: planned stoppage based on time and resource constraints.
Baseline Data	
15	A table showing baseline demographic and clinical characteristics for each group: see Table 3.1 in text.
Numbers Analyzed	
16	For each group, number of participants: Ethnic treatment: 456; Religion treatment: 456; control: 399.

(continued)

Section/ Topic	Checklist Item
Outcomes and Estimation	
17a	For each primary and secondary outcome, results for each group, and the estimated effect size and its precision: means and 95% confidence intervals reported for each group in text and in Figure 3.3. In the logit analysis included in Appendix D, coefficients represent marginal effects.
17b	For binary outcomes, presentation of both absolute and relative effect sizes is recommended: see Figure 3.3.
Ancillary Analyses	
18	Results of any other analyses performed, including subgroup analyses and adjusted analyses: results disaggregated by country and enumeration area are presented in Table 3.3.
Harms	
19	All important harms or unintended effects in each group: no harms were reported, aside from fatigue during the course of trials.
Limitations	
20	Trial limitations, addressing sources of potential bias and imprecision, if relevant: outcomes are susceptible to social desirability bias, though that should not differ systematically across treatment types. There is no reason to suspect spillover in treatment effects.
Generalizability	
21	Generalizability (external validity, applicability) of the trial findings: findings are consistent across two national contexts, suggesting generalizability. Findings are also consistent with observational data from committed ethnic and religious group members, suggesting external validity.
22	Interpretation: the experimental effects are statistically moderate but clear. The study adequately balanced benefits and harms to subjects.
Other Information	
23	Registration number and name of trial registry: not applicable.
24	Where the full trial protocol can be accessed, if available: not applicable.
25	Sources of funding: research was supported by the National Science Foundation.

Appendix C

Thanks again for listening to 107.9 FM, the best new station on Ghanaian radio. In the latest news . . .

A special report has just been issued to chronicle the role of <u>tribes and ethnic</u>[1] groups in Ghana during the past year. Despite small disturbances in different parts of the country and some ongoing fundamental differences, the report suggests that the <u>Asante</u>, <u>Fante</u>, <u>Ewe</u>, <u>Mole-Dagbane</u>, and other <u>tribes</u> of Ghana have contributed positively to society in recent months.

<u>Tribal</u> leaders were especially proactive in calling for peace and for dialogue across the ethnicities. One example comes from a <u>Mamproussi</u> living in Accra, who is quoted as saying that his leader told him that a good <u>Mamproussi</u>, no matter where he is living in Ghana, will prefer peace to violence and good elections to fraudulent ones. Many of the calls for peace from <u>tribal</u> leaders were also aired in the media.

The report notes that it was not only the <u>tribal</u> *leaders* who promoted peace and dialogue. *Common members* of different <u>tribes</u> also took the initiative in many cases to educate people of other <u>tribes</u> about their own groups. <u>Asante</u> shared their views with <u>Ewes</u>. <u>Ewes</u> engaged in dialogue with groups of <u>Fante</u> youth. <u>Ga</u>, <u>Guan</u>, <u>Mole-Dagbon</u>, <u>Grusi</u>, <u>Akyem</u>, and others were mentioned in the report as having an important role to play in Ghanaian society.

The report talks, for example, of two young men from different <u>ethnic</u> groups who happen to be good friends. One of the young men was an

---

[1] Underlining is used to indicate the terms that were altered in the ethnic and religious broadcasts.

Ashanti and one was an Ewe, but they felt comfortable visiting each other's homes, and they even had opportunities to meet the tribal leaders from each other's community. Koffi, as one of them was called, had this to say about his friendship with the other one, Eyram: "Our ethnic backgrounds are important to both of us; after all, it's a critical part of who we are as people. But the nice thing about having a friend who is a proud Ewe is that we can learn from each other about our ethnic customs, practices, and so on. This makes me a more informed member of the country, because as you know we have many different tribes here."

Eyram added this comment: "When I met the chief in Koffi's village, I was nervous at first because I didn't know if he would respect me. We had a nice conversation, and while we don't agree on everything, I can see that he cares about his community just like my chief cares about my community. He inspired me to be an active Ewe."

One thing that emerged in the report was the agreements and disagreements between major ethnic groups on matters of national policy. One area of disagreement between tribal groups in some parts of the country is education policy. For example, Akans and Ewes agree that a strong education system is important for Ghana, but they disagree over the language of the teaching. Should everything be done in English, or should the language of different tribal groups be included in the instruction of our youth? This is a complicated issue, and individual Ashanti, Fante, Ewe, Grusi, Ga, Akyem, and others can all have different views. The report notes that this important issue across tribes is unlikely to be resolved soon.

One lady who was interviewed for the report said that she felt frustrated with the schooling that her child is receiving. "How can I raise my child to respect his ethnic ancestors if he never hears anything in his language all day long at school? This makes me worried that we are forgetting about our ethnic roots and history in this country." However, another lady who was interviewed had a different opinion: "The school is not the place to be teaching our children tribe languages or about ethnic groups in this country. That is for the family and the community to do. I prefer for my child to read good books and get a good education at school, and we will spend time at home to make sure he knows about his tribe." It is clear in the report that the modern education system in Ghana has a complex relationship with ethnicity, and yet both are very important aspects of our country and our future.

Finally, the report notes that some ongoing ethnic tensions exist. Strangers who hear Twi, Ewe, or Dagombe dialogue in a bus, for example, are not always comfortable with it. Many Ghanaians note that they prefer to be friends with people in their own <u>tribe</u>, and that sometimes they do not trust people of other <u>tribes</u>. Thus, if one of Ghana's <u>tribes</u> feels discriminated against on a wide scale, it is possible that we could see open <u>ethnic</u> group disagreements in the future.

In general, however, Ghanaians are proud of their <u>ethnic</u> groups, and most people recognize some benefits from the <u>ethnic</u> diversity. For example, the report discussed the importance of inviting the representatives from all major <u>ethnic</u> groups to take part in formal government ceremonies. In the distant past, this would not have happened: perhaps only the <u>Ashantis</u> would be invited, or only the <u>Ewes</u>. Nowadays, leaders from all major <u>tribes</u> are there to perform their <u>customs</u> and offer their best wishes to the government. This is why you can see <u>Akan</u>, <u>Ewe</u>, and others taking part in civic events, and it is why Ghana has a reputation as a country with a very rich and diverse <u>ethnic</u> population.

The report on ethnic groups in Ghana concludes by asking all Ghanaians to think about the role that <u>ethnicity</u> plays in their lives. Is your <u>ethnicity</u> important in your relationships, in your work, and in your community? Do you have many friends who are from a different <u>tribe</u> than you? What other policy issues does <u>ethnicity</u> affect in your opinion? We would love to hear your thoughts about the issue of <u>ethnic</u> groups in Ghana, so give us a call and we'll try to get you on the air. In the meantime, keep listening right here on 107.9 FM ...

TRANSCRIPT OF RADIO REPORT: RELIGION TREATMENT

Thanks again for listening to 107.9 FM, the best new station on Ghanaian radio. In the latest news ...

A special report has just been issued to chronicle the role of <u>religious</u> groups in Ghana during the past year. Despite small disturbances in different parts of the country and some ongoing fundamental differences, the report suggests that the <u>Christian</u> and <u>Muslim</u> communities in Ghana have contributed positively to society in recent months.

<u>Muslim</u> and <u>Christian</u> leaders were especially proactive in calling for peace and for dialogue across the religions. One example comes from a <u>Muslim</u> living in Accra, who is quoted as saying that his leader told him that a good <u>Muslim</u>, no matter where he is living in Ghana, will prefer peace to violence and good elections to fraudulent ones. Many of the calls for peace from <u>religious</u> leaders were also aired in the media.

The report notes that it was not only the Muslim and Christian *leaders* who contributed to Ghanaian society. Christian and Muslim *community members* also took the initiative in many cases to educate people of other religions about their own groups. Tidjaniyya Muslims have shared their views with Christians. Charismatic Christians engaged in dialogue with groups of Muslim youth. Amhadiyya Muslims, Pentecostals, Orthodox Muslims, Mainline Christians, traditional African religions, and others were mentioned in the report as having an important role to play in Ghanaian society.

The report talks, for example, of two young men from different religious groups who happen to be good friends. One of the young men was a Muslim and one was a Christian, but they felt comfortable visiting each other's homes, and they even had opportunities to meet the religious leaders from each other's community. David, as one of them was called, had this to say about his friendship with the other one, Ibrahim: "Our religions are important to both of us; after all, it's a critical part of who we are as people. But the nice thing about having a friend who is a proud Muslim is that we can learn from each other about our religious customs, practices, and so on. This makes me a more informed member of the country, because as you know we have many different religions here."

Ibrahim added this comment: "When I met the preacher at David's church, I was nervous at first because I didn't know if he would respect me. We had a nice conversation, and while we don't agree on everything, I can see that he cares about his community just like my imam cares about my community. He inspired me to be an active Muslim."

One thing that emerged in the report was the agreements and disagreements between major religious groups on matters of national policy. One area of disagreement between Muslims and Christians in some parts of the country is education. Christians and Muslims agree that a strong education system is important for Ghana, but they disagree over the content of the teaching. Should everything be done in secular terms, or should the content of different religious groups be included in the moral instruction of our youth? This is a complicated issue, and individual Catholics, Protestants, Charismatics, Ahmadiyyas, Wahhabis, other Muslims, and traditional religionists can all have different views. The report notes that this important issue across religious groups is unlikely to be resolved soon.

One lady who was interviewed for the report said that she felt frustrated with the schooling that her child is receiving. "How can I raise my child to be God-fearing if he never hears anything about religion all day long at school? This makes me worried that we are forgetting about our religious roots and history in this country." However, another lady who was interviewed had a different opinion: "The school is not the place to be teaching our children about religious groups in this country. That is for the family and the community to do. I prefer for my child to read good books and get a good education at school, and we will spend time at home to make sure he knows about his religion." It is clear in the report that the modern education system in Ghana has a complex relationship with religion, and yet both are very important aspects of our country and our future.

Finally, the report notes that some ongoing religious tensions exist. Strangers who hear Muslim or Christian dialogue in a bus, for example, are not always comfortable with it. Many Ghanaians note that they prefer to be friends with people in their own religion, and that sometimes they do not trust people of other religions. Thus, if one of Ghana's religious groups feels discriminated against on a wide scale, it is possible that we could see open religious disagreements in the future.

In general, however, Ghanaians are proud of their religious groups, and most people recognize some benefits from the religious diversity. For example, the report discussed the importance of inviting the representatives from all major religions to take part in formal government ceremonies. In the distant past, this would not have happened: perhaps only the Christians would be invited, or only the traditional Religionists. Nowadays, leaders from all religious groups are there to say prayers and offer their best wishes to the government. This is why you can see Muslims as well as Christians taking part in civic events, and it is why Ghana has a reputation as a country with a very rich and diverse religious population.

The report on religious groups in Ghana concludes by asking all Ghanaians to think about the role that religion plays in their lives. Is your religion important in your relationships, in your work, and in your community? Do you have many friends who are from a different religion than you? What other policy issues does religion affect in your opinion? We would love to hear your thoughts about the issue of religious groups in Ghana, so give us a call and we'll try to get you on the air. In the meantime, keep listening right here on 107.9 FM . . .

Appendix D

Multivariate Regression Results

	(1) Prefers Moral Candidate	(2) Prefers Moral Community	(3) Willing to Pay Bribe
Religion	0.04*	0.08***	−0.14***
treatment	(0.02)	(0.02)	(0.03)
Ethnic treatment	−0.08*	−0.01	0.04
	(0.03)	(0.03)	(0.03)
Ghana resident	0.04	0.02	0.11***
	(0.06)	(0.04)	(0.02)
Northern	0.06	−0.01	−0.03*
resident	(0.06)	(0.05)	(0.02)
Urban	0.01	−0.02	−0.03
	(0.01)	(0.04)	(0.02)
Male	−0.06***	−0.04	0.06†
	(0.02)	(0.03)	(0.04)
Age	−0.01***	0.01***	−0.01*
	(0.00)	(0.00)	(0.01)
Education	−0.01	0.05*	−0.10***
	(0.01)	(0.02)	(0.03)
Standard of	0.01	−0.05	−0.01
living	(0.03)	(0.03)	(0.02)
Muslim	−0.01	0.03	−0.01
	(0.02)	(0.03)	(0.02)
(Pseudo) R²	0.02	0.05	0.08
N	1256	1273	1246
Pr (Religion = Ethnic)	0.0004	0.0010	0.0000

Notes: Logit estimations with standard errors in parentheses. $^†p < .10$, $^*p < .05$, $^{**}p < .01$, $^{***}p < .001$. Coefficients represent marginal effects. Religious group fixed effects calculated but not shown (except for Muslim); the omitted religious category is Protestant.

Appendix E

Descriptive Statistics

	Burkina Faso Respondents	Côte d'Ivoire Respondents	p-value of the Difference
Percentage urban	50	52	0.828
Percentage male	53	51	0.727
Percentage aged 18–27	35	35	0.994
Percentage aged 28–45	34	35	0.877
Percentage aged 46 and up	31	30	0.866
Percentage married	65	60	0.451
Average number of years of schooling	3.7	3.5	0.828
Living standards[a]			
Percentage whose standard of living is "high"	8	15	0.114
Percentage whose standard of living is "medium"	67	58	0.198
Percentage whose standard of living is "low"	25	27	0.805
Religion/religious practice			
Percentage Muslim	37	66	0.000
Percentage Catholic	36	11	0.000
Percentage Protestant	4	6	0.488
Percentage Animist	22	15	0.172
Percentage identifying with "no religion"	1	2	0.551
Percentage who never participate in religious services	9	22	0.016
Percentage who participate in religious services daily	31	16	0.018
Migration			
Average number of years spent living in survey town	25	20	0.050

(*continued*)

(continued)

	Burkina Faso Respondents	Côte d'Ivoire Respondents	*p*-value of the Difference
Percentage born in research town/village	52	26	**0.000**
Percentage from nearby villages (<150 km)	17	20	0.611
Percentage internal migrants (>150 km)	15	13	0.613
Percentage migrants from across BF/CI border	13	35	**0.001**
Percentage migrants from a third country	1	5	0.125
Ethnicity			
Percentage Lobi	35	27	0.215
Percentage Gouin	22	1	**0.001**
Percentage Mossi	19	9	**0.055**
Percentage Senefou	1	21	**0.002**
Percentage Dioula	5	10	0.169
Percentage from other ethnic group	18	32	**0.025**
Sample size	100	97	

[a] Living standards are coded into three categories (high, medium, and low) based on a combination of subjective characterizations by the enumerator and information gleaned from survey questions about asset ownership (e.g., radio, television, bicycle, cell phone, moped, car, animals, and fields).

Note: Significant differences (*p*-values ≤ .10) are in bold.

Appendix F

Determinants of Religion as the Primary Self-Identification Choice

	Religion Most Important Identification	Religion Most Important Identification	Religion among Top Two Identifications	Will Marry Different Religion	Closer to Co-Nationalist Than Co-Religionist
Lives in Côte d'Ivoire	0.12*	0.12	0.32*	−0.27*	−0.32*
	(0.07)	(0.08)	(0.09)	(0.09)	(0.10)
Lives in urban survey site	0.01	0.01	−0.10	0.21*	0.01
	(0.09)	(0.09)	0.13	(0.13)	(0.14)
Male	−0.04	−0.04	−0.08	0.25*	0.04
	(0.05)	(0.05)	(0.08)	(0.08)	(0.09)
Aged 18–27	0.11	0.11	0.05	0.20**	0.10
	(0.09)	(0.09)	(0.11)	(0.09)	(0.12)
Aged 28–45	0.21*	0.21*	0.17*	0.07	−0.01
	(0.09)	(0.09)	(0.10)	(0.08)	(0.11)
Married	−0.03	−0.03	0.07	0.14	0.31*
	(0.06)	(0.06)	(0.09)	(0.09)	(0.10)
Years of schooling	−0.01	−0.01	−0.01	0.03*	0.02
	(0.01)	(0.01)	(0.01)	(0.01)	(0.01)
Standard of living	−0.03	−0.03	0.04	0.05	0.04
	(0.05)	(0.05)	(0.07)	(0.06)	(0.08)
Muslim	−0.02	−0.02	0.24	0.08	−0.12
	(0.10)	(0.13)	(0.17)	(0.17)	(0.19)
Catholic	−0.10	−0.10	0.17	0.05	0.10
	(0.08)	(0.08)	(0.20)	(0.16)	(0.19)
Traditional religionist	−0.14*	−0.14*	−0.13	0.25*	0.09
	(0.06)	(0.06)	(0.18)	(0.10)	(0.20)
Born in nearby village (<150 km)	−0.07	−0.07	−0.05	0.05	0.10
	(0.06)	(0.06)	(0.11)	(0.13)	(0.12)
Internal migrant (>150 km)	0.15	0.15	0.27*	−0.34*	−0.12
	(0.13)	(0.13)	(0.15)	(0.17)	(0.16)
Born across border	0.06	0.05	0.05	−0.01	−0.03
	(0.08)	(0.08)	(0.11)	(0.10)	(0.12)
Born in third country	0.39	0.39	0.48*	0.12	−0.07
	(0.27)	(0.27)	(0.21)	(0.15)	(0.26)

(*continued*)

(*continued*)

	Religion Most Important Identification	Religion Most Important Identification	Religion among Top Two Identifications	Will Marry Different Religion	Closer to Co-Nationalist Than Co-Religionist
Lives in Côte d'Ivoire * Muslim		0.01 (0.12)			
Ethnic group fixed effects	Yes	Yes	Yes	Yes	Yes
Pseudo R^2	0.19	0.19	0.18	0.27	0.19
Observations	190	190	190	189	180

Notes: Logit estimations with coefficients reported as marginal effects. Standard errors in parentheses. * $p < .10$. The omitted age category is 46 years or older. "Standard of living" is coded 1 for "low," 2 for "medium," 3 for "high." The omitted religious group is Protestant. The omitted migrant variable is Lifelong Resident. Ethnic group fixed effects include dummy variables for membership in the Dioula, Gouin, Lobi, Mossi, or Senoufo tribes. The omitted category is Other Ethnic Group.

Bibliography

Adams, Martin, S. Sibanda, and Steven Turner. 1999. "Land Tenure Reform and Rural Livelihoods in Southern Africa." *ODI Natural Resource Perspectives*, Working paper no. 39.

Adepoju, Aderanti. 2002. "Issues and Recent Trends in International Migration in Sub-Saharan Africa." *International Social Science Journal* 52, 165: 383–394.

Adibe, Jideofor. 2012. "Boko Haram: One Sect, Conflicting Narratives." *African Renaissance: Terrorism in Africa* 9, 1: 47–64.

Afigbo, A. E. 1978. "The Missions, the State, and Education in South-Eastern Nigeria, 1956–1971." In Edward Fasholé-Luke, Richard Gray, Adrian Hastings, and Godwin Tasie, eds., *Christianity in Independent Africa*. Bloomington: Indiana University Press, pp. 176–192.

African Elections Database. 2010. "Côte d'Ivoire: Presidential Elections." http://africanelections.tripod.com/ci.html#2000_Presidential_Election.

Afrik News. 2010. "Ivory Coast at the Threshold of a Civil War?" February 12. www.afrik-news.com/article16936.html.

Afrobarometer. 2001. "Merged Round 1 Data." www.afrobarometer.org/data/merged-round-1-data-12-countries-1999-2001.

Agence France Press. 2003. "Ivory Coast Conflict Underlines Ethnic, Religious Divisions." January 15.

Agence France-Presse. 2010. "Nigerian Islamist Sect Threatens to Widen Attacks." March 29.

Aghedo, Iro, and Oarhe Osumah. 2012. "The Boko Haram Uprising: How Should Nigeria Respond?" *Third World Quarterly* 33, 5: 853–869.

Akindès, Francis. 2003. "Côte d'Ivoire: Socio-Political Crises, 'Ivoirité', and the Course of History." *African Sociological Review* 7, 2: 11–28.

Alagappa, Muthia. 1995. *Political Legitimacy in Southeast Asia: The Quest for Moral Authority*. Stanford, CA: Stanford University Press.

Alesina, Alberto, et al. 2003. "Fractionalization." *Journal of Economic Growth* 8, 2: 155–194.

Alesina, Alberto, William Easterly, and Janina Matuszeski. 2011. "Artificial States." *Journal of the European Economic Association* 9: 246–277.

Alger, Chadwick F. 2002. "Religion as a Peace Tool." *Ethnopolitics* 1, 4: 94–109.

Alimba, N. Chinyere. 2014. "Probing the Dynamic of Communal Conflict in Northern Nigeria." *African Research Review* 8, 1: 177–204.

AllAfrica. 2009. "Côte d'Ivoire: Coup d'Etat de 1999, Rébellion de 2002 – Les Faits qui Confondent Ouattara." April 2. http://fr.allafrica.com/stories/200904020802.html.

Almond, Gabriel, R. Scott Appleby, and Emmanuel Sivan. 2003. *Strong Religion: The Rise of Fundamentalisms around the World*. Chicago, IL: University of Chicago Press.

Alpine, Robin W., and James Pickett. 1993. *Agriculture, Liberalization, and Economic Growth in Ghana and Côte d'Ivoire: 1960–1990*. Paris: OECD Development Centre.

Amnesty International. 2015. "Nigeria: Horror in Numbers." June 3. www.amnesty.org/en/latest/news/2015/06/nigeria-horror-in-numbers/.

Amselle, Jean-Loup. 1985. "Ethnies et Espaces: Pour une Anthropologie Topologique." In J. L. Amselle and E. M'Bokolo, eds., *Au Cœur de L'Ethnie: Ethnies, Tribalisme et Etat en Afrique*. Paris: La Decouverte, pp. 11–48.

Anderson, Allan. 2013. *An Introduction to Pentecostalism: Global Charismatic Christianity*, 2nd ed. Cambridge: Cambridge University Press.

André, Catherine, and Jean-Philippe Platteau. 1998. "Land Relations under Unbearable Stress: Rwanda Caught in the Malthusian Trap." *Journal of Economic Behavior and Organization* 34: 1–47.

An-Na'im, Abdullahi Ahmed. 1993. "Constitutional Discourse and the Civil War in the Sudan." In M. W. Daly and Ahmad Sikainga, eds., *Civil War in the Sudan*. London: British Academic Press, pp. 97–116.

Arceneaux, Kevin. 2010. "The Benefits of Experimental Methods for the Study of Campaign Effects." *Political Communication* 27, 2: 199–215.

Arrioloa, Leonardo R. 2009. "Patronage and Political Stability in Africa." *Comparative Political Studies* 42, 10: 1339–1362.

Badie, Bertrand. 1987. *Les Deux Etats: Pouvoir et Société en Occident et en Terre d'Islam*. Paris: Fayard.

Badru, Pade. 1998. *Imperialism and Ethnic Politics in Nigeria, 1960–1996*. Asmara: Africa World Press.

Bakary, Tessy D. 1997. "Political Polarization over Governance in Côte d'Ivoire." In I. William Zartman, ed., *Governance as Conflict Management: Politics and Violence in West Africa*. Washington, DC: Brookings Institution, pp. 49–94.

Baldwin, Kate. 2014. "When Politicians Cede Control of Resources: Land, Chiefs, and Coalition-Building in Africa." *Comparative Politics* 46, 3: 253–271.

Baldwin, Kate, and John D. Huber. 2010. "Economic versus Cultural Differences: Forms of Ethnic Diversity and Public Goods Provision." *American Political Science Review* 104, 4: 644–662.

Banegas, Richard. 2006. "Côte d'Ivoire: Patriotism, Ethnonationalism, and Other African Modes of Self-Writing." *African Affairs* 105, 421: 535–552.

Banegas, Richard, and Bruno Losch. 2002. "La Côte d'Ivoire au Bord de l'Implosion." *Politique Africaine* 87: 139–161.

Banks, Antoine J., and N. A. Valentino. 2012. "Emotional Substrates of White Racial Attitudes." *American Journal of Political Science* 56, 2: 286–297.

Bar, Shmuel. 2004. "The Religious Sources of Islamic Terrorism." *Policy Review* 125.

Barkan, Joel D., Michael L. McNulty, and M. A. O. Ayeni. 1991. "Hometown Voluntary Associations, Local Development, and the Emergence of Civil Society in Western Nigeria." *The Journal of Modern African Studies* 29, 3: 457–480.

Barrett, David B. 1968. *Schism and Renewal in Africa: An Analysis of Six Thousand Contemporary Religious Movements*. Oxford: Oxford University Press.

Barth, Fredrik. 1969. *Ethnic Groups and Boundaries: The Social Organization of Culture Difference*. Oslo: Universitetsforlaget.

Bassett, Thomas J. 2003. "'Nord Musulman et Sud Chretien': Les Moules Médiatiques de la Crise Ivoirienne." *Afrique Contemporaine* 206, 2: 13–27.

Bates, Robert H. 1974. "Ethnic Competition and Modernization in Contemporary Africa." *Comparative Political Studies* 6, 4: 457–484.

Bates, Robert H. 1983. "Modernization, Ethnic Competition, and the Rationality of Politics in Contemporary Africa." In D. Rothchild and V. Olorunsola, eds., *State versus Ethnic Claims: African Policy Dilemmas*. Boulder, CO: Westview Press, pp. 152–171.

BBC (British Broadcasting Corportation). 1998. "Millions Dead in Sudan Civil War." December 11. http://news.bbc.co.uk/2/hi/africa/232803.stm.

BBC (British Broadcasting Corporation). 2011. "Nigeria's 'Taliban' Enigma." July 31. http://news.bbc.co.uk/2/hi/8172270.stm.

BBC (British Broadcasting Corporation). 2015a. "Anti-Boko Haram Force to Cross Borders to Fight." July 29. www.bbc.com/news/world-africa-33702738.

BBC (British Broadcasting Corporation). 2015b. "Nigeria's Boko Haram Pledges Allegiance to Islamic State." March 7. www.bbc.com/news/world-africa-31784538.

Beinart, Peter. 1996. "The Jews of South Africa." *Transition* 71: 60–79.

Bentley, Arthur F. 1908. *The Process of Government: A Study of Social Pressures*. Chicago, IL: University of Chicago Press.

Berger, Peter L. 1967. *The Sacred Canopy: Elements of a Sociological Theory of Religion*. New York: Open Road Media.

Berger, Peter L., ed. 1999. *The Desecularization of the World: Resurgent Religion and World Politics*. Grand Rapids, MI: Eerdmans.

Berry, Sara. 2008. "Ancestral Property: Land, Politics, and the Deeds of the Ancestors in Ghana and Cote d'Ivoire." In Janine M. Ubink and Kojo Amanor, eds., *Contesting Land and Custom in Ghana: State, Chief, and Citizen*. Leiden, Netherlands: Leiden University Press, pp. 27–54.

Bigagaza, Jean, Carolyne Abong, and Cecile Mukarubuga. 2002. "Land Scarcity, Distribution, and Conflict in Rwanda." In Jeremy Lind and Kathryn Sturman, eds., *Scarcity and Surfeit: The Ecology of Africa's Conflicts*. Pretoria: Institute for Security Studies, pp. 50–82.

Birnir, Johanna. 2007. *Ethnicity and Electoral Politics*. Cambridge: Cambridge University Press.

Blattman, Christopher. 2009. "From Violence to Voting: War and Political Participation in Uganda." *American Political Science Review* 103, 2: 231–247.

Blattman, Christopher, and Jeannie Annan. 2016. "Can Employment Reduce Lawlessness and Rebellion? A Field Experiment with High-Risk Men in a Fragile State." *American Political Science Review* 110, 1: 1–17.

Blattman, Christopher, and Edward Miguel. 2010. "Civil War." *Journal of Economic Literature* 48, 1: 3–57.

Bleck, Jaime, and Nicholas van de Walle. 2011. "Parties and Issues in Francophone West Africa: Towards a Theory of Non-Mobilization." *Democratization* 18, 5: 1125–1145.

Blench, Roger. 2006. *Archeology, Language, and the African Past*. Lanham, MD: Altamira Press, Rowman & Littlefield.

Boafo-Arthur, Kwame. 2003. "Chieftancy in Ghana: Challenges and Prospects in the 21st Century." *African and Asian Studies* 2, 2: 125–153.

Boone, Catherine. 2014. *Property and Political Order in Africa: Land Rights and the Structure of Politics*. New York: Cambridge University Press.

Bormann, Nils-Christian, Lars-Erik Cederman, and Manuel Vogt. 2013. "Ethnonationalist Cleavages in Civil Wars: Allah's Wrath or Babel's Legacy?" EPSA Paper 647, European Political Science Association.

Bosch, Elana, et al. 2000. "Genetic Structure of North-West Africa Revealed by STR Analysis." *European Journal of Human Genetics* 8: 360–366.

Bouquet, Christian. 2007. "Le Mauvais Usage de la Democratie en Côte d'Ivoire." *L'Espace Politique* Issue 3: http://espacepolitique.revues.org/index894.html.

Brass, Paul R. 1997. *Theft of an Idol: Text and Context in the Representation of Collective Violence*. Princeton, NJ: Princeton University Press.

Bratton, Michael. 2007. "Formal versus Informal Institutions in Africa." *Journal of Democracy* 18, 3: 96–110.

Brégand, Denise. 2007. "Muslim Reformists and the State in Benin." In B. Soares and R. Otayek, eds., *Islam and Muslim Politics in Africa*. New York: Palgrave MacMillan, pp. 121–136.

Brubaker, Rogers. 2004. *Ethnicity without Groups*. Cambridge, MA: Harvard University Press.

Campbell, Aidan. 1997. "Ethical Ethnicity: A Critique." *Journal of Modern African Studies* 35, 1: 53–79.

Chandra, Kanchan. 2004. *Why Ethnic Parties Succeed: Patronage and Ethnic Head Counts in India*. Cambridge: Cambridge University Press.

Chandra, Kanchan. 2006. "What Is Ethnic Identity and Does It Matter?" *Annual Review of Political Science* 9: 397–424.

Chandra, Kanchan. 2012. *Constructivist Theories of Ethnic Politics*. Oxford: Oxford University Press.

Chappell, David A. 1989. "The Nation as Frontier: Ethnicity and Clientelism in Ivoirian History." *The International Journal of African Historical Studies* 22, 4: 671–696.

Chimee, Ihediwa Nkemjika. 2013. "The Nigerian-Biafran War, Armed Conflicts, and the Rules of Engagement." In Toyin Falola, Roy Doron, and Okpeh O. Okpeh, eds., *Warfare, Ethnicity, and National Identity in Nigeria*. London: Africa World Press, pp. 111–137.

Chirot, Daniel. 2006. "The Debacle in Côte d'Ivoire." *Journal of Democracy* 17, 2: 63–77.

CIA World Factbook. 2015. "Africa: Côte d'Ivoire, Ghana. People: Religions." www.cia.gov/library/publications/the-world-factbook/.

CIA World Factbook. 2016. "People and Society: Rwanda." www.cia.gov/library/publications/the-world-factbook/geos/rw.html.

Cisse, Cheik C. 2004. "Côte d'Ivoire: Aux Origines d'une Crise." *Recherches Africaines* Issue 3. www.recherches-africaines.net/document.php?id=236.

Clarke, Peter B. 1982. *West Africa and Islam*. London: Edward Arnold.

Clendenen, Clarence C. 1972. "Tribalism and Humanitarianism: The Nigerian-Biafran Civil War." In Robin Higham, ed., *Civil Wars in the Twentieth Century*. Lexington: University of Kentucky Press, pp. 163–183.

Cogneau, Denis, and Alexander Moradi. 2014. "Borders That Divide: Education and Religion in Ghana and Togo since Colonial Times." *Journal of Economic History* 74, 3: 694–729.

Cohen, Abner. 2013. *Custom and Politics in Urban Africa: A Study of Hausa Migrants in Yoruba Towns*. London: Routledge Press.

Cohen, Ronald, and John Middleton. 1971. *From Tribe to Nation in Africa*. Scranton, PA: Chandler Press.

Coleman, James S. 1990. *Foundations of Social Theory*. Cambridge, MA: Belknap Press.

Collett, Moya. 2006. "Ivoirian Identity Constructions: Ethnicity and Nationalism in the Prelude to Civil War." *Nations and Nationalism* 12, 4: 613–629.

Collier, Paul, and Anke Hoeffler. 2004. "Greed and Grievance in Civil War." *Oxford Economic Papers* 56, 4: 563–595.

Collins, Robert O. 2008. *A History of Modern Sudan*. New York: Cambridge University Press.

Cook, David. 2011. "Boko Haram: A Prognosis." Research note. Baker Institute for Public Policy, Rice University.

Cornwall, Marie, et al. 1986. "The Dimensions of Religiosity: A Conceptual Model with an Empirical Test." *Review of Religious Research* 27, 3: 226–244.

Cox, Harvey. 1995. *Fire from Heaven: The Rise of Pentecostal Spirituality and the Reshaping of Religion in the Twenty-first Century*. Cambridge, MA: Da Capo Press.

Cox, Harvey. 2010. *The Future of Faith*. New York: HarperOne.

Crook, Richard C. 1989. "Patrimonialism, Administrative Effectiveness, and Economic Development in Côte d'Ivoire." *African Affairs* 88, 351: 205–228.

Crook, Richard C. 1990. "State, Society, and Political Institutions in Côte d'Ivoire and Ghana." *IDS Bulletin* 21, 4: 24–34.

Cruise O'Brien, Conor B. 1977. "A Versatile Charisma: The Mouride Brotherhood, 1967–1975." *European Journal of Sociology* 18, 1: 84–106.

Daddieh, Cyril. 2001. "Elections and Ethnic Violence in Côte d'Ivoire: The Unfinished Business of Succession and Democratic Transition." *African Issues* 29, 1–2: 14–19.

Daly, M. W., and Ahmad Alawad Sikainga, eds. 1993. *Civil War in the Sudan*. London: British Academic Press.

de St. Jorre, John. 1972. *The Brothers' War: Biafra and Nigeria*. Boston: Houghton Mifflin.

de Waal, Alex. 1993. "Some Comments on Militias in the Contemporary Sudan." In M. W. Daly and Ahmad Sikainga, eds., *Civil War in the Sudan*. London: British Academic Press, pp. 142–156.

de Waal, Alex. 2007. "Sudan: What Kind of State? What Kind of Crisis? Occasional Paper No. 2. Crisis States Research Center, London School of Economics.

Deng, Francis M. 1973. "Dynamics of Identification: A Basis for National Integration in the Sudan." *Africa Today* 20, 3: 19–26.

Deng, Francis M. 1993. "Hidden Agendas in the Peace Process." In M. W. Daly and Ahmad Sikainga, eds., *Civil War in the Sudan*. London: British Academic Press, pp. 186–215.

Deng, Francis. 1995. *War of Visions: Conflict of Identities in the Sudan*. Washington, DC: The Brookings Institution.

Deng, Francis M. 2001. "Sudan – Civil War and Genocide: Disappearing Christians in the Middle East." *Middle East Quarterly* (Winter): 13–21.

Deng, Francis M. 2006. "Sudan: A Turbulent Nation in Search of Itself." *Annals of the American Academy of Political and Social Science* 603: 155–162.

Diamond, Larry J. 1988. *Class, Ethnicity, and Democracy in Nigeria: The Failure of the First Republic*. Syracuse, NY: Syracuse University Press.

Doron, Roy. 2013. "We Are Doing Everything We Can, Which Is Very Little: The Johnson Administration and the Nigerian Civil War, 1967–1970." In Toyin Falola, Roy Doron, and Okpeh O. Okpeh, eds., *Warfare, Ethnicity, and National Identity in Nigeria*. London: Africa World Press, pp. 139–159.

Douglass, William A. 1988. "A Critique of Recent Trends in the Analysis of Ethnonationalism." *Ethnic and Racial Studies* 11, 2: 192–206.

Dowd, Robert A. 2015. *Christianity, Islam, and Liberal Democracy: Lessons from Sub-Saharan Africa*. Oxford: Oxford University Press.

Dozon, Jean-Pierre. 2000. "La Côte d'Ivoire entre Democratie, Nationalisme, et Ethnonationalisme." *Politique Africaine* 78: 45–62.

Droit Afrique. 2010. "Côte d'Ivoire: Loi Relatif au Domaine Foncier Rurale." www.droit-afrique.com/images/textes/Côte_Ivoire/RCI%20-%20Domaine%20foncier%20rural.pdf.

Druckman, James N., Donald P. Green, James H. Kuklinski, and Arthur Lupia. 2011. *Cambridge Handbook of Experimental Political Science*. New York: Cambridge University Press.

Dunning, Thad. 2008. "Improving Causal Inference: Strengths and Limitations of Natural Experiments." *Political Research Quarterly* 61 (June): 282–293.

Dunning, Thad. 2012. *Natural Experiments in the Social Sciences: A Design-Based Approach*. New York: Cambridge University Press.

Dunning, Thad, and Lauren Harrison. 2010. "Cross-Cutting Cleavages and Ethnic Voting: An Experimental Study of Cousinage in Mali." *American Political Science Review* 104, 1: 21–39.

Dunning, Thad, and Janhavi Nilekani. 2013. "Ethnic Quotas and Political Mobilization: Caste, Parties, and Distribution in Indian Village Councils." *American Political Science Review* 107, 1: 35–56.

Durkheim, Emile. 1912 [1995]. *The Elementary Forms of the Religious Life.* Trans. Karen E. Fields. New York: Free Press.

Dustmann, Christian, and Ian Preston. 2001. "Attitudes to Ethnic Minorities, Ethnic Context and Location Decisions." *The Economic Journal* 111: 353–373.

Easterly, William, and Ross Levine. 1997. "Africa's Growth Tragedy: Policies and Ethnic Divisions." *Quarterly Journal of Economics* 112, 4: 1203–1250.

Economist. 2000. "Côte d'Ivoire – Destroying the Inheritance: Disqualifying a Northern Politician Has Set the North against the South." December 7. www.economist.com/node/443321.

Economist. 2012. "Still Too Tribal." June 9.

Edgerton, Robert B. 1995. *The Fall of the Asante Empire: The Hundred-Year War for Africa's Gold Coast.* New York: Simon & Schuster.

Edmonds, Martin. 1972. "Civil War and Arms Sales: The Nigerian-Biafran War and Other Cases." In Robin Higham, ed., *Civil Wars in the Twentieth Century.* Lexington: University of Kentucky Press, pp. 203–216.

Eifert, Ben, Edward Miguel, and Daniel Posner. 2010. "Political Competition and Ethnic Identification in Africa." *American Journal of Political Science* 54, 2 (April): 494–510.

Elizabeth, Isichei. 1976. *A History of the Igbo People.* London: Macmillan.

Englebert, Pierre, Stacy Tarango, and Matthew Carter. 2002. "Dismemberment and Suffocation: A Contribution to the Debate on African Boundaries." *Comparative Political Studies* 35 (December): 1093–1118.

Eprile, Cecil. 1974. *War and Peace in the Sudan, 1955–1972.* London: David & Charles.

Esteban, Joan, and Debraj Ray. 2008. "On the Salience of Ethnic Conflict." *American Economic Review* 98, 5: 2185–2202.

Evans-Pritchard, E. E. 1940. *The Nuer: A Description of the Modes of Livelihood and Political Institutions of a Nilotic People.* Oxford: Oxford University Press.

Evening Standard. 2012. "Nigerian Religious Killings Spiral." June 19.

Fafchamps, Marcel. 2001. "Networks, Communities, and Markets in Sub-Saharan Africa: Implications for Firm Growth and Investment." *Journal of African Economies* 10, 2: 109–142.

Falola, Toyin. 1997. "Nigeria in the Global Context of Refugees: Historical and Comparative Perspectives." In Paul E. Lovejoy and Pat Williams, eds., *Displacement and the Politics of Violence in Nigeria.* Leiden, Netherlands: Brill, pp. 5–21.

Falola, Toyin. 1998. *Violence in Nigeria: The Crisis of Religious Politics and Secular Ideologies.* Rochester, NY: University of Rochester Press.

Falola, Toyin. 1999. *The History of Nigeria.* Westport, CT: Greenwood Press.

Falola, Toyin. 2001. *Violence in Nigeria: The Crisis of Religious Politics and Secular Ideologies.* Rochester, NY: University of Rochester Press.

Falola, Toyin, and Matthew M. Heaton. 2008. *A History of Nigeria.* Cambridge, UK: Cambridge University Press.

Famhi, Monica. 2012. "Is Identity the Root Cause of Sudan's Civil Wars?" Unpublished manuscript.

Fauré, Yves. 1993. "Democracy and Realism: Reflections on the Case of Côte d'Ivoire." *Africa* 63, 3: 313–329.

Fearon, James D., and David Laitin. 2000a. "Violence and the Social Construction of Ethnic Identity." *International Organization* 54, 4 (Autumn): 845–877.

Fearon, James D., and David Laitin. 2000b. "Ordinary Language and External Validity: Specifying Concepts in the Study of Ethnicity." Paper prepared for the LiCEP meeting, October 20–22, University of Pennsylvania.

Finke, Roger, and Laurence R. Iannaccone. 1993. "Supply-Side Explanations for Religious Change." *Annals of the American Academy of Political and Social Science* 527: 27–39.

Ford, Neil. 2003. "Côte d'Ivoire: Divide and Reap Chaos." *African Business* November 1. www.allbusiness.com/africa/1134782-1.html.

Fox, Jonathan. 2004. "The Rise of Religious Nationalism and Conflict: Ethnic Conflict and Revolutionary Wars, 1945–2001." *Journal of Peace Research* 41, 6: 715–731.

Fox, Jonathan. 2007. "The Increasing Role of Religion in State Failure: 1960–2004." *Terrorism and Political Violence* 19, 3: 395–414.

Fox, Jonathan. 2012. "The Religious Wave: Religion and Domestic Conflict from 1960 to 1999." *Civil Wars* 14, 2: 141–158.

Franck, Raphaël, and Ilia Rainer. 2012. "Does the Leader's Ethnicity Matter? Ethnic Favoritism, Education, and Health in Sub-Saharan Africa." *American Political Science Review* 106, 2: 294–324.

Francois, Patrick, Ilia Rainer, and Francesco Trebbi. 2015. "How Is Power Shared in Africa?" *Econometrica* 83, 2: 565–603.

Fukuyama, Francis. 2011. *The Origins of Political Order: From Prehuman Times to the French Revolution.* New York: Farrar, Straus and Giroux.

Gasana, James K. 2000. "Natural Resource Scarcity and Violence in Rwanda." In Richard Matthew, Mark Halle, and Jason Switzer, eds., *Conserving the Peace: Resources, Livelihoods, and Scarcity.* Winnepeg: International Institute of Sustainable Development, pp. 199–246.

Geertz, Clifford. 1973. *The Interpretation of Cultures: Selected Essays by Clifford Geertz.* New York: Basic Books.

Gerber, Alan S., and Donald P. Green. 2000. "The Effects of Canvassing, Telephone Calls, and Direct Mail on Voter Turnout: A Field Experiment." *American Political Science Review* 94, 3 (Sept.): 653–663.

Gifford, Paul. 1994. "Some Recent Developments in African Christianity." *African Affairs* 93: 513–534.

Gifford, Paul. 2004. *Ghana's New Christianity: Pentecostalism in a Globalising African Economy.* London: Hurst & Co.

Goody, Jack. 1962. *Death and the Ancestors: A Study of the Mortuary Customs of the LoDagaa of West Africa.* London: Routledge Press.

Gould, Michael. 2012. *The Struggle for Modern Nigeria: The Biafran War 1967–1970.* London: I. B. Tauris.

Green, Donald P., and Alan S. Gerber. 2003. "The Underprovision of Experiments in Political Science." *The Annals of the American Academy of Political and Social Science* 589: 94–112.

Green, Elliott D. 2006. "Ethnicity and the Politics of Land Tenure Reform in Central Uganda." *Commonwealth and Comparative Politics* 44, 3: 370–388.

Grim, Brian J., and Roger Finke. 2007. "Religious Persecution in Cross-National Context: Clashing Civilizations or Regulated Religious Economies?" *American Sociological Review* 72 (August): 633–658.

Grossman, Guy. 2015. "Renewalist Christianity and the Political Saliency of LGBTs: Theory and Evidence from Sub-Saharan Africa." *Journal of Politics* 77, 2: 337–351.

Groves, Charles P. 1954. *Planting of Christianity in Africa*, vol. II. London: Lutterworth Press.

Gurr, Ted Robert. 1970. *Why Men Rebel*. Princeton, NJ: Princeton University Press.

Habyarimana, James, Macartan Humphreys, Daniel Posner, and Jeremy Weinstein. 2007. "Why Does Ethnic Diversity Undermine Public Goods Provision?" *American Political Science Review* 101, 4: 709–725.

Hall, Rodney Bruce. 1997. "Moral Authority as a Power Resource." *International Organization* 51, 4 (Autumn): 591–622.

Hamdi, Mohamed E. 1998. *The Making of an Islamic Leader: Conversations with Hasan Al-Turabi*. Boulder, CO: Westview Press.

Harden, Blaine. 1990. *Africa: Dispatches from a Fragile Continent*. Boston: Houghton Mifflin.

Hardin, Russell. 1995. *One for All: The Logic of Group Conflict*. Princeton, NJ: Princeton University Press.

Hartill, Lane. 2002. "In Time of Crisis, Ivoirians Turn their Eyes toward Heaven." *Christian Science Monitor*, November 25.

Hassan, Yusuf F. 1973. *The Arabs and the Sudan*. Khartoum: Khartoum University Press.

Hassner, Ron E. 2013. *War on Sacred Grounds*. Ithaca, NY: Cornell University Press.

Hastings, Adrian. 1994. *The Church in Africa, 1450–1950*. Oxford: Oxford University Press.

Head, William, and Earl H. Tilford, Jr., eds. 1996. *The Eagle in the Desert: Looking Back on U.S. Involvement in the Persian Gulf War*. Westport, CT: Praeger.

Helmke, Gretchen, and Steven Levitsky. 2004. "Informal Institutions and Comparative Politics: A Research Agenda." *Perspectives on Politics* 2, 4: 725–740.

Hintjens, Helen M. 2001. "When Identity Becomes a Knife: Reflecting on the Genocide in Rwanda." *Ethnicities* 1, 1: 25–55.

Hogg, Michael A. 2006. "Social Identity Theory." In Peter James Burke, ed., *Contemporary Social Psychological Theories*. Palo Alto, CA: Stanford University Press, pp. 111–136.

Holy Bible, New International Version. 1984 (reprint). Old and New Testaments. Biblica.

Horowitz, Donald L. 1985. *Ethnic Groups in Conflict*. Berkeley, CA: Berkeley University Press.

Hugon, Philippe. 2003. "La Côte d'Ivoire: Plusieurs Lectures pour une Crise Annoncée." *Afrique Contemporaine* 206, 2: 105–127.

Humphreys, Macartan. 2011. "Ethnicity and the Politics of AIDS." *Perspectives on Politics* 9, 4: 873–877.

Huntington, Samuel. 1993. "The Clash of Civilizations?" *Foreign Affairs* 72, 3: 22–49.

Huntington, Samuel. 1996. *The Clash of Civilizations and the Remaking of World Order*. New York: Simon & Schuster.

Hunwick, John. 1996. "Sub-Saharan African and the Wider World of Islam: Historical and Contemporary Perspectives." *Journal of Religion in Africa* 26, 3: 230–257.

Hutchinson, Sharon E. 2001. "A Curse from God? Religious and Political Dimensions of the Post-1991 Rise of Ethnic Violence in South Sudan." *Journal of Modern African Studies* 39, 2: 307–331.

Huth, Paul K. 1988. "Extended Deterrence and the Outbreak of War." *American Political Science Review* 82, 2: 423–443.

Iannacconne, Laurence R., Roger Finke, and Rodney Starke. 1997. "Deregulating Religion: The Economics of Church and State." *Economic Inquiry* 35, 2: 350–364.

Insoll, Timothy. 2003. *The Archeology of Islam in Sub-Saharan Africa*. Cambridge: Cambridge University Press.

Ivoire Business. 2009. "Affaire 'Alassane est bel et bien Burkinabé.'" December 11. www.ivoirebusiness.net/article.php?id=4592.

Iyengar, Shanto. 2013. "Laboratory Experiments in Political Science." In James N. Druckman, Donald Green, James Kuklinski, and Arthur Lupia, eds., *Cambridge Handbook of Experimental Political Science*. New York: Cambridge University Press, pp. 73–88.

Iyengar, Shanto, Mark D. Peters, and Donald R. Kinder. 1982. "Experimental Demonstrations of the 'Not-So-Minimal' Consequences of Television News Programs. *American Political Science Review* 76, 4: 848–858.

James, William. 1890 [1950]. *The Principles of Psychology*, vol. I. New York: Dover Press.

Johnson, Douglas H., and Gerard Prunier. 1993. "The Foundations and Expansion of the Sudan People's Liberation Army." In M. W. Daly and Ahmad Sikainga, eds., *Civil War in the Sudan*. London: British Academic Press, pp. 117–141.

Johnson, Hildegard Binder. 1967. "The Location of Christian Missions in Africa." *Geographical Review* 57, 2: 168–202.

Jok, J. M., and Sharon E. Hutchinson. 1999. "Sudan's Prolonged Civil War and the Militarization of Neur and Dinka Ethnic Identities." *African Studies Review* 42, 2: 125–145.

Kalyvas, Stathis N. 2000. "Commitment Problems in Emerging Democracies: The Case of Religious Parties." *Comparative Politics* 32, 4 (July): 379–398.

Kalyvas, Stathis N. 2006. *The Logic of Violence in Civil War*. New York: Cambridge University Press.

Kane, Ousame, and Jean-Louis Triaud. 1998. *Islam et Islamistes au Sud du Sahara*. Paris: Karthala.

Kaoma, Kapya J. 2009. "The Marriage of Convenience: The U.S. Christian Right, African Christianity, and Postcolonial Politics of Sexual Identity." In Meredith L. Weiss and Michael J. Bosia, eds., *Global Homophobia: States, Movements, and the Politics of Oppression*. Champaign: University of Illinois Press, pp. 75–102.

Kaplan, Robert D. 2003. "Infectious Chaos in West Africa." *New York Times*, January 12.

Karsh, Efraim, and Inari Rautsi. 2002. *Saddam Hussein: A Political Biography*. New York: Grove Press.

Kasfir, Nelson. 1979. "Explaining Ethnic Political Participation." *World Politics* 31 (April): 365–388.

Kastfelt, Niels. 1994. *Religion and Politics in Nigeria: A Study in Middle Belt Christianity*. London: British Academic Press.

Kastfelt, Niels. 2005. "Religion and African Civil Wars: Themes and Interpretations." In Niels Kastfelt, ed., *Religion and African Civil Wars*. New York: Palgrave Macmillan, pp. 1–27.

Kellows, Christine L., and H. Leslie Steeves. 1998. "The Role of Radio in the Rwandan Genocide." *Journal of Communication* 48, 3: 107–128.

Kessler, David F. 1982. *The Falashas: A Short History of the Ethiopian Jews*. London: Frank Cass.

Khalid, Mansour. 2003. *War and Peace in Sudan: A Tale of Two Countries*. London: Kegan Paul.

Kirk-Greene, A. H. M. 1971a. *Crisis and Conflict in Nigeria*, vol. I. London: Oxford University Press.

Kirk-Greene, A. H. M. 1971b. *Crisis and Conflict in Nigeria*, vol. II. London: Oxford University Press.

Kirwin, Matthew. 2006. "The Security Dilemma and Conflict in Côte d'Ivoire." *Nordic Journal of African Studies* 15, 1: 42–52.

Klor, Esteban F., and Moses Shayo. 2010. "Social Identity and Preferences over Redistribution." *Journal of Public Economics* 94: 269–278.

Klusener, Rainer. 2005. "Islam in Rwanda." Working paper, United States Institute of Peace. www.usip.org/muslimworld/bulletin/2005/may.html.

Kohler, Jessica. 2003. "From Miraculous to Disastrous: The Crisis in Côte d'Ivoire." Working paper, Centre for Applied Studies in International Negotiations (CASIN).

Konate, Siendou A. 2004. "The Politics of Identity and Violence in Côte d'Ivoire." *West Africa Review* Issue 5. www.westafricareview.com/issue5/konate.htm.

Lacina, Bethany. 2006. "Explaining the Severity of Civil Wars." *Journal of Conflict Resolution* 50, 2: 276–289.

Laitin, David. 1978. "Religion, Political Culture, and the Weberian Tradition." *World Politics* 30, 4: 563–592.

Laitin, David D. 1982. "The Shari'a Debate and the Origins of Nigeria's Second Republic." *Journal of Modern African Studies* 20, 3: 411–430.

Laitin, David D. 1986. *Hegemony and Culture: Politics and Religious Change among the Yoruba*. Chicago, IL: University of Chicago Press.

Laitin, David D. 1998. *Identity in Formation: The Russian-Speaking Populations of the Near-Abroad*. Ithaca, NY: Cornell University Press.

Laitin, David. 2000. "Language Conflict and Violence: The Straw That Strengthens the Camel's Back." *Archives Européennes de Sociologie* 41, 1: 97–137.

Langer, Arnim. 2008. "When Do Horizontal Inequalities Lead to Conflict? Lessons from a Comparative Study of Ghana and Côte d'Ivoire." In Frances

Stewart, ed., *Horizontal Inequalities and Conflict: Understanding Group Violence in Multiethnic Societies.* New York: Palgrave Macmillan, pp. 163–189.

Law, Robin. 1991. "Religion, Trade, and Politics on the Slave Coast: Roman Catholic Missions in Alladah and Whydah in the Seventeenth Century." *Journal of Religion in Africa* 21, 1: 42–77.

Lawry, Stephen W. 1990. "Tenure Policy toward Common Property Natural Resources in Sub-Saharan Africa." *Natural Resources Journal* 30: 403–422.

Le Pape, Marc. 2003. "Les Politiques d'Affrontement en Côte d'Ivoire, 1999–2003." *Afrique Contemporaine* 206, 2: 29–39.

Le Pape, Marc, and Claudine Vidal, eds. 2002. *Côte d'Ivoire, L'Année Terrible: 1999-2000.* Paris: Karthala.

Leach, Justin D. 2013. *War and Politics in Sudan: Cultural Identities and the Challenges of the Peace Process.* London: I. B. Tauris & Co.

Lentz, Carola. 1995. "'Tribalism' and Ethnicity in Africa: A Review of Four Decades of Anglophone Research." *Cahiers des Sciences Humaines* 31, 2: 308–328.

Lentz, Carola, and Paul Nugent, eds. 2000. *Ethnicity in Ghana: The Limits of Invention.* New York: St. Martin's Press.

Lester, David, Bijou Yang, and Mark Lindsay. 2004. "Suicide Bombers: Are Psychological Profiles Possible?" *Studies in Conflict and Terrorism* 27: 283–295.

Levan, Carl A. 2013. "Sectarian Rebellions in Post-Transition Nigeria Compared." *Journal of Intervention and Statebuilding* 7, 3: 335–352.

Levtzion, Nehemia. 1994. *Islam in West Africa: Religion, Society, and Politics to 1800.* Brookfield, VT: Ashgate.

Levtzion, Nehemia, and Randall L. Pouwels. 2012. *History of Islam in Africa.* Athens: Ohio University Press.

Lewis, Bernard. 1990. "The Roots of Muslim Rage." *Atlantic Monthly* 266, 3: 47–56.

Lichbach, Mark I. 1998. *The Rebel's Dilemma.* Ann Arbor: University of Michigan Press.

Lieberman, Evan S., and Gwyneth H. McClendon. 2013. "The Ethnicity–Policy Preference Link in Sub-Saharan Africa." *Comparative Political Studies* 46: 574–602.

Lijphart, Arend. 1975. *The Politics of Accommodation: Pluralism and Democracy in the Netherlands.* Berkeley: University of California Press.

Lindenfeld, David F. 2005. "Indigenous Encounters with Christian Missionaries in China and West Africa, 1800–1920: A Comparative Study." *Journal of World History* 16, 3: 327–369.

Lindhardt, Martin, ed. 2014. *Pentecostalism in Africa: Presence and Impact of Pneumatic Christianity in Postcolonial Societies.* Leiden, Netherlands: Brill.

Lipsky, Michael. 1968. "Protest as a Political Resource." *American Political Science Review* 62, 4: 1144–1158.

Livingston, David. 1868. *Missionary Travels and Researches in South Africa.* New York: Harpers Press.

Loada, Augustin. 2006. "L'élection présidentielle du 13 novembre 2005: Un plébiscite par défaut." *Politique Africaine* 101 (March–April) : 19–41.

Longman, Timothy. 2010. *Christianity and Genocide in Rwanda*. Cambridge: Cambridge University Press.

Lydon, Ghislaine. 2009. *On Trans-Saharan Trails: Islamic Law, Trade Networks, and Cross-Cultural Exchange in Nineteenth-Century Western Africa*. New York: Cambridge University Press.

Lyman, Princeton N., and Stephen J. Morrison. 2004. "The Terrorist Threat in Africa." *Foreign Affairs* 83, 1: 75–86.

Maccoby, Michael. 1981. *The Leader: A New Face for American Management*. New York: Simon & Schuster.

MacEachern, Scott. 2000. "Genes, Tribes, and African History." *Current Anthropology* 41, 3: 357–384.

MacLean, Lauren M. 2004. "Mediating Ethnic Conflict at the Grassroots: The Role of Local Associational Life in Shaping Strong Political Values in Côte d'Ivoire and Ghana." *Journal of Modern African Studies* 42: 589–617.

MacLean, Lauren M. 2010. *Informal Institutions and Citizenship in Rural Africa: Risk and Reciprocity in Ghana and Côte d'Ivoire*. New York: Cambridge University Press.

Mafeje, Archie. 1971. "The Ideology of Tribalisms." *Journal of Modern African Studies* 9, 2: 253–261.

Mang, Henry G. 2013. "Land and Labor Migrations in Central and Southern Plateau: Observing Latent Potentials for Conflict Due to Ideologies of Identities." In Toyin Falola, Roy Doron, and Okpeh O. Okpeh, eds., *Warfare, Ethnicity, and National Identity in Nigeria*. London: Africa World Press, pp. 275–295.

Marshall, Kathryn. 2010. "Côte d'Ivoire in Crisis: Faith in Action." Wash. Post, *On Faith*. http://newsweek.washingtonpost.com/onfaith/georgetown/2010/05/a_plea_for_peace_Côte_divoire_in_crisis.html.

Martin, Jean-Clément. 1998. *Contre-Révolution, Révolution, et Nation en France, 1789–1799*. Paris: Editions du Sueil.

May, Glenn Anthony. 1991. *Battle for Batangas: A Philippine Province at War*. New Haven, CT: Yale University Press.

Mazrui, Ali A. 1975. "The Resurrection of the Warrior Tradition in African Political Culture." *Journal of Modern African Studies* 13, 1: 67–84.

McCauley, John F. 2013a. "Economic Development Strategies and Communal Violence in Africa: The Cases of Cote d'Ivoire and Ghana." *Comparative Political Studies* 46, 2:182–211.

McCauley, John F. 2013b. "Africa's New Big Man Rule?" *African Affairs* 112, 446: 1–21.

McCauley, John F. 2014. "The Political Mobilization of Ethnic and Religious Identities in Africa." *American Political Science Review* 108, 4: 801–816.

McCauley, John F. 2016. "Ethnicity and Religion as Sources of Political Division in Africa: Evidence from a Dictator Game." Unpublished manuscript.

McCauley, John F., and E. Gyimah-Boadi. 2009. "Religious Faith and Democracy: Evidence from the Afrobarometer Surveys." Afrobarometer Working paper no. 113.

McCauley, John F., and Daniel N. Posner. 2015. "African Borders as Sources of Natural Experiments: Promise and Pitfalls." *Political Science Research and Methods* 3, 2: 409–118.

McCauley, John F., and Daniel N. Posner. 2017. "The Political Sources of Religious Identification: A Study on the Burkina Faso–Côte d'Ivoire Border." *British Journal of Political Science* doi:10.1017/S0007123416000594.

McClendon, Gwyneth H. 2014. "Social Esteem and Participation in Contentious Politics: A Field Experiment at an LGBT Pride Rally." *American Journal of Political Science* 58, 2: 279–290.

McClendon, Gwyneth, and Rachel R. Riedl. 2015. "Religion as a Stimulant of Political Participation: Experimental Evidence from Nairobi, Kenya." *Journal of Politics* 77, 4: 1045–1057.

McGovern, Mike. 2011. *Making War in Côte d'Ivoire.* Chicago, IL: University of Chicago Press.

Michalopoulos, Stelios, and Elias Papaioannou. 2014. "National Institutions and Subnational Development in Africa." *Quarterly Journal of Economics* 129, 1: 151–213.

Michelitch, Kristin. 2015. "Does Electoral Competition Exacerbate Interethnic or Interpartisan Economic Discrimination? Evidence from a Field Experiment in Market Price Bargaining." *American Political Science Review* 109, 1: 43–61.

Miguel, Edward. 2004. "Tribe or Nation? Nation Building and Public Goods in Kenya versus Tanzania." *World Politics* 56 (April): 327–362.

Miles, William, and David Rochefort. 1991. "Nationalism versus Ethnic Identity in Sub-Saharan Africa." *American Political Science Review* 85, 2 (June): 393–403.

Miran, Marie. 2006. "The Political Economy of Civil Islam in Côte d'Ivoire." In H. Weiss and M. Broenig, eds., *Islamic Democracy? Political Islam in Western Africa.* Berlin: Lit Verlag.

Miran-Guyon, Marie. 2012. "Native Conversion to Islam in Southern Côte d'Ivoire." *Journal of Religion in Africa* 42, 2: 95–117.

Mkandawire, Thandika. 2015. "Neopatrimonialism and the Political Economy of Economic Performance in Africa: Critical Reflections." *World Politics* 67, 3: 563–612.

Montalvo, Jose, and Marta Reynal-Queral. 2005. "Ethnic Polarization, Potential Conflict, and Civil Wars." *The American Economic Review* 95, 3: 796–816.

Monteil, Vincent. 1964. *L'Islam Noir: Une Religion à la Conquête de l'Afrique.* Paris: Editions de Seuil.

Morton, Rebecca B., and Kenneth C. Williams. 2010. *Experimental Political Science and the Study of Causality: From Nature to the Lab.* New York: Cambridge University Press.

Mu'azzam, Ibrahim, and Jibrin Ibrahim. 2000. Religious Identity in the Context of Structural Adjustment in Nigeria." In Attahiru Jega, ed., *Identity Transformation and Identity Politics Under Structural Adjustment in Nigeria.* Stockholm: Nordiska Africainstitutet, pp. 62–85.

Mueller, G. H. 1980. "The Dimensions of Religiosity." *Sociological Analysis* 41, 1: 1–24.

Mueller, John E. 1994. *Policy and Opinion in the Gulf War.* Chicago, IL: University of Chicago Press.

Muller, Jerry Z. 2008. "Us and Them: The Enduring Power of Ethnic Nationalism." *Foreign Affairs* (March/April): 18–35.

Munson, Lestor. 2016. "America's Biggest Challenge in Africa." *Foreign Policy*, April 15.

Nafziger, Wayne E. 1972. "Economic Aspects of the Nigerian Civil War." In Robin Higham, ed., *Civil Wars in the Twentieth Century*. Lexington: University of Kentucky Press, pp. 184–202.

Nayar, M. G. Kaladharan. 1975. "Self-Determination beyond the Colonial Context: Biafra in Retrospect." *Texas International Law Journal* 10, 2: 321–346.

N'Diaye, Boubacar. 2005. "Not a Miracle After All ... Côte d'Ivoire's Downfall: Flawed Civil-Military Relations and Missed Opportunities." *Scientia Militaria* 33, 1: 89–118.

New York Times. 2000. "Dictator Gone, Violence Erupts in Ivory Coast." October 27.

New York Times. 2001. "Rising Muslim Power in Africa Causes Unrest in Nigeria and Elsewhere." November 1.

New York Times. 2004. "Since '94 Horror, Rwandans Turn toward Islam." April 6.

New York Times. 2015. "A New Approach to South Sudan." July 28.

Njoh, Ambe J. 2006. *Tradition, Culture, and Development in Africa: Historical Lessons for Modern Development Planning*. Farnham, UK: Ashgate.

Nordås, Ragnhild. 2007. "Identity Polarization and Conflict: State Building in Côte d'Ivoire and Ghana." Working paper prepared for the Conference on Polarization and Conflict. Gaillac, June 7–9.

Nordås, Ragnhild. 2014. "Religious Demography and Conflict: Lessons from Côte d'Ivoire and Ghana." *International Area Studies Review* 17, 2: 146–166.

Norris, Pippa, and Ronald Inglehart. 2004. *Sacred and Secular: Religion and Politics Worldwide*. Cambridge: Cambridge University Press.

O'Brien, Richard P. 1994. *Catholicism*, new edition. New York: Harper Collins.

Olivier de Sardan, Jean-Pierre. 1999. "A Moral Economy of Corruption in Africa? *Journal of Modern African Studies* 37, 1: 25–52.

Omeje, Kenneth. 2004. "The State, Conflict, and Evolving Politics in the Niger Delta, Nigeria." *Review of African Political Economy* 31, 101: 425–440.

Omenka, Nicholas I. 2010. "Blaming the Gods: Christian Religious Propaganda in the Nigeria-Biafra War." *The Journal of African History* 51, 3: 367–389.

Onaiyekan, John. 1983. "Tribal Religion in General." In E. A. Adegbola, ed., *Traditional Religion in West Africa*. Ibadan: Daystar Press, pp. 238–241.

Onu, Godwin. 2001. *Ethnicity and Conflict Management: A Case Study of the MASSOB Movement in Nigeria*. UNESCO/ENA working paper. MOST Etho-Net Publications.

Onuoha, Freedom C. 2010. "The Islamist Challenge: Nigeria's Boko Haram Crisis Explained." *African Security Review* 19, 2: 54–67.

Onuoha, Freedom C. 2014. "Boko Haram and the Evolving Salafi Jihadist Threat in Nigeria." In Marc-Antoine Pérouse de Montclos, ed., *Boko Haram: Islamism, Politics, and Security, and the State in Nigeria*. Leiden: African Studies Centre, pp. 158–191.

Opp, Karl-Dieter. 1989. *The Rationality of Political Protest*. Boulder, CO: Westview Press.

Osaghae, Eghosa E., and Rotimi T. Suberu. 2005. "A History of Identities, Violence, and Stability in Nigeria." CRISE working paper WP06. Oxford Department of International Development.

Palmer-Fernandez, Gabriel, ed. 2004. *Encyclopedia of Religion and War*. New York: Routledge.

Pearce, Susanna. 2005. "Religious Rage: A Quantitative Analysis of the Intensity of Armed Conflicts." *Terrorism and Political Violence* 17: 333–352.

Penn, Elizabeth Maggie. 2008. "Citizenship versus Ethnicity: The Role of Institutions in Shaping Identity Choice." *The Journal of Politics* 70, 4: 956–973.

Podeh, Elie. 1994. "In the Service of Power: The Ideological Struggle in the Arab World during the Gulf War." *Conflict Quarterly* 14, 4 (Fall).

Poggo, Scopas S. 2009. *The First Sudanese Civil War: Africans, Arabs, and Israelis in the Southern Sudan, 1955–1972*. New York: Palgrave Macmillan.

Posen, Barry. 1993. "The Security Dilemma and Ethnic Conflict." *Survival* 35, 1: 27–47.

Posner, Daniel N. 2004. "The Political Salience of Cultural Difference: Why Chewas and Tumbukas Are Allies in Zambia and Adversaries in Malawi." *American Political Science Review* 98, 3 (August): 1–17.

Posner, Daniel N. 2005. *Institutions and Ethnic Politics in Africa*. New York: Cambridge University Press.

Pritchard, John. 1973. "The Prophet Harris and Ivory Coast." *Journal of Religion in Africa* 5, 1: 23–31.

Prunier, Gérard. 1995. *The Rwanda Crisis: History of a Genocide*. New York: Columbia University Press.

Pulinckx, Olivier. 2001. "Côte d'Ivoire, Poudrière Identitaire." Prévention Génocides Productions. www.olivier-pulinckx.eu/documentaires/.

Putnam, Robert, and David Campbell. 2010. *American Grace: How Religion Is Reshaping our Civic and Political Lives*. New York: Simon & Schuster.

Rambo, Lewis R. 1993. *Understanding Religious Conversion*. New Haven, CT: Yale University Press.

Reese, Scott S. 2014. "Islam in Africa/Africans and Islam." *Journal of African History* 55, 1: 17–26.

Reforme. 2005. "Un Président 'Très Chrétien.'" No. 3153. January 12. www.reforme.net/archive2/article.php?num=3153&ref=1058.

Reinikka, Ritva. 2006. "Using Micro-Surveys to Measure and Explain Corruption." *World Development* 34, 2: 359–370.

Reuters 2014. "Census Sparks Resurgence in Cote d'Ivoire's Identity Politics." March 17. UK edition.

Reynolds, Jonathan T. 1997. "The Politics of History: The Legacy of the Sokoto Caliphate in Nigeria." In Paul E. Lovejoy and Pat Williams, eds., *Displacement and the Politics of Violence in Nigeria*. Leiden, Netherlands: Brill, pp. 50–65.

Richards, Paul. 1996. *Fighting for the Rain Forest: War, Youth, and Resources in Sierra Leone*. Oxford: James Currey.

Roberts, T. D., et al. 1973. *Area Handbook for Ivory Coast*. Washington, DC: American University–Foreign Area Studies Press.

Roger, Jacques. 2010. "Côte d'Ivoire: Le RDR, L'Ivoirité, Alassane D. Ouattara et sa Rebellion en Côte d'Ivoire." Ivoirenews, March 21. http://ivoirenews.net/info24/tld/5520.html.

Rothchild, Donald. 1997. *Managing Ethnic Conflict in Africa: Pressures and Incentives for Cooperation*. Washington, DC: Brookings Institution Press.

Roubaud, Francois. 2003. "La Crise Vue d'en Bas à Abidjan: Ethnicité, Gouvernance et Démocratie." *Afrique Contemporaine* 206, 2: 57–85.

Sachs, Natan B. 2010. "Shame and Religious Prosociality." Unpublished manuscript, Stanford University.

Sacks, Nicholas. 1992. *Lectures on Conversation*. Oxford: Blackwell Press.

Sambanis, Nicholas. 2001. "Do Ethnic and Non-ethnic Civil Wars Have the Same Causes?" *Journal of Conflict Resolution* 45, 3: 259–282.

Sambanis, Nicholas, and Moses Shayo. 2013. "Social Identification and Ethnic Conflict." *American Political Science Review* 107, 2: 294–325.

Sanneh, Lamin. 1994. "Translatability in Islam and Christianity in Africa: A Thematic Approach." In Thomas Blakely, W.V. Beek, and D. Thompson, eds., *Religion in Africa: Experience and Expression*. London: James Curry, pp. 23–45.

Sanneh, Lamin. 2003. *Whose Religion Is Christianity? The Gospel Beyond the West*. Cambridge: Wm. B. Eerdmans.

Sanneh, Lamin. 2015. *Piety and Power: Muslims and Christians in West Africa*. Eugene, OR: Orbis Books.

Schultz, Kenneth F., Douglas Altman, and David Moher, for the CONSORT Group. 2010. "CONSORT 2010 Statement: Updated Guidelines for Reporting Parallel Group Randomized Trials." *Annals of Internal Medicine* 152, 11: ePub.

Sharkey, H. 2004. "Sudan: Oil and War." In C. Legum, ed., *Africa Contemporary Record 1998–2000*. New York: Holmes and Meier.

Shayo, Moses. 2009. "A Model of Social Identity with an Application to Political Economy: Nation, Class, and Redistribution." *American Political Science Review* 103, 2: 147–174.

Sikainga, Ahmad Alawad. 1993. "Northern Sudanese Political Parties and the Civil War." In M. W. Daly and Ahmad Sikainga, eds., *Civil War in the Sudan*. London: British Academic Press, pp. 78–96.

Simon, Herbert. 1985. "Human Nature in Politics: The Dialogue of Psychology with Political Science." *American Political Science Review* 79: 293–304.

Simpson, John. 1991. *From the House of War: John Simpson in the Gulf*. London: Vintage Books.

Smelser, Neil J. 2007. *The Faces of Terrorism: Social and Psychological Dimensions*. Princeton, NJ: Princeton University Press.

Soares, Benjamen F., and René Otayek, eds. 2007. *Islam and Muslim Politics in Africa*. New York: Palgrave Macmillan.

Soudan, F. 2003. "French, Go Home?" *Jeune Afrique Intelligent*. February 8.

Southall, Aidan. 1970. "The Illusion of Tribe." *Journal of Asian and African Studies* 5: 28–50.

Staniland, Martin. 1975. *The Lions of Dagbon: Political Change in Northern Ghana*. Cambridge: Cambridge University Press.

Stark, Rodney. 2001. *One True God: Historical Consequences of Monotheism.*
Princeton, NJ: Princeton University Press.

Stark, Rodney, and Laurence R. Iannaccone. 1994. "A Supply-Side Reinterpret-
ation of the 'Secularization' of Europe." *Journal for the Scientific Study of
Religion* 33, 3: 230–252.

Stewart, Frances, ed. 2008. *Horizontal Inequalities and Conflict: Understanding
Group Violence in Multiethnic Societies.* New York: Palgrave Macmillan.

Svensson, Isak. 2007. "Fighting with Faith: Religion and Conflict Resolution in
Civil Wars." *Journal of Conflict Resolution* 51, 6: 930–949.

Tajfel, Henri, and J. C. Turner. 1979. "An Integrative Theory of Intergroup
Conflict." In W. G. Austin and S. Worchel, eds., *The Social Psychology of
Intergroup Relations.* Monterey, CA: Brooks/Cole, pp. 33–47.

Tajfel, Henri, and J. C. Turner. 1986. "The Social Identity Theory of Inter-group
Behavior," in S. Worchel and L. W. Austin, eds., *Psychology of Intergroup
Relations.* Chicago, IL: Nelson-Hall Press.

Telegraph. 2010. "Jacob Zuma Fathers 20th Child with Friend's Daughter." 31 January 31. www.telegraph.co.uk/news/worldnews/africaandindianocean/southafrica/
7120593/Jacob-Zuma-fathers-20th-child-with-friends-daughter.html.

Tilly, Charles. 1964. *The Vendée.* Cambridge, MA: Harvard University Press.

Toft, Monica D. 2005. *The Geography of Ethnic Violence: Identity, Interests, and
the Indivisibility of Territory.* Princeton, NJ: Princeton University Press.

Toft, Monica Duffy. 2007. "Getting Religion? The Puzzling Case of Islam and
Civil War." *International Security* 31, 4: 97–131.

Toungara, Jeanne Maddox. 2001. "Ethnicity and Political Crisis in Côte
d'Ivoire." *Journal of Democracy* 12, 3: 63–72.

Touré, M. 2000. "Immigration en Côte d'Ivoire: La Notion de 'Seuil Tolérable'
Relève de la Xénophobie." *Politique Africaine* 78: 75–93.

Trimingham, J. Spencer. 1970. *A History of Islam in West Africa.* Oxford: Oxford
University Press.

Uche, Chibuike. 2008. "Oil, British Interests, and the Nigerian Civil War." *The
Journal of African History* 49, 1: 111–135.

Uchendu, Egodi. 2010. "Being Igbo and Muslim: The Igbo of Southeastern
Nigeria and Conversions to Islam, 1930s to Recent Times." *The Journal of
African History* 51, 1: 63–87.

U.S. Department of State. 2001. *Côte d'Ivoire: Country Report on Human Rights
Practices.* www.state.gov/g/drl/rls/hrrpt/2000/af/index.cfm?docid=773.

U.S. Department of State. 2003. "2003 Report on International Religious Freedom: Côte d'Ivoire." www.state.gov/g/drl/rls/irf/2003/23701.htm.

Uzokwe, Alfred. 2003. *Surviving in Biafra: The Story of the Nigerian Civil War.*
New York: Writers Advantage Press.

Vaïsse, Justin. 2003. "The Crisis in Côte d'Ivoire." U.S.–France Analysis Series,
the Brookings Institution. www.vaisse.net/BiblioJustin/Articles/Biblio Justin-
Briefvaisse-IvoryCoast_mars2003.pdf.

Vanderlinden, Jacques. 2007. "What Kind of Law Making in a Global World?
The Case of Africa." *Louisiana Law Review* 67: 1043–1072.

Vanguard. 2009. "Boko Haram Resurrects, Declares Total Jihad." August 14.
www.vanguardngr.com/2009/08/boko-haram-ressurects-declares-total-jihad/.

Varshney, Ashutosh. 2002. *Ethnic Conflict and Civil Life: Hindus and Muslims in India*. New Haven, CT: Yale University Press.

Vertovec, Steven. 2000. *The Hindu Diaspora: Comparative Patterns*. London: Routledge.

Vickers, Michael. 1970. "Competition and Control in Modern Nigeria: Origins of the War with Biafra." *International Journal* 25, 3: 603–633.

Vüllers, Johannes. 2011. "Fighting for the Kingdom of God? The Role of Religion in the Ivoirian Crisis." GIGA Working Paper No. 178.

Wakoson, Elias N. 1993. "The Politics of Southern Self-Government, 1972–83." In M. W. Daly and Ahmad Sikainga, eds., *Civil War in the Sudan*. London: British Academic Press, pp. 27–50.

Walls, A. F. 1978. "Religion and the Press in 'the Enclave' in the Nigerian Civil War." In Edward Fasholé-Luke, Richard Gray, Adrian Hastings, and Godwin Tasie, eds., *Christianity in Independent Africa*. Bloomington: Indiana University Press, pp. 207–215.

Wantchekon, Leonard. 2003. "Clientelism and Voting Behavior: Evidence from a Field Experiment in Benin." *World Politics* 55 (April): 399–422.

Washington Post. 2000. "Ethnic, Religious Rifts to Test Ivorian Leader; Abidjan Killings in Wake of Vote Points Up Problem." October 29.

Waugh, Auberon, and Suzanne Cronjé. 1969. *Biafra: Britain's Shame*. London: Michael Joseph.

Weber, Max. 1922 [1991]. *The Sociology of Religion*. Boston: Beacon Press.

Weber, Christopher, and Matthew Thorton. 2012. "Courting Christians: How Political Candidates Prime Religious Considerations in Campaign Ads." *The Journal of Politics* 74, 2: 400–413.

Weinstein, Jeremy M. 2007. *Inside Rebellion: The Politics of Insurgent Violence*. New York: Cambridge University Press.

Wilkinson, Steven I. 1999. "Ethnic Mobilization and Ethnic Violence in Post-Independence India." Working paper prepared for the SSRC-Macarthur Foundation workshop, May 19–21, University of Chicago.

Williams, Pat A. T. 1997. "Religion, Violence, and Displacement in Nigeria." In Paul E. Lovejoy and Pat Williams, eds., *Displacement and the Politics of Violence in Nigeria*. Leiden, Netherlands: Brill, pp. 33–49.

Williams, Pat, and Toyin Falola. 1995. *Religious Impact on the Nation State*. Brookfield VT: Ashgate.

Wissler, Clark. 1923. *Man and Culture*. New York: Thomas Y. Crowell.

World Christian Database. 2006. "Ivory Coast, Religious Change Over Time." Data – Countries and Regions. www.worldchristiandatabase.org/wcd/about/country.asp.

World Christian Database. 2014. "Peoples and Languages." www.worldchristiandatabase.org/wcd/.

World Christian Database. 2016. "Africa; Religious Change over Time." www.worldchristiandatabase.org/wcd/.

Yongo-Bure, B. 1993. "The Underdevelopment of the Southern Sudan since Independence." In M. W. Daly and Ahmad Sikainga, eds., *Civil War in the Sudan*. London: British Academic Press, pp. 51–77.

Young, Crawford. 1976. *The Politics of Cultural Pluralism*. Madison: University of Wisconsin Press.

Zinnbauer, Brian, et al. 1997. "Religion and Spirituality: Unfuzzying the Fuzzy." *Journal for the Scientific Study of Religion* 36, 4: 549–564.

Zubaida, Sami. 1993. *Islam, the People, and the State: Political Ideas and Movements in the Middle East.* New York: Palgrave Macmillan.

Zulaika, Joseba. 1988. *Basque Violence: Metaphore and Sacrament.* Reno: University of Nevada Press.

Index

Abbud, Ibrahim, 145
Abidjan, 3, 120, 127–8
Abobo, 130
Abyssinians, 32
Achebe, Chinua, 162–3
Action Group (AG), 158–9
actors
  in conflict, 8–9
  rhetoric of, 8–9
Addis Ababa Agreement, 139–40, 148
Adekunle, Benjamin, 163
Africa. *See also specific countries*
  Chandra on, 41
  Christianity in, 10–11, 15
  ethnic groups in, 7, 10–11, 28–31, 39–40
  Islam in, 10–11, 15, 32–3
  mobilizational differences in, 10
  religion in, 7, 10–11
African diaspora, 31
AFRISTAT. *See l'Observatoire économique et statistique d'Afrique subsaharienne*
Afrobarometer, 52–3, 62–4, 133
  observational analyses of, 183–5
AG. *See* Action Group
Ahlu Sunnah wal Jama'aah (ASWAJ), 82–3, 85
  in Ghana, 83–4
Akan, 24–5, 30–1, 118–20, 137–8
Almond, Gabriel R., 82
An-Na'im, Abdullahi Ahmed, 148–9
Anuak, 141
Anya-Nya movement, 146–7
Anyi, 118–19

Arab Muslims, 74
Arabistes, 32–3
Arceneaux, Kevin, 53
Asante Kroye Kuo, 84–5
Asanteman Nkoso Kuo, 84–5
ascetism, 16–17, 43
Ashantehene, 84–5
Ashanti, 14–15, 82–5
  in Kumasi, 85
ASWAJ. *See Ahlu Sunnah wal Jama'aah*
atheism, 96
attendance, 78
al-Azhari, Ismail, 145

Ba'athists, 96–7
Badru, Pade, 164
Baha'i, 33
Baldwin, Kate, 42–3
Bambara, 118
Baoulé, 118–19, 122–3, 125
Barkan, Joel D., 49
Barrett, David B., 38–9
al-Bashir, Omar Hassan, 149
Bassett, Thomas J., 126
Bates, Robert H., 31
Bedié, Henri Konan, 123–5, 131, 138, 172
  protestors, 126–7
  rule of, 125–6
behavioral differences, 19
Belgium, 100–1
belonging, 42
Bété, 118–19